The Child Molester

An Integrated Approach to
Evaluation and Treatment

BRUNNER/MAZEL CLINICAL PSYCHIATRY SERIES

Series Editor: John G. Howells, M.D., F.R.C.Psych., D.P.M.

This Series aims to provide the clinician with information from the developing areas of psychiatry. Each volume in the Series constitutes a ready update of its subject by an acknowledged authority with the purpose of enhancing clinical practice.

BRUNNER/MAZEL CLINICAL PSYCHIATRY SERIES NO. 1

The Child Molester

An Integrated Approach to Evaluation and Treatment

By

George W. Barnard, M.D.

A. Kenneth Fuller, M.D.

Lynn Robbins

Theodore Shaw

BRUNNER/MAZEL *Publishers* • **NEW YORK**

Library of Congress Cataloging-in-Publication Data

The Child molester : an integrated approach to evaluation and
treatment / by George W. Barnard . . . [et al.].
    p.   cm. — (Brunner/Mazel clinical psychiatry series; no. 1)
    Includes bibliographies and index.
    ISBN 0-87630-526-5
    1. Child molesting.   I. Barnard, George W.   II. Series.
    [DNLM: 1. Child Abuse, Sexual. 2. Paraphilias—diagnosis.
3. Paraphilias—therapy.   WM 610 C536]
    RC560.C46C47 1989
    616.85′83—dc19
    DNLM/DLC
    for Library of Congress   88-19466
                                     CIP

Published by
BRUNNER/MAZEL, INC.
19 Union Square
New York, New York 10003

Foreword

The problem of child sexual abuse runs so deeply through our social and cultural structures as to defy scientifically based quantitative description. More apt descriptions of its pervasiveness are found in commonly used metaphors referring to child sexual abuse statistics as "tip of the iceberg" or in images of society being engulfed and rocked by a "tidal wave of sexual abuse."

Gradually, as girls and boys and women and men have disclosed the painful and bottled-up secrets of their sexual abuse, society has begun to respond to the problem more comprehensively. Along with restorative therapeutic interventions for survivors, prevention efforts have broadened to include the treatment of offenders. Mental health and other professionals have become increasingly convinced of the potential for molesters of children to learn to control their sexually inappropriate and aggressive behaviors.

This new social and clinical awareness is not universal; it is, in fact, surprisingly uneven. Despite the development of an impressive specialized sex-offender treatment discipline in the last few decades, some states remain in the grip of the negative "nothing works with child molesters so let's lock 'em up and throw away the key" punishment model that has influenced social control policies since the 1970s. In such states, few or no specialized evaluation and treatment services are offered; where services are available, generally they are not provided by public agencies. At the other end of the spectrum, many states, equally revulsed but not impeded by the actions of those who would rob children of their innocence and childhood, offer a range of specialized services to such offenders, both juvenile and adult. Their goal is to reduce the potential for molesters to reoffend.

The development of specialized evaluation and treatment for sex offenders has not been guided systematically by any public or educational policy-oriented process and testing. Therapeutic interventions have, in fact, evolved outside the traditional institutions most commonly associated with treatment. Only rarely can this new discipline be found in the curricula of schools of medicine, psychology, nursing, public and mental health, and social work. Rather, theory is continuing to develop out of practice—eclectic practice hammered out in treatment programs in the private and public sectors by social workers, psychologists, mental health workers, correctional personnel, probation and parole agents, child protection service workers, and victim/survivor specialists. While this has been a productive and creative process, it is time to integrate what has been learned thus far into the curricula of institutions that teach and train professionals. *The Child Molester: An Integrated Approach to Evaluation and Treatment* is a valuable book that can contribute significantly to this process. In addition to its pedagogical usefulness, the authors have provided a comprehensive overview of the various special issues and interventions involved in evaluating and treating child molesters. The book is distinctive also for its detailed presentation of a residential adult evaluation and treatment program model.

Fortunately, the authors have not limited themselves to factual information about the evaluation and treatment of child molesters but have included their insights on the clinical implications for the therapists who treat these complex and difficult clients. More needs to be said about this new breed of treatment specialists, a largely unappreciated group of dedicated professionals working on emotionally charged issues with clients whom society would prefer to punish and ignore. As a result of this book, may their numbers increase, may their skills be strengthened, and may they be cherished for their contribution to the safety of children everywhere.

Fay Honey Knopp
Director
Safer Society Program
Orwell, VT

Contents

Figures

Tables

Authors

George W. Barnard, M.D.
Department of Psychiatry
University of Florida
Gainesville, Florida

A. Kenneth Fuller, M.D.
Archbold Mental Health Center
Thomasville, Georgia
and
Department of Psychiatry
University of Florida
Gainesville, Florida

Lynn Robbins
Department of Psychiatry
University of Florida
Gainesville, Florida

Theodore Shaw
Director, Sex Offender Treatment Unit
North Florida Evaluation and Treatment Center
Gainesville, Florida

Acknowledgments

We extend our appreciation to all the individuals who have contributed to the realization of this book. Foremost to receive our thanks is Sandra Barnard, who contributed many hours of very helpful editorial assistance.

We thank John Adams, M.D., Chairman and Professor of the Department of Psychiatry of the University of Florida, and Dennis Gies, Administrator of North Florida Evaluation and Treatment Center (NFETC) in Gainesville, Florida, for their cooperation and support of our efforts in developing a psychosocial assessment laboratory and a behaviorally oriented treatment program in the Sex Offender Treatment Unit at NFETC. We also thank Susanne Casey, Health and Rehabilitative Services District Administrator, for her willingness to back the project. We extend special appreciation to Gustave Newman, M.D., Clinical Director at NFETC, for his support of the project at all phases of development. Gary Dunham and William Baxter, administrative staff at NFETC, have always been enthusiastic supporters of our endeavors and we wish to thank them for their assistance. David Hutchinson, former head of the Sex Offender Treatment Unit at NFETC, was the initial force behind our project to assess objectively sex offenders. We are grateful to him for sharing with us his enthusiasm for the development of an effective assessment and treatment program.

We extend our warm appreciation for the cooperation and helpfulness of the staff of the Sex Offender Treatment Unit at NFETC: to Harry Spears for his energetic effort to implement the psychosocial assessment laboratory; to therapists Harlon Brody, Jay Keister, Astrid Hastay, and David Cunningham who have been active participants in our weekly staff conferences; and to Alvin Butler,

Assistant Director of the Sex Offender Unit, Gerald Kish, laboratory coordinator, Regis Gates, and Ellen Young whose work behind the scenes assured that the laboratory functioned properly in its day-to-day operations. In our work with both the administrative and treatment staff at NFETC we have been greatly impressed with the humane orientation which is fundamental to all aspects of the treatment program for sex offenders. In addition to this basic humaneness, they display a sincere desire to see advancements in the state of the art of assessment and treatment of sex offenders.

Psychologists Roger Blashfield, Ph.D., and Sheryl Fellows, Ph.D., provided invaluable advice in test selection and in establishing testing procedures in the laboratory; and Ernest J. Bordini, Ph.D., contributed to the development of an interpretative computer program for the laboratory.

We are greatly appreciative of the creativity of Gary Bennett who wrote the interactive computer programs used in the laboratory. Without his brilliance, perseverance, and loyalty, we would never have seen the project through to completion.

We thank Fay Honey Knopp, Stephen J. Hucker, M.D., and Roger Blashfield, Ph.D., for taking time from their busy schedules to review the book and give their most helpful comments. Other persons who have contributed significantly to the book by reading and commenting on various chapters are Gustave Newman, M.D.; Ross A. McElroy, Jr., M.D.; Maria I. Vera, M.S.W.; Robert J. Bartucci, M.D.; Patrick Atkins, M.D.; Patricia Barnard; Angela Fuller; Linda Provus McElroy, Ph.D.; William G. Slaughter, M.D.; and Robert Garrison, Ed.D.

To all those who have helped with the library work and the typing we acknowledge our gratitude: Janet Madden, Sarah Connelly, Carrie Euston, Michelle Deal, Elease Coleman, Michelle Rapp, Nancy Vick, and Susan Statum.

Introduction

Child sexual abuse has reached the magnitude where ignoring it is no longer justifiable or even possible. The criminal justice system is flooded with cases of sexual offenders. Although historically the child molester has engendered strong moral opposition and often harsh legal penalties, in recent years there has been a gradual, but dramatic, shift in the attitude in which both the subject and the perpetrator of child sexual abuse are viewed. Encouraging signs indicate that people are beginning to recognize that these offenders are desperately in need of medical, psychological, and psychiatric treatment. In response to this shift in attitude, it is important that the public health, criminal law, and legislative sectors work together to find practical and effective approaches to the problem.

The criminal justice system is looking toward the medical profession for help, both in the prevention and treatment of child sexual abuse. Mental health clinicians have been unduly slow to recognize that sexual offenders need their care. Until recently, these clinicians have in practice tended to dismiss the child molester as criminal, hopeless, or at best, unpleasant, unrewarding, and untreatable.

Within the last 10 years, research efforts have introduced new ideas, fresh approaches, and deeper insights into the treatment and understanding of child molestation. These new research efforts come in response to the urgent need for clinicians, uneducated in the treatment of sex offenders, to provide effective treatment in both inpatient and outpatient clinical settings. However, the literature is expanding so rapidly that even clinicians specialized in the area of child sexual abuse have difficulty assessing the relevance of the research findings and the worth of the proliferating treatment modalities.

This book is intended to help clinicians in their endeavors to treat persons who sexually molest children by providing a comprehensive overview of the subject. *The Child Molester: An Integrated Approach to Evaluation and Treatment* comprises three sections. These are: Part I, Etiology, Assessment, Diagnosis, and Treatment; Part II, A Model Residential Evaluation and Treatment Program for Sex Offenders; and Part III, Legal, Ethical, and Treatment Issues. The first part provides the clinician with comprehensive information on child molesters—the factors that are important in the development of their sexual deviancy and some considerations involved in the assessment, diagnosis, and treatment of their condition.

Part II includes a description of a computerized psychosexual assessment laboratory and a model for an eclectic residential treatment program. This section also contains a clinical interview of a child molester at the close of the inpatient phase of his treatment. The interview covers the sexual events of his early childhood, his first engagement in molesting behavior, and his subsequent history of molestation. His treatment history and his insight into both his pathology and the treatment process are presented. A six-month follow-up interview provides insight into problems confronting the treated sex offender when attempting to resettle into the community.

The legal and ethical issues having direct implications for clinicians are included in Part III. The fiduciary relationship between the clinician and the patient as defined by the law is discussed, as are the right to refuse treatment, confidentiality issues, and the duty to warn and protect third parties. The examination process and forensic report writing are also covered in this section. An example of a forensic report is given. The final chapter looks at the emotional and treatment problems confronting the clinician in establishing the patient-therapist relationship and the treatment environment when evaluating and treating child molesters.

Throughout this book, *he* is predominantly used to embrace both genders for ease of reading; it does not indicate the gender of the molester, victim, or the clinician.

Because the book is oriented toward practical rather than academic considerations, readers are urged to consult appropriate psychiatric and psychological literature for additional information. This book is offered with the hope that it will be of genuine use to practicing clinicians in their assessment and treatment of the child molester.

The Child Molester

An Integrated Approach to Evaluation and Treatment

I. ETIOLOGY, ASSESSMENT, DIAGNOSIS, AND TREATMENT

CHAPTER 1
Overview of the Problem

"My first molestation was at about 15 when I molested a six-year-old boy next door. . . . I was looking for someone who had a sexual interest, where I could play the role of the teacher about sex, and they could play the role of the student. . . . I was committing mutual oral sex acts with adolescent boys and a few girls. Over 35 years—from the time I was 15 until about age 50—I had around 280 victims. Only about 30 or so were female. . . . I was fairly convinced that what I had done was really okay and that the law was really wrong. I was convinced that I was really helping the kids. The sexual gratification was there, but the benefit that I was giving them was offsetting that. . . ." R.I., a child molester (see Chapter 8)

EXTENT OF THE PROBLEM

Incidence

No one can say with accuracy how many child molesters exist, although estimates of the number of cases of child sexual abuse in the United States range from 100,000 to 500,000 cases per year.[5,9] However, these figures may underreport the problem, and they do not indicate whether the incidence of child abuse is increasing or decreasing—although most investigators are convinced that acts of child molestation are steadily rising.[6] There are a variety of reasons why reliable statistics are not available. Primarily, consistent standards have not been applied to most epidemiological studies, and the respondents' typical and frequent use of denial mechanisms to conceal that any deviant sexual behavior has occurred hamper the accuracy of these studies. Perhaps the greatest difficulty is detecting and confirming that child molestation has indeed occurred.

Prevalence

According to the American Humane Association, in 1985 there were an estimated 123,000 reported cases of child sexual abuse in the United States.[2] Recently, some ambitious and quite comprehensive investigations have been undertaken which indicate not only that this high incidence rate does accurately reflect the current prevalence of child sexual abuse, but also that the social and mental health implications of these data are overwhelming.

Gaining insight into the pervasiveness of child sexual abuse can perhaps best be gleaned by examining the findings of several of the most recent and representative studies.

In her investigation, Russell, a professor of sociology at Mills College, studied more than 900 randomly selected women, age 18 or older, from the San Francisco area.[12,13] Overall, 38% in her survey reported that they had had at least one experience of sexual abuse before age 18, and 28% reported at least one such experience prior to the age of 14. It is interesting to note that less than 6% of these cases of child molestation were ever reported to the police.

One study includes a biracial examination of the prevalence of child sexual abuse among Afro-American and White-American women in Los Angeles. Wyatt[15] studied a sample of women who ranged from 18–36 years old. Out of the 248 women examined, 62% reported at least one incident of child molestation before the age of 18. While 57% of the Afro-American women reported some form of sexual abuse, a larger 67% of the White-American women claimed that they were sexually molested.

Studies of child sexual abuse have not been limited solely to the United States. Mrazek, Lynch, and Bentovim[11] mailed questionnaires to nearly 1,600 family doctors, police surgeons, pediatricians, and child psychiatrists to determine the frequency of child molestation in the United Kingdom. A range from 16% (among family doctors) to 56% (among police surgeons) responded that they had seen cases of child sexual abuse. Mrazek, Lynch, and Bentovim have estimated that about one child in 6,000 per year and three children in 1,000 over the entire span of childhood have been recognized as being abused sexually in the United Kingdom.

In a survey of a nationally representative sample of Great Britain, 2,019 men and women over the age of 14 years were interviewed.[4]

Ten percent reported sexual abuse before the age of 16, and the majority of these individuals felt that they had been harmed by the experience. Baker and Duncan, the authors of this study, have estimated that there are over four-and-a-half million adults in Great Britain who have been sexually abused, and among the current population of children they project that 1,117,000 children will be sexually victimized before they reach the age of 15.

Overall, the percentage of persons who have experienced sexual abuse in their childhood is reported in the various studies to be between 10% and 60%. The divergences in response rates may be due to a variety of reasons. Although many methodological differences and other factors have influenced the discrepancies between prevalence rates, an assessment by Wyatt and Peters[16] has noted the following variables in research orientations: the upper age limit assessed for child sexual abuse; the criteria used to define a given sexual experience as abusive; the inclusion or exclusion of experiences involving age peers; and the use of different criteria to determine incidents that occurred during adolescence.

Self-Report of Child Molesters

The work of Abel and his colleagues[1] has helped illuminate the enormous effect that sexual abusers have had on their young victims. Abel's group conducted structured clinical interviews with over 400 nonincarcerated child molesters to determine the onset and frequency of the subjects' sex offenses. Working under a federal contract, the researchers were protected by a government certificate of confidentiality that exempted them from the requirements of reporting patients for sexual crimes. Because of this exemption, the research findings have been highly regarded; it is believed that these results were not biased by the child molester's fear of legal repercussions. However, Abel et al.'s findings have not yet been replicated or confirmed independently.

Abel and his colleagues[1] concluded that child molesters come from every segment of society, appearing in representative numbers in every religious, ethnic, educational, and socioeconomic group.

They regard as their most impressive finding the astoundingly high frequency of paraphilic acts committed by the sex offenders. To sum up their findings, both the number of victims and the total number of molestations must be taken into account. The molesters who targeted boys outside the home had a surprisingly high number of victims (150.2) compared with those who molested girls outside the home (19.8), with those who molested boys inside the home

(1.7), or with those who molested girls inside the home (1.8). The mean number of pedophilic acts per offender disclosed by the nonincarcerated sex offenders in their study reflected the greater frequency of offenses committed by those child molesters who targeted boys outside the home: nonincest male targets—281.7; nonincest female targets—23.2; incest male targets—62.3; and incest female targets—81.3. Based on these figures, Abel and his group recommended that treatment efforts be directed at those child molesters who target boys outside the home when only limited evaluation and treatment resources are available. Treatment of this group of molesters, they reasoned, would result in the greatest reduction in child molestations.

MYTHS AND REALITIES

The general public and many professionals have subscribed to a number of myths and misconceptions about child molesters. The child molester is often imagined to be a stranger, a dirty old man, a crazy man, a retardate, an alcoholic, a drug addict, a brutal sex fiend, or someone predisposed to antisocial behavior. Although it is quite clear that case examples support each of these types, these cases prove to be the exception rather than the rule.

The research results of Abel and his associates[1] show that nonincarcerated sex offenders come from every socioeconomic stratum and are usually well educated. Their potentially deviant interests and fantasies have surfaced by 12 or 13 years of age. According to Lanyon's assessment, "the child molester is most commonly a respectable, otherwise law-abiding person, who may escape detection for exactly that reason"[8] (p. 177). Although many myths remain that blur the vision of clinicians, much of the information that they learned during their training years has been questioned, reexamined, and in large part, altered.

SCOPE OF THE PROBLEM

Treating child molestation as solely a symptom to be cured by incarceration becomes impossible in light of the following study. A report[10] given in 1984 on treatment programs for sex offenders in the State of Florida noted that although 6,039 persons were arrested for sexual abuse, well over 10,000 sex offenses were actually reported in Florida during 1982. Only 10.1% (612) of the total number arrested for sexual abuse were sentenced to prison that year; 9% (545) were merely placed on probation. The criminal justice system is also increasingly mandating that all types of sex offenses, including child sexual abuse, be treated in clinical settings on an outpatient basis. The fact remains that most of these sex offenders are not in the prison system. They are living in the community, and are free to continue committing sex offenses.

Clinicians in the public health community must recognize that victim treatment is needed not only to reduce psychological trauma, but also to provide preventative intervention. Overwhelming evidence indicates that some child sexual abuse victims continue to act out this victimization in adult life as abusers. As many as 50%–60% of incarcerated sex offenders have reported that they themselves were victims of sexual abuse as children.[7]

DEFINITION OF CHILD MOLESTATION

Although a variety of definitions for child molestation have been offered, no single definition is universally accepted. Because of the varying manifestations and purported causes of child sexual abuse, and because of the divergent viewpoints among investigators of child molestation, it seems unlikely that any one definition will ever be endorsed completely by everyone interested in child sexual abuse. However, there is enough agreement among those involved in the clinical and legal aspects of child sexual abuse to support the accuracy of the following broad definition: child molesters can be defined as "older persons whose conscious sexual desires and responses are directed, at least in part, toward dependent, developmentally immature children and adolescents who do not fully comprehend these actions and are unable to give informed consent"[8] (p. 176). Typically, child molestation is associated with seriously risking the child's well-being and further psychological, moral, and/or social development.

Although some practitioners in the field have limited their definition of child molesters to those who only direct their sexual desires and behavior toward prepubertal children, others have included both prepubertal and postpubertal children in their definition. Some definitions require that a child molester's total sexual interest be directed toward children, while others require that any sexual contact with, or interest in, the child, however transitory, be viewed as child sexual abuse.

The Council on Scientific Affairs of the American Medical Association has recommended that child sexual abuse be defined as the sexual "exploitation of a child for the gratification or profit of an adult"[5] (p. 798), noting that child sexual abuse often does not involve sexual intercourse or physical force. According to the Council, sexual abuse ranges from exhibitionism and fondling, to intercourse or use of a child in the production of pornography.

One other distinction is also worth noting: not only is there disagreement among the myriad definitions of *child molestation*, but the term *pedophilia* also adds confusion. Frequently, *pedophilia*, which literally means *love of children*, is equated synonymously, but erroneously, with child sexual abuse. Whereas *pedophile* and *pedophiliac* imply that a mental disorder is present in the individual, *child molester* refers to the perpetrator of a more general sexual maltreatment of children and does not connote that a mental illness exists. According to one diagnostic definition, pedophilia exists if there are "sexual deviations in which an adult engages in sexual activity with a child of the same or opposite sex"[14] (p. 196). A more delineated definition specifies the following criteria:

A. Over a period of at least six months, recurrent intense sexual urges and sexually arousing fantasies involving sexual activity with a prepubescent child or children (generally age 13 or younger).
B. The person has acted on these urges, or is markedly distressed by them.
C. The person is at least 16 years old and at least 5 years older than the child or children in A.[3] (p. 285)

According to the new revision of DSM-III,[3] a person meeting these criteria may be considered a pedophile. In short, pedophilia is a mental disorder that can be subsumed under the term *child molester*—all pedophiles are child molesters, but not all child molesters are diagnostically viewed as pedophiles.

Child molestation has immense social, psychological, and forensic consequences. It is a long-standing problem, as is made evident in the next chapter.

REFERENCES

1. Abel, G. G., Becker, J. V., Mittelman, M., Cunningham-Rathner, J., Rouleau, J. L., & Murphy, W. D. (1987). Self-reported sex crimes of nonincarcerated paraphiliacs. *Journal of Interpersonal Violence, 2*, 3.

2. American Humane Association (1987). Children's Divsion, 9725 E. Hampden Avenue, Denver, Colorado 80231 (personal communication.)
3. American Psychiatric Association (1987). *Diagnostic and Statistical Manual of Mental Disorders, Third Edition, Revised (DSM-III-R)*. Washington, D. C.: American Psychiatric Association.
4. Baker, A. W., & Duncan, S. P. (1985). Child sexual abuse: A study of prevalence in Great Britain. *Child Abuse & Neglect, 9*, 457.
5. Council on Scientific Affairs of the American Medical Association (1985). AMA diagnostic and treatment guidelines concerning child abuse and neglect. *Journal of the American Medical Association, 254*, 796.
6. Finkel, K. C. (1987). Sexual abuse of children: An update. *Canadian Medical Association Journal, 136*, 245.
7. Finkelhor, D. (1984). *Child Sexual Abuse: New Theory and Research.* New York: Free Press.
8. Lanyon, R. I. (1986). Theory and treatment in child molestation. *Journal of Consulting & Clinical Psychology, 54*, 176.
9. Moore, D. S. (1984). A literature review on sexual abuse research. *Journal of Nurse-Midwifery, 29*, 395.
10. Moore, H. A., & Zusman, J. (1984). *Report on Sex Offenders and Their Victims: Summary and Recommendations in Conjunction with the Governor's Task Force on Sex Offenders and Their Victims.* Tampa: Florida Mental Health Institute.
11. Mrazek, P. J., Lynch, M. A., & Bentovim, A. (1983). Sexual abuse of children in the United Kingdom. *Child Abuse and Neglect, 7*, 147.
12. Russell, D. E. H. (1983). The incidence and prevalence of intrafamilial and extrafamilial sexual abuse of female children. *Child Abuse & Neglect, 7*, 133.
13. Russell, D. E. H. (1986). *The Secret Trauma.* New York: Basic Books.
14. World Health Organization (1977). Section V—Mental Disorders. *International Statistical Classification of Diseases, Injuries, and Causes of Death, 9th Revision.* Geneva: World Health Organization.
15. Wyatt, G. E. (1985). The sexual abuse of Afro-American and White-American women in childhood. *Child Abuse & Neglect, 9*, 507.
16. Wyatt, G. E., & Peters, S. D. (1986). Issues in the definition of child sexual abuse in prevalence research. *Child Abuse & Neglect, 10*, 231.

CHAPTER 2
Historical
Perspectives

Recently, a number of disturbing cases of incest within middle-class suburban families have been dramatized in television documentaries. Several politicians and celebrities have also openly acknowledged that they were sexually abused as children. Not only has the press sensationalized incidents of child sexual abuse allegedly committed by staff members in various day-care centers, but there has been a provocative trend in many school systems to educate children about the prevention of sexual violation by older persons. All of this current controversy reflects an important shift in consciousness: people are beginning to recognize that child molestation is not a crime restricted to the ghetto; it is a form of victimization that can and does occur "right next door" by apparently affluent, well-educated, and, often, well-respected individuals in the community.

From a modern-day perspective, child sexual abuse is a deeply rooted problem that has been around for centuries[6] and is only now coming out in the open.[14] However, child molestation has not always rallied such publicity and alarm. For instance, abuse of children—including castration and infanticide—was common from antiquity until the fourth century A.D.[6,14] Likewise, sexuality between an adult male and a young boy held a very different significance in ancient Greece.[8,16] Viewing such an act as "deviant behavior" is an attitude colored by our contemporary value system.

ANTIQUITY

The sexual *use* of children in ancient Greece and Rome was an accepted practice.[6,8,16] Despite the use of children as sexual objects, Licht,[21] the noted historian of sexual manifestations in Greece, pointed out that sexual abuse and sexual perversions were actually rare in this ancient culture. In ancient Greece, pederasty, or anal intercourse, was a central factor in the upbringing of boys. It had a deeply religious significance and was regarded as a normal precursor to marriage.[9] Typically, an older male mentor assumed responsibility for the behavior and upbringing of a young male noble. This bond was formal and carried with it the blessings of the parents, the Greek city state, and their religious institutions. The Greeks believed that pederasty empowered the youth with the mentor's masculine qualities; it was thought that the young passive recipient would "take in" the older male's essence. When the youth reached puberty and developed secondary sexual characteristics, this homosexual relationship was terminated. He was then expected to marry and have children. Thereafter, homosexuality with grown men was proscribed.

Similarly, in ancient Rome, homosexuality between an older male and a young boy was not considered to be a sexual perversion, nor did it connote antisocial behavior. At that time, the code of sexual ethics allowed young boys, as well as girls and women, to be violated, raped, and sold in prostitution and slavery. Boys were castrated as preparation for the popular brothel because, according to the belief of that period, intercourse with castrated youngsters was especially arousing.[6,14]

The roots of the Judeo-Christian tradition have historically influenced sexual attitudes. The social climate on which the Judeo-Christian tradition is predicated was accepting of sexual contact between men and young girls. Brown[6] succinctly states the law of sexual validity and implies the rationalizations that early child molesters used to justify their actions and the punishment they faced:

During the time that the Bible and Talmud came into being, sex between men and very young girls in marriage, concubinage, and slavery was condoned. . . . The Talmud states that a female child of "three years and one day" could be betrothed by sexual intercourse with her father's permission. If she was subjected to intercourse prior to three years and one day, it was considered to be of no consequence. The reason for the invalidity of this act was that another law stated that a female under three years and one day was too immature to have sexual validity and therefore had no virginity to lose. However, once she reached the age of three and one day, she would "recover her virginity and be like other virgins." . . . One way to try and understand this lack of concern for the female child is to remember that she was considered to be property that had monetary value; she had no human attributes or qualities. The law of sexual validity also applied to boys, except the age was nine. A similar concept concerning sexual validity stated that children were totally innocent of all notions of pleasure and pain. This concept thus allowed those who were molesting children to use this as a defense against admitting that their abuse was harming the child and to allow them to continue with their business. (pp. 23–24)

THE MIDDLE AGES AND RENAISSANCE

With the spread of Christianity, child-rearing practices and attitudes gradually changed. During the Middle Ages "the child had no special status. . ."[14] (p. 11). Sexual use of children extended into the Renaissance period. For example, upper-class Europeans had the freedom to sexually exploit servant girls and young chambermaids well into the nineteenth century.[6]

Laws prohibiting physical and sexual abuse of children slowly emerged with the influence of Christian doctrine, which became extremely punitive, and the Renaissance moralists. Greenland[13] reports that criminal laws prohibiting sexual intercourse with girls under a certain age have existed for over 700 years in Great Britain. However, since children were considered property, the laws generally were not enforced.[6] More often than not, the victim was considered to be in the wrong and the child molester went unpunished.

At the close of the Renaissance period, adults began to empathize with children, who were considered to be separate, emotional beings. As attitudes changed toward the sexual use (now abuse) of children, the need for classification, treatment, and legal intervention arose.

NINETEENTH-CENTURY THOUGHT

Krafft-Ebing

The first orthodox medical textbook on psychosexual disorders, *Psychopathia Sexualis*,[15] was published by Krafft-Ebing, a German contemporary of Kraepelin and Freud. During the 19th century, Krafft-Ebing was a major contributor to the understanding of psychopathology; however, to modern readers he is usually associated with his writings about sexual deviation. It was Krafft-Ebing who coined the terms *sadism* and *masochism*. To understand the extent of respect that this author received among his contemporaries, it is worth noting that not until Sigmund Freud received the support and recommendation of Krafft-Ebing, who was then a prominent Professor of Psychiatry in Vienna, did the famous Freud become elected as Professor of Psychiatry there, too.[25]

During the compilation of several revisions of *Psychopathia Sexualia*,[19] Krafft-Ebing collected, classified, and presented all his available data on sexual disorders. Krafft-Ebing classified *Paedophilia Erotica*, or "unchastity with individuals under the age of 14," in a special Pathology section, which contained the most serious sexual deviations that brought patients into conflict with legal authorities.[15] Although he discussed *Paedophilia Erotica* in the forensic section of the book, Krafft-Ebing ranked it among his sexual *Paradoxies*—what he referred to as deviant sexual impulses that appear in childhood and/or advanced age.

Krafft-Ebing noted that acts of pedophilia could be committed by persons who otherwise had a normal sex life, and that even individuals with very strong pedophilic tendencies often did not act on these sexual urges. However, according to Krafft-Ebing, in the strictest sense *Paedophile Pervertee* refers to an individual who is *only* stimulated by sexual intercourse with children; to be a fully classified pedophile the individual must not feel any sexual attraction toward adults.

The implications inherent in Krafft-Ebing's distinction are important. Based on the broad and widely accepted definition of child molestation endorsed earlier in Chapter 1, only a portion—perhaps 30%-40%—of the child sexual abusers currently designated as molesters would be classified under Krafft-Ebing's *Paedophile Pervertee*.

Nearly one hundred years ago, Krafft-Ebing noted the same difficulty in documenting the frequency and distribution of pedophilia that researchers involved in methodological issues struggle with today; the problem has always been in defining the boundaries of sexual deviation. Krafft-Ebing did observe, however, that the use of children to gratify sexual impulses had a surprisingly frequent occurrence. He also noted that the sexual predispositions of pedophiles varied from case to case. According to Krafft-Ebing, among these various manifestations one male pedophile might express his deviancy by persuading a child to participate in masturbatory manipulations, whereas another might merely press his erect penis against a child to have genital contact with the child's body. He noted that female pedophiles generally tended to seduce small boys, and less frequently small girls, into cunnilingus; however, it was by no means exceptional for an 8–to–10-year-old boy to be seduced into performing sexual intercourse.

Krafft-Ebing perceived no single cause why *Paedophilia Erotica* emerged.[15] He believed that impotence or sexual anxiety are two factors that prompted a man to choose children as his sexual targets and that the sexual pressure to perform with an adult female was alleviated by interacting with children. He noted that external factors such as lacking an attractive appearance or possessing bodily infirmities could play a part in individual cases. He also believed that an individual who came into frequent contact with children, particularly in the course of earning a livelihood (e.g., someone in the teaching profession), had a higher risk of becoming a pedophile.

Krafft-Ebing's observations[15] that *Paedophilia Erotica* appeared in conjunction with other perversions—most notably sadism, exhibitionism, or homosexuality—has recently been confirmed by Abel and his colleagues. In Abel's sample of child molesters,[1] many displayed additional deviant behaviors. For instance, Abel noted that 29.7% of these child molesters exposed themselves to both child and adult victims; 16.8% had raped adults; 13.8% engaged in voyeurism (peeping behavior); and 8.6% admitted to frottage (touching and rubbing against another person).

Krafft-Ebing recorded a number of individual case histories of *Paedophilia Erotica.* The following case report[15] summarizes a male pedophile's predisposition toward young girls:

Man cursed by heredity; since puberty, which set in late (at 24), sensual feelings for 5–10 year old girls. At the very sight of such girls he may already begin ejaculation while on touching them he experiences a formal sexual affect with only summary memory for the course thereof. Patient had been tolerably satisfied by marital sex congress and was able to master his urge towards young girls, until severe neurasthenia gained the upper hand over him and drove him into criminal courses. (p. 90)

Another summary[15] highlights the case of a female pedophile who felt impelled to have sexual relations with her young nephew:

29 years old, cursed by heredity, a lady the prey of phobias and fixed ideas. Suffered for 8 years with a violent impulsion to sexual congress with one of her nephews. Her desire was principally concentrated on the eldest, when he was about 5 years old, and was transferred at times to the younger as he grew up. The sight of the child in question sufficed to provoke an orgasm. She succeeded however in withstanding this to her inexplicable impulse. She had no taste at all for adults. (pp. 90–91)

In general, Krafft-Ebing believed that the treatment of psychosexual disorders was difficult, worrisome, and frequently unsuccessful. For Krafft-Ebing, the most effective treatment of pedophilia was simply to eliminate all contact that the potential child molester had with young persons, noting that it was particularly important that the child molester not be employed in professions involving contact with children.

Havelock Ellis

At the turn of the century the famous sexologist, Havelock Ellis, argued that *Paedophilia,* or "the sexual love of children," was not a separate deviation at all, but could be sustained under classification called the "parts of the body." He included pedophilia with such abnormalities as lameness, squinting, pitting of small pox, *Presbyophilia, Necrophilia,* and *Zoophilia.*[9] Ellis conceded that medicolegally it would be convenient to regard pedophilia as a separate deviation. However, he pointed out that there was no "congenital" basis for an individual to feel exclusive sexual attraction toward unripe children. According to Ellis, pedophilia was often associated with the impotence of senility, noting also that it occasionally occurred as a luxurious specialty of a few overly refined persons. He believed, however, that pedophilia was more commonly a general, indiscriminating sexual tendency among those who possessed weak minds.

Sigmund Freud

Like Krafft-Ebing, Sigmund Freud also speculated on the nature of pedophilia. In *Studies on Hysteria,*[5] which Freud wrote with Breuer, child sexual trauma was cited to explain the origin of the symptoms of hysteria. In "Aetiology of Hysteria"[11] Freud further stated: "I therefore put forward the thesis that at the bottom of every case of hysteria there are *one or more occurrences of pre-*

mature sexual experience, occurrences which belong to the earliest years of childhood . . ." (p. 203). Because of the strong sexual taboos and the Victorian emphasis on "family" as a sacred institution, Freud's attempt to expose acts of child molestation among parents was considered extremely radical.[22,24,26] His revolutionary theory aroused a great deal of controversy and objection among many of his colleagues, teachers, and patients.[22] After several attempts to respond to the barrage of criticism, Freud eventually abandoned this theory.

However, it is believed that a dream at the time of his own father's death caused Freud to discount the validity of recollections of child sexual abuse and prompted him to perceive such stories as fantasy.[25,26] By the mid-1920s Freud had changed his emphasis from infantile sexual trauma to infantile sexual fantasies. In 1924, in a footnote to the 1896 paper, "Further Remarks on the Neuro-Psychoses of Defence,"[11] he stated the following:

> This section is dominated by an error which I have since repeatedly acknowledged and corrected. At that time I was not yet able to distinguish between my patients' phantasies about their childhood years and their real recollections. As a result, I attributed to the aetiological factor of seduction a significance and universality which it does not possess. (p. 168)

The importance of this shift cannot be denied. In so doing, Freud arrived at his psychodynamic understanding of neuroses. However, as a result of this retraction many psychoanalysts abandoned the distinction between real versus fantasized traumatic events, and subsequently the primary focus in psychoanalysis became sexual fantasies.

RECENT DEVELOPMENTS

Psychoanalytic Influence

In 1954, Karpman published the first book entirely devoted to sex offenders.[17] In his book, Karpman reviewed the classical psychoanalytic literature from Freud's time up to the early 1950s and reported several cases of pedophilia along with their psychodynamic interpretations. According to Karpman, there are two types of *Paedophiliacs:* the first group developed deviant behavior as a result of the trauma of weaning; the second group developed the perversion because of a strong identification with the mother and a rivalry with the father.

Unlike Ellis, who attributed the majority of cases of pedophilia to the condition of senility or persons with "weak" minds, Karpman noted that the increasing number of senile pedophiles merely corresponded with the increasing longevity of this age group. Although he recognized that other factors were involved, Karpman conceded, however, that sexual abuse was frequently caused by conditions external to any psychopathology—for example, many molesters were simply ignorant about sexuality. For instance, Karpman noted that many "ignorant people" believed that a sexual relationship with a female child could restore potency or cure venereal disease. Like Krafft-Ebing, he noted that these external factors merely combined with an aggressive sexual drive. Overall, he described young *Paedophiliacs* as frequently passive, immature, insensitive, and lacking in courage, which prevented them from establishing sexual contact with their peers.

However, Karpman noted that child molesters had some fundamental organic or functional psychopathological characteristics in common that prevented them from seeking sexual gratification with age-appropriate mates. Echoing Krafft-Ebing, Karpman contended that practically all child molesters were impotent or were particularly afflicted with anxiety in regard to their sexual potency.

Development as a Field of Study

In his historical survey of sexual psychopathology, Rada[23] discussed two events that have particularly influenced the study of sexuality: publication of Kinsey and colleagues' *Sexual Behavior in the Human Male*,[18] and the enactment of "sexual psychopath statutes in various states throughout the country"[23] (p. 4). Whereas Kinsey's book established the area of sexual behavior as a suitable field for research, the sexual psychopath law helped to identify sex offenders who were particularly dangerous and prone to repeating their sexual offenses, and to place them in institutions where they could receive appropriate treatment. Since the time of Rada's survey, the majority of states in the United States have instituted statutory regulations regarding sexual psychopathic behavior, and a number of large institutions have been established to study and rehabilitate sex offenders.

Since the advent of behaviorism in the 1950s, relatively atheoretical, behavioral approaches have been applied to sexual deviations. Generally, behaviorists make no assumptions about the cause of abnormal behavior, regarding treatability as purely a pragmatic matter. In contrast to psychoanalysts, learning theorists do not assume that a particular form of psychopathology underlies deviant sexual behavior. They recommend interventions to bring about symptomatic changes which depend primarily on developing adaptive sexual functioning and eliminating the deviant urges, thoughts, and feelings.

Psychoanalysts like Krafft-Ebing, Ellis, and Freud believed that "all sexual deviant behaviors are theoretically and etiologically similar and that they represent a single type of psychopathology"[20] (p. 176). Deviant behavior was best understood as a form of character disorder, a view referred to by several current researchers in the field.[7,23]

Given that the primary thrust of the 1960s was the attempt to delineate the hypothesized personality and character disorder associated with sex offenders, it is not surprising that the American Psychiatric Association's nomenclature (DSM-II)[2] classified several sexual deviations juxtaposed to personality (character) disorders. Pedophilia was among these. In the subsequent (DSM-III)[3] and current revision (DSM-III-R),[4] pedophilia, along with other sexual deviations, was moved from this section and included within the subgroups of psychosexual disorders. Pedophilia is currently listed as a paraphilia, a category of conditions in which sexual arousal consistently and preferentially is either (1) related to the use of a nonhuman object, (2) involves a real or simulated suffering or humiliation, or (3) depends upon nonconsenting partners. The shift in the classification of pedophilia from a personality disorder to a psychosexual disorder indicates the difficulty in universal classification of sexually deviant behavior, and reflects the uncertainty involved in determining appropriate treatment approaches.

Penile Plethysmograph

A premier advance over the past two decades has been the development of a physiological measure for sexual arousal. Plethysmography has been used by reputable investigators in psychosexual assessment laboratories in the United States and Canada since the pioneering work of Freund in the 1960s.[12] Recording the sex offender's erection responses to nondeviant and deviant stimuli represents a useful assessment and treatment monitoring device that enhances clinical evaluation of child molesters and rapists.

Objective physiological assessment of sexual arousal has stimulated research and enhanced the application of the behavioral

Table 2.1
DSM-III-R Diagnostic Criteria for 302.20 Pedophilia

A. Over a period of at least six months, recurrent intense sexual urges and sexually arousing fantasies involving sexual activity with a prepubescent child or children (generally age 13 or younger).
B. The person has acted on these urges, or is markedly distressed by them.
C. The person is at least 16 years old and at least 5 years older than the child or children in A.
   Note: Do not include a late adolescent involved in an ongoing sexual relationship with a 12- or 13-year-old.
Specify: same sex, opposite sex, or **same and opposite sex.**
Specify if limited to incest.
Specify: exclusive type (attracted only to children), or **nonexclusive type.**

Reprinted with permission from the *Diagnostic and Statistical Manual of Mental Disorders, Third Edition, Revised*, p. 285. Copyright 1987 American Psychiatric Association.

therapies to paraphilic disorders. However, it is not without its shortcomings. Although the penile plethysmograph is useful as an assessment instrument indicating deviant arousal patterns, it is not a truth serum, a fortune teller, or a crystal ball. Perhaps one of the most serious limitations on the use of the plethysmograph is the inhibitory response of the subject. Some individuals become anxious with the test and do not become aroused to any type of stimuli—deviant or nondeviant. Others do not want their deviant arousal patterns known and are successful in their attempt to avoid sexual arousal. This means that the examiner can remark only on the stimuli to which the subject has responded with arousal. Nothing can be said about the stimuli that produced or evoked no arousal response.

We are not aware of any research findings claiming that abnormal sexual arousal patterns alone are an accurate predictor of future sex offenses. Although these individuals may be at greater risk for committing sexual abuse or child molestation, deviant sexual arousal patterns cannot be used exclusively for predicting dangerousness or determining release from a prison or a treatment program.

Current Trends

In recent years child molestation has been viewed with increasing concern. Child molesters are seen to vary widely in terms of who they are and what they do. The emotional impact on the victim has become a major social issue.[10]

In Lanyon's recent review of the current understanding on child molestation,[20] he acknowledges that there has been an increase in available research literature describing child molesters and their treatment. Lanyon concludes that child molestation is not always based in character disorder and must be treated with this understanding. According to Lanyon, psychoanalytic psychotherapy has been a relatively unsuccessful treatment strategy, whereas behavior modalities have had a relatively high success rate and are gaining in popularity. He suggests that it is important to distinguish among the types of subcategories of sex abusers; for example, Lanyon recommends the family systems approach for incest offenders, although he cautions that adequate empirical data are not yet available.

In general, the medical, psychiatric, and psychological professions have been unduly slow in recognizing child molestation as an illness. Most clinicians have had little training in treating child molesters. As society—and clinicians—have begun to accept more fully their responsibilities toward child sexual abuse, change has come about. The last 10 years have led to a regrouping and reappraisal. The recognition of child molestation as a field worthy of study has yielded the development of new research, fresh treatment approaches, and specialized methods of assessment. This reassessment has brought a more realistic, integrated, and multifaceted comprehension of this complex condition.

REFERENCES

1. Abel, G. G. Mittelman, M. S., & Becker, J. (1985). Sexual offenders: Results of assessment and recommendations for treatment. In M. H. Ben-Aron, S. J. Hucker, & C. D. Webster (Eds.), *Clinical Criminology: Current Concepts.* Toronto: M & M Graphics.
2. American Psychiatric Association (1968). *Diagnostic and Statistical Manual of Mental Disorders, Second Edition (DSM-II).* Washington, D. C.: American Psychiatric Association.
3. American Psychiatric Association (1980). *Diagnostic and Statistical Manual of Mental Disorders, Third Edition (DSM-III).* Washington, D. C.: American Psychiatric Association.
4. American Psychiatric Association (1987). *Diagnostic and Statistical Manual of Mental Disorders, Third Edition, Revised (DSM-III-R).* Washington, D. C.: American Psychiatric Association.
5. Breuer, J., & Freud, S. (1955). Studies on hysteria (1893–1895). In J. Strachey (Ed.), *The Complete Psychological Works of Sigmund Freud, Vol II.* London: Hogarth Press.

6. Brown, N. (1985). Historical perspective on child abuse. In A. Downer (Ed.), *Prevention of Child Sexual Abuse: A Trainer's Manual*. Seattle, WA: Seattle Institute for Child Advocacy Committee for Children.
7. Burgess, A., Groth, A. N., Holmstrom, L., & Sgroi, S. (1978). *Sexual Assault of Children and Adolescents*. Lexington, MA: D. C. Heath.
8. Dickes, R. (1981). Historical and Cultural Perspectives. In R. C. Simons & H. Pardes (Eds.), *Understanding Human Behavior in Health and Illness*. Baltimore: Williams & Wilkins.
9. Ellis, H. (1933). *Psychology of Sex*. London: Pan Books Ltd.
10. Finkelhor, D. (1987). The sexual abuse of children: Current research reviewed. *Psychiatric Annals, 17*(4), 233.
11. Freud, S. (1955). Further remarks on the neuro-psychoses of defence. In J. Strachey (Ed.), *The Complete Psychological Works of Sigmund Freud, Vol. III*. London: Hogarth Press, pp. 162–185.
12. Freund, K. (1967). Diagnosing homo- or heterosexuality and erotic age-preference by means of a psychophysiological test. *Behavioral Research and Therapy, 5*, 339.
13. Greenland, C. (1983). Sex law reform in an international perspective: England, Wales and Canada. *Bulletin of the American Academy of Law and Psychiatry, 11*(4), 309.
14. Group for the Advancement of Psychiatry (1982). The history of child treatment in western culture. *The Process of Child Therapy*. New York: Brunner/Mazel, pp. 9–46.
15. Hartwich, A. (1959). *Aberrations of Sexual Life after the "Psychopathia Sexualis" of Dr. R. V. Krafft-Ebing* (translated by A. V. Burbury). London: Staples Press.
16. Jones, G. P. (1982). The social study of pederasty: In search of a literature base: an annotated bibliography of sources in English. *Journal of Homosexuality, 8*(1), 61–85.
17. Karpman, B. (1954). *The Sexual Offender and His Offenses: Aetiology, Pathology, Psychodynamics and Treatment*. New York: Julian Press.
18. Kinsey, A., Pomeroy, W., & Martin, C. (1948). *Sexual Behavior in the Human Male*. Philadelphia: Saunders.
19. Krafft-Ebing, R. V. (1901). *Psychopathia Sexualia . . . Eine Medicinisch-Gerichtiiche Studie*. Stuttgart: Ferdinand Enke.
20. Lanyon, R. I. (1986). Theory and treatment in child molestation. *Journal of Consulting & Clinical Psychology, 54*(2), 176.
21. Licht, H. (1931). *Sexual Life in Ancient Greece* (translated by J. H. Freese). London: Routledge.
22. Peters, J. J. (1976). Children who are victims of sexual assault and the psychology of offenders. *American Journal of Psychotherapy, 30*, 398.
23. Rada, R. T. (1978). Sexual psychopathology: Historical survey and basic concepts. In R. T. Rada (Ed.), *Clinical Aspects of the Rapists*. New York: Grune & Stratton.
24. Rome, H. P. (1987). Personal reflections: Child abuse as a psychosocial issue. *Psychiatric Annals, 17*(4), 225.
25. Stewart, R. L. (1985). Psychotherapies. In H. I. Kaplan & B. J. Sadock (Eds.), *Comprehensive Textbook of Psychiatry/IV, Vol. 2*. Baltimore: Williams & Wilkins, p. 1335.
26. William Alanson White Institute (1986). Incest—fact or fiction? New York: The William Alanson White Institute of Psychiatry, Psychoanalysis and Psychology.

CHAPTER 3
Etiology and Typology

ETIOLOGY

The etiological factors that relate to child molestations have been subject to wide speculation and controversy. Typically, various attempts to attribute child molestation to a single causative model have enjoyed enthusiastic but fleeting acceptance. However, research is currently making a directed effort to bring new understanding to the issue of what causes an individual to become sexually aroused by children. Most authorities now agree that there is no single cause, but a complicated interplay of organic, psychological, cultural, environmental, and sociological factors.

The following section presents some of the prevalent, if not controversial, theories on the origin and development of child molestation and includes some of the evidence for these explanations (see Table 3.1). Emphasis has been given, however, to those theories that are directly relevant to practicing clinicians. Before examining the etiology of aberrant sexual arousal, we offer a brief review of physiology of normal sexual response.

PHYSIOLOGY OF SEXUAL AROUSAL

Normal sexual arousal varies from person to person and is influenced by a combination of experiential, genetic, hormonal, and neurological factors. The normal sequence of sexual response in adult men and women—appetitive, excitement, orgasm, and resolution phases—involves physiological responses to sexual stimulation[3] (see Figure 3.1).

Table 3.1
Summary of Empirical Evidence for Explanations of Pedophilia

Theory	Evidence
Emotional congruence	
Children attractive because of lack of dominance	One positive study
Arrested development/immaturity	Some support from psychologic testing, but inferences are weak
Low self-esteem	Some support from psychologic testing, but inferences are weak
Mastery of trauma through repetition	Several studies show frequent histories of sexual abuse in offenders' backgrounds
Identification with aggression	Several studies show frequent histories of sexual abuse in offenders' backgrounds
Narcissism	Untested
Male socialization to dominance	Untested
Sexual arousal	
Heightened arousal to children	Clear experimental evidence, except for incest offenders
Conditioning from early childhood experience	Several studies show frequent histories of sexual abuse in offenders' backgrounds
Modeling from earlier childhood experiences	Several studies show frequent histories of sexual abuse in offenders' backgrounds
Hormonal abnormalities	Mixed evidence
Misattribution of arousal	Untested
Socialization through child pornography or advertising	Untested
Blockage	
Difficulty relating to adult females	Generally positive evidence
Inadequate social skills	Some support from uncontrolled studies
Sexual anxiety	Some support from uncontrolled studies
Unresolved oedipal dynamics	Family problems evident, but not necessarily the ones oedipal theory would predict
Disturbances in adult sexual romantic relationships	Suggestive evidence from uncontrolled studies

(continued)

Table 3.1 *(continued)*

Theory	Evidence
Repressive norms about sexual behavior	Suggested by two studies
Disinhibition	
Impulse disorder	True for some small group of offenders, but not for all
Senility	Negative
Mental retardation	Negative
Alcohol	Present in great many instances, exact role unclear
Failure of incest avoidance mechanism	Two studies show higher rates of abuse in stepfather families
Situational stress	Only anecdotal evidence
Cultural toleration	Untested
Patriarchal norms	Untested

From "Explanations of pedophilia: Review of empirical research," by S. Araji & D. Finkelhor (1985), *Bulletin of American Academy of Psychiatry & the Law, 13*, 19. Reprinted by permission.

Fantasies about sexual activity and a desire to have sexual as well as other forms of psychological stimulation constitute the *appetitive* phase of sexual response.[3] A complex interplay between prenatal and postnatal psychosexual development, state of mind, attitude toward sexuality, and biological factors (e.g., higher cortical central nervous system functions, chemical messengers, genetic predisposition) mediates the appetitive phase.[36,44]

The *excitement* phase consists of the feelings of pleasure associated with sexual activity and the accompanying physiological changes.[3] Psychological stimulation (appetitive influence, pornography, or presence of desired object) and physiological stimulation (stroking, kissing, caressing) bring on the excitement phase. This phase is characterized by penile tumescence and erection in the male and vaginal lubrication, breast changes and hardening of the clitoris in the female.[36]

Orgasm is a subjective sense of the peaking of sexual pleasure, release of tension, and contractions of involved muscles and organs.[3] A slight clouding of consciousness is associated with orgasm. The peripheral nervous system mediates much of this phase.[36] For example, in men the parasympathetic system activates the process

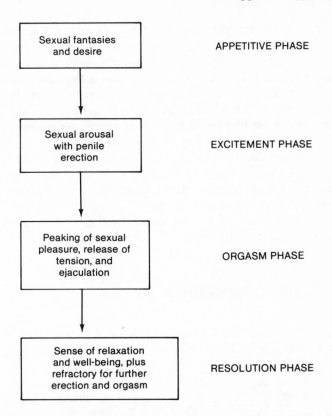

Figure 3.1. The four phases of the complete sexual cycle for males.

of erection via the pelvic splanchnic nerves. Ejaculation occurs through the sympathetic nervous system's hypogastric plexus.

In the *resolution* phase, a sense of general relaxation is accompanied by emotional well-being and muscular relaxation.[3] Unlike women during this phase, men have a refractory period for which they are physiologically unable to produce further erection or orgasm. This refractory period is capitalized on by several treatment strategies presented later.

The normal sexual response cycle is a true psychophysiological experience influenced by a large array of incompletely understood forces. The first three phases seem to be influenced by neurotransmitters, such as monoamines, like norepinephrine and dopamine.[14,44] All of these phases are mediated, at least in part, by brain structures that have extensive frontal lobe and limbic connections.[44]

The base of the frontal lobe interconnects with the thalamus, hypothalamus, and other parts of the limbic system.[14,44] The hypothalamus converts impulses from higher cortical areas into endocrine or hormonal responses. Appetitive stimulation under certain conditions causes the hypothalamus to release luteinizing hormone-releasing hormone (LHRH), which stimulates the anterior pituitary gland to secrete luteinizing hormone (LH) and follicular stimulation hormone (FSH).[14] These chemical messengers, LH and FSH, are associated with an increased release of testosterone from the male testis. Testosterone is the most important hormone in the maintenance of, and the determining factor in, male sexual behavior.[14]

A feedback system controls the release of these hormones, which comprise the hypothalamic-pituitary-gonadal axis. Testosterone inhibits or produces a negative feedback effect on the release of LHRH and the pituitary's response to LHRH.[14] In short, an ample amount of testosterone turns off the system that would produce more testosterone (see Figure 3.2).

ORGANIC OR PHYSIOLOGICAL FACTORS

For nearly one hundred years, it was thought that organic factors played a causative role in child molestation. In Chapter 2, several

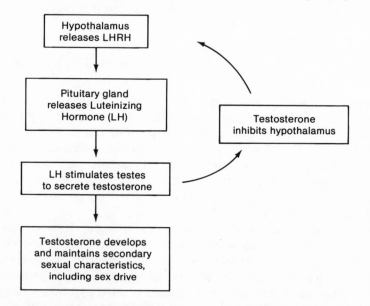

Figure 3.2. Negative feedback mechanism operating between the hypothalamus, pituitary gland, and testes controlling the release and level of testosterone.

of the earlier hypotheses that related pedophilia to organic origins were discussed. Krafft-Ebing[37] noted that pedophilia was commonly the result of a child molester's hypersexuality, whereas Havelock Ellis[20] observed that child molestation arose from debilitating mental diseases (e.g., senile dementia). Ellis further believed that the lowered intellectual abilities found in mental retardation contributed to child-molesting behavior. In each of these cases, it was felt that an organic impairment decreased the individual's ability to assess a situation and to use good judgment.

Although the oversimplified hypotheses of Krafft-Ebing and Ellis have long been discounted, a number of other theories that focus on neurological, endocrine, and genetic factors have related child molestation to various physiological or organic causes. Here are several of the most common hypotheses that are currently proposed.

Neural Mechanisms

Our understanding of the neurological basis for sexual preference is limited and largely based on animal studies.[54] Unfortunately, animal studies are not necessarily applicable to humans. Berlin[10] mentioned several animal studies which seem to have some bearing on human sexuality.

Miller and his colleagues[44] described eight cases of hypersexuality or altered sexual preference following brain injury. One patient presented with pedophilia (i.e., repeated sexual proposals toward his seven-year-old daughter and public sexual advances toward other youngsters) and impotence. He had a dramatic shift from heterosexual orientation to "an almost single-minded preoccupation with children." This change was associated with a tumor (infiltrating glioma) of the midbrain-hypothalamic region. Miller and his group[44] suspect that this hypothalamic lesion contributed to the altered sexual object choice.

The observation by Lilly et al.[40] that bilateral temporal lobe dysfunction (i.e., the human Klüver-Bucy Syndrome) is associated with altered sexual orientation was supported by the Miller et al. report.[44] They concluded that specific sexual changes may be produced by brain damage and that paraphilic behavior may be the first manifestation of brain injury. Specifically, lesions of the limbic system—dysfunction of the hypothalamus and temporal lobe—are associated with altered sexual orientation. Hypersexual behavior is associated with basal frontal or diencephalic injury. In the past, child-molesting behavior has been associated with seizure disorders, postencephalitic parkinsonism, suprasellar meningiomas, and postanoxic encephalopathy.[44] Further support for brain dysfunction leading to child sexual abuse is provided by Henn, Herjanic, and Vanderpearl.[33] These researchers documented "organic psychosyndromes" in 14.4% and mental retardation in 13.5% of 111 child molesters who had been arrested.

In addition to structural lesions of the brain, alterations in neurotransmitters may affect sexual behavior.[14,44] For instance, increased dopamine may be involved in sexual preference and increased libido.[44] According to Bradford,[14] the effect of neurotransmitters supports the belief that sexual behavior is dependent on male hormones. The neurochemistry of aggressive sexual behavior is complex. Multiple neurotransmitters and peptides are possibly involved in increasing or diminishing the frequency and intensity of sexual offenses. Despite recent discoveries in neurochemistry and neuroanatomy, our understanding is far from complete.

Endocrine Factors

In the past decade, the study of sexual arousal patterns has related specific erotic stimuli to physiological sexual responses.[7] Although this research has provided useful information, it has also left many unanswered questions. For instance, most researchers who study sexual arousal patterns gear their procedures toward determining the age and gender preference of child molesters (see, e.g., reference 24, 49); the main thrust has not been in assessing whether or not child molestation is a physiological aberration.

Despite this lack of emphasis, several recent studies have implicated endocrine abnormalities as a potential etiological factor. In addition to such elements as structural brain damage, genetic anomalies, and epileptic disturbances,[10] child molestation has also been linked to such endocrine abnormalities as hypogonadism and hypergonadism.[14] It is known that testosterone regulates normal male sexual arousal and that a clear relationship exists between testosterone level and male sexual development and behavior. Because of the complex interplay of hormones like testosterone in sexual functioning, researchers began to investigate whether differences, even subtle ones, occur in a child molester's hormonal patterns. Although the few studies that have been done show that there is little evidence to support that plasma testosterone levels are invariably altered in perpetrators of child sexual abuse,[25,50] several studies have suggested that testosterone levels, if either too low or too high, may be a causative factor.

A study by Rada, Laws and Kellner[50] indicated that the plasma testosterone levels in child molesters fall within the normal limits, albeit at a *lower mean level* than normal controls or rapists. In a separate study by Gurnani and Dwyer,[32] preexisting data for testosterone levels in 23 outpatient pedophiles and incest offenders and 16 control subjects were examined. Controlling for age, stress, alcohol, and medication, Gurnani and Dwyer found that serum testosterone levels in child molesters were *significantly lower* than the control group. Gurnani and Dwyer inferred that hyposexuality may be a critical factor in identifying some child sex offenders.

However, a study by a group of researchers headed by Schiavi[54] approached the relevance of testosterone level from a slightly different perspective. They selected 4,591 men at least 184 cm in height who represented the top 15.9% of the height distribution of the original sample (all men born in Copenhagen during the period 1944 to 1947). Out of these 4,591 men, they found 12 XYY and 16 XXY men with ages ranging from 26 to 31 years. All the XYY and 14 of the XXY men were individually matched with a control. Fifteen subjects (five from the XYY group, two from the XXY group and eight from the control groups) having a history of criminal convictions had testosterone levels significantly higher than those without any convictions. The authors concluded that a significant positive relationship exists among XY controls as well as all subjects between plasma testosterone level and criminal convictions.

Although most endocrinological approaches have focused on assessing testosterone levels,[50] a recent investigation by Gaffney and Berlin[25] compared endocrine studies by infusing subjects with luteinizing hormone-releasing hormone (LHRH). Three groups of men were included in the study: men with pedophilia, men with nonpedophilic paraphilias, and normal male controls. The pedophile group showed a much higher elevation of luteinizing hormone in response to LHRH than did the other two groups. After analyzing the data, the authors concluded that a hypothalamic-pituitary-gonadal dysfunction exists in some pedophiles. Although the significance of a link between plasma testosterone levels and child molestation remains controversial, the Gaffney and Berlin study suggests that seeking to identify specific biological markers to ascertain sexual orientation may be of use in identifying child molesters.

Genetic Factors

Proponents of the theory that child molestation is caused by genetic abnormalities make the observation that pedophilia seems to occur in certain families; this inclination leads them to believe that there may be an inherited *tendency toward* pedophilia. They further support their hypothesis by citing the increased incidence of pedophilia among patients with Klinefelter's Syndrome, a sex chromosome abnormality manifesting as the 47XXY genotype.[10,14] This syndrome surfaces as specific clinical features in patients, which include small testicular development, hypogonadism, infertility, a tall physical structure, gynecomastia, personality dysfunction, and commonly, intellectual impairment. Hypothalamic abnormalities as well as low plasma testosterone levels and raised LH and FSH levels[10,14] have also been documented in this group. This hormonal profile is similar to postmenopausal females.[10] The predisposition of individuals with Klinefelter's Syndrome toward specific characteristics and hormonal abnormalities suggest that their child-molesting behavior is also genetically transmitted. However, this correlation alone is not conclusive proof that genetic factors are responsible for all child-molesting behavior.

PSYCHOLOGICAL FACTORS

Although it is generally agreed that a psychological basis contributes to the development of child-molesting behavior, attempts to define these psychopathological factors are hindered by the fact that most child abusers are evaluated only after becoming involved with the judicial system. By the time of the evaluation, their sexual abuse of children may have been a chronic pattern, occurring over a long period of time. This duration makes it extremely difficult to isolate specific developmental factors. The problem of assessing the psychopathological development is further complicated by the evaluator's inability to distinguish whether the current psychological functioning of the molester is related to the child-molesting behavior or to pressures that arise from incarceration and/or criminal charges. Despite these limitations, two theories in particular have offered important insight into the pathogenesis of child sexual abuse. In practice, there is generally some overlap between psychodynamic and learning theory disciplines; however, here is a brief distillation of each approach.

Psychodynamic Factors

Although there are many variations in the basic theme, according to the classical psychodynamic orientation all sexually deviant behavior is considered both as being etiologically similar and as having the same psychopathology.[39] Based on this viewpoint, sexually deviant behavior is believed to be caused by early emotional, physical and/or sexual trauma, the impact of which is so devastating that it subsequently results in emotional immaturity or an arrest in development.[31,57] Because of this developmental arrest, as the individual grows older he begins to rely on children as sex objects to relieve sexual anxiety, feelings of low self-esteem, and family problems.[30,38] The molesting behavior is then reinforced through repeated child molestations and becomes habitual, during which time the molester experiences a decrease in his intrapsychic discomfort. However, this reliance on children as sexual targets reflects much deeper and usually unrecognized patterns of character pathology. It is believed that the level of psychological adjustment or ego functioning prior to the particular trauma that initiated the molesting behavior is related to the severity of the character pathology. A defective superego or impaired moral conscience is also considered a precondition for an individual who sexually abuses children.[27]

Early analysts, including Sigmund Freud, presented the thesis that perversions like child molestation resulted when infantile sexual impulses, not transformed during puberty, continued into adult life.[27,57] However, believing that the perverted behavior arose from unresolved oedipal dynamics, Freud stressed that perversions were not simply the manifestations of infantile sexual impulses surfacing from the *id*, but were the result of defense mechanisms arising from the *ego*.[55] The gratification obtained from molesting children represented an escape from reality.

Subsequent observations have noted that there is frequently a history of sexual abuse in a child molester's background.[7] This consideration has helped to substantiate the theory that a molester's habitual sexual abuse of children is a repeated and unsuccessful attempt to master his own early sexual trauma through a reenactment of the cruel experiences; unable to overcome the anxiety, guilt, and pain of his childhood trauma, the molester identifies with the aggressor in order to project or displace the original conflict onto another victim. Repetition of the molesting behavior occurs when the abuser not only fails to resolve his internal conflict, but feeds the fire of the conflict by duplicating the circumstances of the original trauma.

Bliss and Larson[11,12] hypothesized that early physical, sexual, or psychological abuse could lead to a dissociated state or "spontaneous self-hypnosis" that works with other factors to facilitate sexual assaults. Their group of 33 sex offenders, which included nine pedophiles and six incest offenders, had very high hypnotizability scores.

Child Molesting as a Learned Response

It would be impossible to cover in any great depth all that has been written on learning theories—whole books are devoted to the topic. However, for the purpose of relating what is known about learning to child molestation, it is necessary to address the two basic types of conditioning posed by learning theorists: classical conditioning and operant conditioning.

Classical conditioning, which describes procedures developed by the Russian physiologist Pavlov, refers to training in which one stimulus comes to substitute for another in evoking a response. In classical conditioning, a formerly neutral stimulus (the conditioned stimulus) comes to elicit a response (conditioned response) that initially was produced only by an innate, biological stimulus (unconditioned stimulus).

A typical example of classical conditioning with humans is the excitement phase of the sexual response. Stroking or kissing the penis will automatically elicit penile tumescence; here, obviously, is the unconditioned stimulus—unconditioned response sequence. If the physical caressing is paired with the sight, sound, or presence of prepubertal children over a series of presentations, the sight and sound of children will come to elicit the erection and sexual excitement.

Operant, or instrumental, conditioning views behavior as being dependent upon its consequences. This view has held a central position in the psychology of learning since the work of Thorndike and, more recently, B. F. Skinner.

According to operant conditioning, a reinforcer is any event which, when occurring in close temporal relationship to a response, increases the likelihood that the response will be repeated in the future. Positive reinforcers are any event that strengthens a response when it is presented. Thus, food, candy, positive feeling states, and orgasm are said to be positive reinforcers if their presentation following a response tends to affirm or strengthen that response. For example, a child molester who has not had many affirmative experiences in his life may experience a positive feeling state through sexual contact with a child; this feeling both reinforces the molesting behavior and increases the possibility of its occurring in the future. From another angle, a child who has had sexual experiences that were pleasurable (e.g., with someone his own age) may seek similar sexual contact with this same age group in order to continue experiencing that initial pleasure, even as he grows older. In this instance, the pleasure of the sexual contact acts as a positive reinforcer or as a conditioning force that promotes continued molesting behavior.

A study by McGuire, Carlisle, and Young[43] indicated that the conditioning process does not, however, have to relate to a single, actual sexual encounter, but may be reinforced in cases where an individual masturbates while fantasizing about children. In this instance, the molester's sexual arousal toward children is reinforced by the repeated peaking of sexual pleasure (orgasm) during masturbation.

In the case of negative reinforcement, a response is actually strengthened when the negative reinforcer is removed or terminated. For example, a child molester may be fearful of relating to an adult female, become anxious in her presence, and withdraw from her. He may then molest a child to escape from the distressed state associated with his conflict with adult females. In this case, the response of child molesting is strengthened because it prevents the painful sexual anxiety of relating to peer mates. From another point of view, a child may have sexual contact with an adult that has an aversive or negative effect. As an adult, the memories of the incident, combined with the distressed feelings associated with sexual activity with adults, may cause sexual activity with children to be reinforced. In this instance, the molester learns to terminate or avoid the remembered aversive event by molesting children. He has learned because of a negative reinforcing contingency.

In addition to positive and negative reinforcement, the third learning response that is believed to contribute to the development of child molesting behavior is punishment. Punishment can occur in two ways: through withdrawing positive reinforcement and through presenting an aversive stimulus. Punishment has been found to be much less effective than other behavioral therapies and is usually temporary. The side effects of punishment for sexual activity can cause child-molesting behavior to be shaped. An example in which punishment may be thought to shape the development of future child molesting behavior would be the following:

A 12-year-boy engages in mutual fondling with a girl his own age. This activity is discovered by the boy's mother who registers shock and disapproval. She punishes the boy severely. Later, when the father comes home, she tells him what the boy has done. The father forces the boy to go with him to the girl's parents and apologize. Subsequently, the boy believes that sexual activity with girls is bad and he fears making any contact with them. Over a period of time he develops friendships with boys his own age, and engages in sex play with them without any unpleasant association. He develops a belief set that sex with boys is appropriate; it is associated with pleasure rather than punishment. As he matures, he carries this belief with him into adulthood where he continues his sexual activity with boys.

It is now felt that this internal shaping is a crucial factor in formulating child-molesting behavior. Clinicians have found that there are certain cognitive distortions common to many child molesters. These learned beliefs function as part of a conditioning chain of events that ultimately leads to the child-molesting behavior. The series is depicted as follows:

cognitive distortion→fantasy→cruising behavior to set up a victim→child-molesting behavior

According to Abel, Becker, and Cunningham-Rathner,[1] child molesters have been known to hold the following distorted beliefs:

- A child who does not physically resist really wants sex.
- Having sex with a child is a good way to teach a child about sex.
- A child doesn't tell anyone about having sex with an adult because he or she really enjoys it.
- Society will someday condone sex with children.
- An adult who fondles a child's genitals is not really sexually engaging the child, and so no harm is being done.
- When a child asks about sex, it means that the child wants to see the adult's genitals, or to have sex with the older person.
- The relationship between the child and the adult is enhanced by having sex.

SOCIOLOGICAL FACTORS

A study by Groth, Hobson, and Gary[31] determined that race, religion, intelligence, education, occupation, or socioeconomic status do not differentiate a child molester from the general population. However, Finkelhor[21] found that pedophiles are commonly relatives of their victims. He noted that both the patriarchal family structure and the family's isolation as a social unit are two factors that can be attributed to the high incidence of pedophilia among related family members. Because of these same factors, there is also a high risk of child-molesting behavior among stepfathers or the mothers' live-in boyfriends, who assume the role of adult male authority figures in the household.

Not only has research indicated that pedophilia typically occurs among family members, but there has also been research effort to help distinguish pedophilia from other paraphilic activity. A group of researchers working with Gaffney[26] provided one of the rare studies that did not involve convicted offenders. In this study, the charts of all inpatients (all male) at the Johns Hopkins Biosexual Psychohormonal Clinic during the period of January 1980 to April 1983 were reviewed. All charts not meeting the DSM-III criteria for the paraphilias were discarded. The charts were separated into two groups: pedophiles (n=33) and other paraphilics (n=21); depressives from the same age range were used as controls. Eighteen-and-a-half percent of the male paraphilics reported that they had family members with some form of sexual deviancy, as opposed to the low 3% among the depressives. The prominent sexual disorder noted among the family members of the pedophiles was pedophilia, whereas the sexual deviancy in the families of the other paraphilics was a paraphilia that did not involve children. The authors concluded that pedophilia may be independent of the other paraphilias and may indicate specificity in familial transmission.

A separate study by Abel, Mittelman, and Becker[2] helped to emphasize the high incidence of pedophilic activity subsumed under the broad paraphilic classification. In a group of 411 paraphilic outpatient volunteers, the study disclosed that 232 child sexual abusers had attempted an average of 238.2 child molestations; out of these attempted molestations, an average of 166.9 actual acts of child sexual abuse were inflicted on 75.8 victims. The study also indicated that 16.8% of the child molesters were also involved in rape; however, 50.6% of the rapists had committed child sexual abuse.

The literature on the etiology of child sexual abuse is too vast to survey comprehensively in a brief chapter. We have attempted to describe common causes. The reader is asked to consult the work of Finkelhor,[5,21,22,23] Groth,[29,31] Berlin,[10] and others.[13,16,35]

OBSERVATIONS CONCERNING INCARCERATED SEX OFFENDERS

A recent study by our group[56] compared convicted rapists with convicted child molesters on the basis of a self-report, sharing information about their childhood, and adolescent characteristics. The bulk of the findings of this study provides further evidence that the sex offenders have antecedent factors common in their life histories. Typically, the molester experienced chaos in his home situation. Not only was the notable absence of a close relationship with the father common, but such experiences as abandonment by parents, parental separation or divorce, neglect, physical or sexual abuse, familial violence, frequent arguments, and parental problem drinking were indicated as common characteristics among those child molesters evaluated. The absence of nurturance, physical affection, or examples of healthy sexuality were also reported.

Since this investigation was restricted to incarcerated sex offenders, the study was limited in its ability to generalize about *all* child molesters. However, the following premorbid features were often shared by the child molesters in the study:

- physical and/or sexual abuse
- alcohol or substance abuse
- preoccupation with sexuality
- ignorance, confusion, or guilt about their own sexuality
- societal and peer pressure to be "macho," aggressive, controlling, or violent
- marital stress
- interpersonal deficits
- either no or few friendships while growing up
- the absence of moral development
- feelings of anxiety, powerlessness, fear, inadequacy, anger, and low self-esteem

Although these characteristics are frequently found in child molesters, they should not be viewed as exclusively associated with molesters. Individuals with similar life histories and psychosocial characteristics may have perfectly normal, healthy, and nondeviant sexual interest and behavior throughout their lives.

It is equally important to realize that although some characteristics are common among sex offenders, *individuality* is by far the most impressive feature. Attempts to delineate a stereotyped profile of the "typical child molester" are highly variable, frequently misleading, and, as a rule, ambiguous. There is probably as much divergence of personality structure among child molesters as in those individuals suffering from alcoholism, asthma, or even amputation. The nature of the perversion, its causes, the signs and symptoms, the particular environmental forces and unique circumstances that have molded the individual's life—all of these, and more, contribute to the final analysis. Controlled studies that compare the normal population with child molesters are needed before any definitive statements can be made that adequately profile the "typical child molester."

Rothblum, Solomon, and Albee[51] remind us that scientific research on the classification, etiology, and treatment of mental disorders reflects the attitudes, biases, and expectations of the times and culture. They encourage us to look for the "causes of causes":

> . . . we may find specific personality disorders that identify men who have been guilty of rape or the sexual abuse of children. But we neglect to look for the larger cause in the sexist nature of our society with its emphasis on male domination of females, with the focus in the mass media on male violence and female passivity, and with a pervasive and subtle sexism that is everywhere present. What is the cause of the cause? What causes sexism and what can we do about sexism as a cause of psychopathology? Our research should begin to examine the distribution of sexism and its relationship to the power structure of the industrial society, a power structure that survives through exploitation, patriarchal religion, and militarism. (p. 169)

Rothblum, Solomon, and Albee[51] make a valid, provocative point for future research. Now, however, it is important pragmatically for clinicians to become aware of the general characteristics indicative of a potential child molester. By becoming knowledgeable, the practitioner can be alerted to elucidate additional information during the clinical interview for the purpose of determining whether the individual has committed or has had the urge to commit sexual offenses. In this manner, the evaluator will be able to intervene before more children are needlessly traumatized.

TYPOLOGY

The synthesis of multiple causative and contributive factors found in child-molesting behavior does not lend itself to a simple classification system. For this reason, the classification systems of child molesters are primarily based on clinical descriptions and usually lack scientific evidence for content validity. However, despite limitations, typologies can be clinically useful if clinicians remember that "pure types" rarely, if ever, are found in practice. Most molesters represent composites of the various types. Primarily, classification is based on such criteria as the child molester's motivation and choice of victim, the nature of the molestation, the characteristics of the molester, and the purported causative factors that led to the molestation.

Preference (Fixated) Versus Situational (Regressed)

Groth and his group[31] used the term *fixated* to describe a child molester whose primary sexual objects, since adolescence, have been children. According to Groth,[29] a "fixated child molester is a person who has, from adolescence, been sexually attracted primarily or exclusively to significantly younger people, and this attraction has persisted throughout his life, regardless of what other sexual experiences he has had" (p. 6). Such characteristics as inadequate social skills, sexual anxiety, difficulty in relating to adults, immaturity or arrested psychological development, and an identification with a child's lack of dominance are popular explanations for the fixated, or *preference*, child molester. Fixated child molesters commonly fit the criteria for Pedophilia established in the DSM-III[3] and its revision, the DSM-III-R.[4]

In contrast to the fixated child molester, if the child-molesting behavior begins in adulthood, occurring after the sexual abuser has established primary sexual attraction toward an adult, the molester is classified as a *situational*, or *regressed* type. For the regressed molester, involvement with children is usually isolated or episodic. In such cases, the victim acts as a surrogate for the preferred, but unavailable, adult. The assumption is that sexual development is normal until precipitating stressors intervene to produce the return, or regression, to a previous level of sexual development and object orientation. Such factors as problems in an adult romantic relationship, alcohol or substance abuse, and various situational stresses are catalysts for the regressed sexual behavior.

Conte[17] points out a number of problems with the regressed/fixated typology. (See Table 3.2 for a comparison of these two types.) Based on this typology, Conte notes that the assumptions about child molesters made by law enforcement, social service, and mental health professionals are unwarranted. For instance, the typology makes assumptions regarding the etiology of child molestation and its relationship to normal developmental processes of sexuality that are not supported by research evidence. Although the criminal justice system and clinicians have tended to view these typologies as possessing predictive validity (i.e., fixated offenders

Table 3.2
Typology of Child Molesters

Fixated Type	Regressed Type
1. Primary sexual orientation is to children.	1. Primary sexual orientation is to agemates.
2. Pedophilic interests begin at adolescence.	2. Pedophilic interests emerge in adulthood.
3. No precipitating stress/no subjective distress.	3. Precipitating stress usually evident.
4. Persistent interest and compulsive behavior.	4. Involvements may be more episodic and may wax and wane with stress.
5. Premeditated, pre-planned offenses.	5. Initial offense may be impulsive and not premeditated.
6. Identification: offender identifies closely with the victim and equalizes his behavior to the level of the child and/or may adopt a pseudo-parental role to the victim.	6. Substitution: offender replaces conflictual adult relationship with involvement with a child; victim is a pseudoadult substitute and in incest situations the offender abandons his parental role.
7. Male victims are primary targets.	7. Female victims are primary targets.
8. Little or no sexual contact initiated with agemates; offender is usually single or in a marriage of convenience.	8. Sexual contact with a child coexists with sexual contact with agemates; offender is usually married or common-law.
9. Usually no history of alcohol or drug abuse and offense is not alcohol related.	9. Offense is often alcohol related.
10. Characterological immaturity; poor sociosexual peer relationships.	10. More traditional lifestyle but under-developed peer relationships.
11. Offense = maladaptive resolution of life development (maturation) issues.	11. Offense = maladaptive attempt to cope with specific life stresses.

From "The child molester: Clinical observations," by A. N. Groth, W. F. Hobson, & T. S. Gary (1982). In J. Conte & D. A. Shore (Eds.), *Social Work and Child Sexual Abuse.* New York: Haworth, p. 134. Reprinted by permission.

are looked upon as untreatable, whereas regressed types are perceived as more amenable to therapeutic intervention), there are no predictive studies to support the treatability of one type over the other. Since the typology is formulated on clinical experience with incarcerated offenders, who may be dissimilar to offenders seen in community settings, Conte asserts that it is wrong for decisions to be made about treatment, release into the community, and the probability of reoffending based on this tentative typology.

Incest Versus Nonincest

Incest is generally thought of as a sexual congress between persons who are blood-related—for example, a sexual relationship between a mother and son, a father and daughter, a brother and sister, a mother and daughter; however, more recently, sexual contact with adoptive relatives or stepparents has been included in the definition. In each of these cases, the sexual encounter may be genital intercourse, oral-genital contact, fondling the genitals and breasts, or mutual masturbation.

Incestuous relationships with a child by a blood relative happen enough to evoke concern—the incidence of intrafamilial sexual abuse is an alarmingly high 16%![52] Despite the universality of the incest taboo today, studies support the observation that the incest avoidance mechanism fails in circumstances where intrafamilial sexual abuse occurs.[22,53] Using large-scale surveys of nonclinical populations, one study by Russell[52,53] reported that 16% of her female subjects claimed that they had been sexually molested by a relative; 4.5% of these women indicated that they had been sexually abused by their father before the age of 18. However, sexual abuse by stepfathers occurred *seven times* more frequently than did molestation by biological fathers. One out of six women who lived with a stepfather had been sexually abused by him during her childhood.[28] Perhaps even more frightening than these overwhelming statistics, only 2% of the cases of intrafamilial sexual abuse were ever reported to the police.

Phelan[47] compared incest between 46 biological fathers and their daughters versus 56 stepfathers and their stepdaughters. Eighty percent of abusive biological fathers molested multiple daughters, whereas 75% of stepfathers molested only one daughter. Biological fathers were found to begin sexual advances toward victims of an older age (12–16 years) than stepfathers who began with victims at a younger age (8–11 years). Biological fathers engaged in full intercourse more frequently than did stepfathers.

In studying the long-term effects of incestuous childhood abuse, Herman, Russell, and Trocki[34] found that approximately half of the women surveyed felt that they had recovered from the sexual trauma, although they had previously been upset by the experience. The group reporting the greatest duration of effects from the trauma were those who had been abused by their father or stepfather, or had suffered from a prolonged and forceful or highly intrusive sexual molestation.

There is still much speculation concerning the causative and contributing factors for incest. For further information, interested readers can refer to Mrazek's "The Nature of Incest: A Review of Contributing Factors"[45] and deChesnay's "Father-Daughter Incest: An Overview."[18] Twitchell[58] provides an interesting twist by tracing incest-related literature during the recent past.

Violent Versus Nonviolent

Violence over and above the sexual interaction occurs in 10%–15% of sex offenses against children,[39,46] and whether or not violence has occurred is one way of distinguishing child molesting behavior. Generally, nonviolent offenders coax or pressure children into sexual activity—for example, the child gives sex in exchange for attention, acceptance, recognition, or material gain. Child rapists use threat, intimidation, and physical force, which closely resemble circumstances of rape among adult females. Sadistic acts (paddling, spanking, whipping, beating, burning, cutting, strangulation, torture, mutilation, or killing) may occur during child sexual abuse. A small portion of child molesters probably meet the criteria for classification of Sexual Sadism.[4]

When compared to the other forms of child molestation, child rape is, at best, understood as an intense mingling of aggression and sexual urges, although it is basically viewed more as an act of aggression than a sexual encounter.

Male Versus Female

Although evidence has indicated that child sexual abuse is primarily perpetrated by males, many experts in the field argue that the number of female child molesters is seriously underestimated.[29,48] Because of cultural attitudes that perceive sexual molestation by females as less serious and traumatic than abuse by male perpetrators, it has been suggested that victims of female abuse may be more reluctant to report the offense. It has also been conjectured that, as primary caretakers, women can mask their sexually abusive acts more easily than men.

However, there is an indication that cultural barriers are lifting that have not only inhibited the reporting of sexual molestation by women, but have concealed the high prevalence of child sexual abuse in general.

The increase in reporting all types of child molestation parallels a rise in the proportion of known female offenders. This rise has prompted studies to examine the phenomenon of female perpetrators. Finkelhor[21] noted that sexual abuse by women occurs in roughly 20% of the cases with male victims, and in 5% of the cases with female victims. In their chapter comparing the frequency of sexual abusive acts performed by males as opposed to females, Finkelhor and Russell[23] concluded that sexual abuse by women does, in fact, occur; however, child sexual abuse is primarily perpetrated by men.

Much of the available literature on female perpetrators of child sexual abuse is in the form of case reports (see, e.g., references 6 and 15). The Dallas Incest Treatment Program reports that mothers constitute 4% of their offender population. McCarty[42] reviewed 29 case records of mother-child incest offenders from the Dallas Incest Treatment Program. Three of the 29 cases were dropped from the study because of indeterminate involvement with the child; five who were accomplices in the sexual abuse were kept in the study but evaluated separately; nine were co-offenders with a male partner and 12 were independent offenders, although six of the 12 had a male offender also involved. Biological mothers constituted 90% of this sample. Eleven mothers chose female victims (average age 6.4 years); eight mothers chose male victims (average age 9.6 years); and two were bisexual in victim choice.

In this study the independent mother-offenders were of average intelligence, had a troubled childhood, were sexually abused in childhood, abused drugs, and had an emotional disturbance. Mothers who were co-offenders with a male partner typically were sexually abused in childhood, troubled during childhood, and of borderline intellect.

Marvasti,[41] who has treated several female child molesters, concluded that female sexual abusers are: (1) subtle, nonviolent, nonthreatening; (2) rarely reported or included in public statistics; (3) tend to report themselves, but only after several months of psychotherapy; (4) not motivated by the sense of "power" and "authority" commonly used to explain the psychodynamics of male molesters; (5) less antisocial than male child molesters; and (6) nonpsychotic.

Juvenile Versus Adult

According to the Seattle Institute of Child Advocacy Committee for Children, the majority of sex offenders committed their first offenses as teenagers.[19] Although the reports of abuse by juvenile girls are increasing, like their adult counterparts the vast majority of juvenile sex offenders are males. Babysitting is the most common setting for a juvenile sexual abuser.

In a study to determine the extent and general characteristics of sex offenses committed by adolescents in that state, the Vermont Department of Health collected information on 161 sex offenders.[59] The survey included all of the sex molesters under 20 years of age who were known by caseworkers in 1984. In the sample, over 90% of these juveniles were males. The median age of male offenders was 15 years, whereas the median age for the female perpetrators was 13 years. The ages of the victims ranged from two to 60 years of age, with a median age of seven. The results of the study showed that less than 10% of these offenders victimized persons older than themselves. More than two-thirds of the victims were under 10 years of age, and nearly half were under the age of seven. In the vast majority of the offenses, the male molesters tended to victimize females, whereas the female offenders tended to molest males.

In the Vermont study, several categories of sexual activity emerged: *penetration, oral-genital acts, fondling,* and *noncontact offenses.* Penetration was the most common category, occurring in 60% of the cases. The study indicated that the older the offender, the greater was the likelihood for penetration to happen. In 51% of the offenses the victims were friends or acquaintances; 20% of the molestations occurred between immediate family members; and 9% of the molestations were committed on strangers. Some method of coercion was identified in 81% of the cases: verbal threats were used in 57% of the incidents, physical force was inflicted in 26% of the molestations, and the threat of physical force was exercised in 4% of the offenses. In 8% of the cases a weapon was employed, and in 5% of the offenses the threat to use a weapon was given.

Becker and her co-workers[8] describe 67 adolescent male sex offenders who were largely indigent, inner city, minority youth. The following were among their findings:

- Most had a primary diagnosis of Pedophilia.
- The majority had engaged in nongenital, nondeviant sexual activity prior to deviant behavior.
- Adolescent child molesters used physical coercion but not as much as adolescent rapists.
- 31% denied sex offense.

In a separate report,[9] Becker's group analyzed data from 22 adolescent incest sex perpetrators and found that 77% were defined as pedophiles. By self-report, these subjects had an early onset of sexual behavior (mean age 10.3 years) and had additional DSM-III Axis I diagnoses (e.g., Conduct Disorder [12], Attention Deficit Disorder [five]; and Substance Abuse [four]). As might be expected, prior victimization was present in eight of the 22 subjects.

Since the first instance of child-molesting behavior often begins in early adolescence, these disturbing statistics of the Vermont study and Becker's research reveal that early intervention programs, as well as early identification and effective treatment strategies, are necessary to avoid lifelong patterns of sexually abusive behavior.

Continued research effort must also be directed toward understanding the factors that facilitate child sexual abuse. For instance, the molester's wife may possess features that tend to reinforce the child abuser's impulses; or the molester becomes involved in activities that bring him close to children—for example, the molester is hired as a teacher or volunteers as a scout leader. Also, such situational stresses as deteriorating marital and family relationships, work-related problems, and alcohol abuse have commonly been seen in clinical practice as motivating forces for child-molesting behavior. Whereas Krafft-Ebing and Havelock Ellis associated senile sexuality or impotency as precipitating factors, it is now believed that a complex and variable interplay of biological mechanisms, psychodynamic influences, conditioning, and social factors facilitate child-molesting behavior.

REFERENCES

1. Abel, G. G., Becker, J. V., & Cunningham-Rathner, J. (1984). Complications, consent and cognitions in sex between children and adults. *International Journal of Law & Psychiatry, 7,* 89.
2. Abel, G. G., Mittelman, M. S., & Becker, J. V. (1985). Sexual offenders: Results of assessment and recommendations for treatment. In M. H.

Ben-Aron, S. J. Hucker, & C. D. Webster (Eds.), *Clinical Criminology: Current Concepts.* Toronto: M & M Graphics.

3. American Psychiatric Association (1980). *Diagnostic and Statistical Manual of Mental Disorders, Third Edition (DSM-III).* Washington, D.C.: American Psychiatric Association.

4. American Psychiatric Association (1987). *Diagnostic and Statistical Manual of Mental Disorders, Third Edition, Revised (DSM-III-R).* Washington, D. C.: American Psychiatric Association.

5. Araji, S., & Finkelhor, D. (1985). Explanations of pedophilia: Review of empirical research. *Bulletin of the American Academy of Psychiatry & Law, 13,* 17.

6. Arroyo, W., Eth, S., & Pynoos, R. (1984). Sexual assault of a mother by her preadolescent son. *American Journal of Psychiatry, 141,* 1107.

7. Barnard, G. W., Fuller, A. K., & Robbins, L. (1988). Child molesters. In J. G. Howells (Ed.), *Modern Perspectives in Psychosocial Pathology.* New York: Brunner/Mazel.

8. Becker, J. V., Cunningham-Rathner, J., & Kaplan, M. (1986). The adolescent sexual offender. Demographics, criminal history, victims, sexual behavior and recommendations for reducing future offenses. *Journal of Interpersonal Violence, 1,* 431.

9. Becker, J. V., Kaplan, M. S., & Cunningham-Rathner, J. (1986). Characteristics of adolescent incest sexual perpetrators. *Journal of Family Violence, 1,* 85.

10. Berlin, F. S. (1983). Sex offenders: A biomedical perspective and a status report on biomedical treatment. In J. G. Greer & I. R. Stuart (Eds.), *The Sexual Aggressor: Current Perspectives on Treatment.* New York: Van Nostrand.

11. Bliss, E. L. (1986). *Multiple Personality, Allied Disorders, and Hypnosis.* New York: Oxford University Press.

12. Bliss, E. L., & Larson, E. M. (1985). Sexual criminality and hypnotizability. *Journal of Nervous & Mental Disease, 173,* 522.

13. Boniello, M. J. (1986). The family as "stage" for creating abusive children. *Connections in the Prevention of Child Sexual Abuse, 1,* 4.

14. Bradford, J. M. W. (1985). Organic treatments for the male sexual offender. *Behavioral Science & the Law, 3,* 55.

15. Chasnoff, I. J., Burns, W. J., Schnoll, S. H., Burns, K., Chisum, G., & Kyle-Spore, L. (1986). Maternal-neonatal incest. *American Journal of Orthopsychiatry, 56,* 577.

16. Cohn, A., Finkelhor, D., & Holmes, C. (1985). *Preventing Adults From Becoming Child Sexual Molesters.* Working Paper Number 25. Chicago, IL: National Committee for the Prevention of Child Abuse.

17. Conte, J. R. (1985). Clinical dimensions of adult sexual abuse of children. *Behavioral Sciences & Law, 3,* 341.

18. deChesnay, M. (1985). Father-daughter incest: An overview. *Behavioral Science & Law, 3,* 391.

19. Downer, A. (1985). *Prevention of Child Sexual Abuse: A Trainer's Manual.* Seattle, WA: Seattle Institute for Child Advocacy Committee for Children.

20. Ellis, H. (1933). *Psychology of Sex.* London: Pan Books Ltd.

21. Finkelhor, D. (1984). *Child Sexual Abuse: New Theory and Research.* New York: Free Press.

22. Finkelhor, D. (1980). Risk factors in the sexual victimization of children. *Child Abuse & Neglect, 4,* 265.
23. Finkelhor, D., & Russell, D. (1984). Women as perpetrators. In D. Finkelhor, *Child Sexual Abuse: New Theory and Research.* New York: Free Press.
24. Freund, K. (1967). Diagnosing homo- or heterosexuality and erotic age-preference by means of a psychophysiological test. *Behaviour Research & Therapy, 5,* 209.
25. Gaffney, G. R., & Berlin, F. S. (1984). Is there hypothalamic-pituitary-gonadal dysfunction in pedophilia? *British Journal of Criminology, 145,* 657.
26. Gaffney, G. R., Shelly, F. L., & Berlin, F. S. (1984). Is there a familial transmission of pedophilia? *Journal of Nervous & Mental Disease, 172,* 546.
27. Gillespie, W. H. (1956). The general theory of sexual perversion. *International Journal of Psychoanalysis, 37,* 396.
28. Goldstein, M. J., & Kant, H. S. (1973). *Pornography and Sexual Deviance.* Berkeley, CA: University of California Press.
29. Groth, A. N. (1978). Patterns of sexual assault against children and adolescents. In A. W. Burgess, A. N., Groth, L. L. Holmstrom, & S. M. Sgroi (Eds.), *Sexual Assault of Children and Adolescents.* Lexington, MA: Lexington.
30. Groth, A. N., & Birnbaum, H. J. (1979). Adult sexual orientation and attraction to underage persons. *Archives of Sexual Behavior, 7,* 175.
31. Groth, A. N., Hobson, W. F., & Gary, T. S. (1982). The child molester: Clinical observations. In: J. Conte & D. A. Shore (Eds.), *Social Work and Child Sexual Abuse.* New York: Haworth.
32. Gurnani, P. D., & Dwyer, M. (1986). Serum testosterone levels in sex offenders. *Journal of Offender Counseling, Services & Rehabilitation, 11,* 39.
33. Henn, F. A., Herjanic, M., & Vanderpearl, R. H. (1976). Forensic psychiatry—profiles of two types of sex offenders. *American Journal of Psychiatry, 133,* 696.
34. Herman, J., Russell, D., & Trocki, K. (1986). Long-term effects of incestuous abuse in childhood. *American Journal of Psychiatry, 143,* 1293.
35. Howells, K. (1979). Some meanings of children for pedophiles. In M. Cook & G. Wilson (Eds.), *Love and Attraction: An International Conference.* Oxford, England: Pergamon Press.
36. Kaplan, H. I., & Sadock, B. J. (1985). *Modern Synopsis of Comprehensive Textbook of Psychiatry/IV.* Baltimore: Williams & Wilkins.
37. Krafft-Ebing, R. (1959). *Aberrations of Sexual Life.* London: Staples.
38. Langevin, R., Hucker, S. J., Ben-Aron, M. H., Purins, J. E., & Hook, H. J. (1985). Why are pedophiles attracted to children? Further studies of erotic preference in heterosexual pedophilia. In R. Langevin (Ed.), *Erotic Preference, Gender Identity, and Aggression in Men: New Research Studies.* Hillsdale, NJ: Erlbaum.
39. Lanyon, R. I. (1986). Theory and treatment in child molestations. *Journal of Consulting & Clinical Psychology, 54,* 176.
40. Lilly, R., Cummings, J. L., Benson, D. F., & Frankel, M. (1983). The human Klüver-Bucy Syndrome. *Neurology, 33,* 1141.

41. Marvasti, J. A. (1987). Women who commit incest. *Psychiatry '87*, Mt. Royal, NJ: Health Science Network. August issue, p. 8.
42. McCarty, L. M. (1986). Mother-child incest: Characteristics of the offender. *Child Welfare, 65*, 447.
43. McGuire, R. J., Carlisle, J. M., & Young, B. G. (1965). Sexual deviations as conditioned behaviour: A hypothesis. *Behaviour Research and Therapy, 2*, 185.
44. Miller, B. L., Cummings, J. L., McIntryre, H., Ebers, G., & Grode, M. (1986). Hypersexuality or altered sexual preference following brain injury. *Journal of Neurology, Neurosurgery, & Psychiatry, 49*, 867.
45. Mrazek, P. B. (1981). The nature of incest: A review of contributing factors. In P. Mrazek & H. Kempe (Eds.), *Sexually Abused Children and Their Families*. New York: Pergamon Press.
46. Mrazek, P. J., Lynch, M. A., & Bentovim, A. (1983). Sexual abuse of children in the United Kingdom. *Child Abuse & Neglect, 7*, 147.
47. Phelan, P. (1986). The process of incest: Biologic father and stepfather families. *Child Abuse & Neglect, 10*, 531.
48. Plummer, K. (1981). Pedophilia: Constructing a sociological baseline. In M. Cook & K. Howells (Eds.), *Adult Sexual Interest in Children*. London: Academic Press.
49. Quinsey, V. L., Chaplin, T. C., & Carrigan, W. F. (1979). Sexual preferences among incestuous and nonincestuous child molesters. *Behavior Therapy, 10*, 562.
50. Rada, R. T., Laws, D. R., & Kellner, R. (1976). Plasma testosterone levels in the rapist. *Psychosomatic Medicine, 38*, 257.
51. Rothblum, E. D., Solomon, L. J., & Albee, G. W. (1986). A sociopolitical perspective of DSM-III. In T. Millon & G. L. Klerman (Eds.), *Contemporary Directions in Psychopathology: Toward the DSM-IV*. New York: Guilford Press.
52. Russell, D. E. H. (1983). The incidence and prevalence of intrafamilial and extrafamilial sexual abuse of female children. *Child Abuse & Neglect, 7*, 133.
53. Russell, D. E. H. (1984). The prevalence and seriousness of incestuous abuse: Stepfathers vs. biological fathers. *Child Abuse & Neglect, 8*, 15.
54. Schiavi, R. C., Theilgaard, A., Owen, D. R., & White, D. (1984). Sex chromosome anomalies, hormones and aggressivity. *Archives of General Psychiatry, 41*, 93.
55. Socarides, C. W. (1959). Meaning and content of a pedophilia perversions. *Journal of the American Psychoanalytic Association, 7*, 84.
56. Tingle, D., Barnard, G. W., Robbins, L., Newman, G., & Hutchinson, D. (1986). Childhood and adolescent characteristics of pedophiles and rapists. *International Journal of Law & Psychiatry, 9*, 108.
57. Tollison, C. D., & Adams, H. E. (1978). *Sexual Disorders: Treatment, Theory, and Research*. New York: Gardner Press.
58. Twitchell, J. B. (1987). *Forbidden Partners: The Incest Taboo in Modern Culture*. New York: Columbia University Press.
59. Vermont Department of Health (1985). Adolescent sex offenders— Vermont, 1984. Morbidity and Mortality Weekly Report. *Journal of the American Medical Association, 255* (2), 181.

CHAPTER 4

Assessment and Diagnosis

*Roderick L. Hall, Ph.D.**

Trends in the assessment of sex offenders, a rationale for comprehensive assessment procedures, and related diagnostic issues are discussed in this chapter. In addition to these more theoretical applications, the typical psychological assessment battery currently used in evaluating sex offenders at North Florida Evaluation and Treatment Center (NFETC) and a case example are also provided to demonstrate the value of a comprehensive assessment in the treatment of sex offenders.

As most readers are aware, in clinical psychology and psychiatry there are two major schools of thought, the psychodynamic and the behavioral. The psychodynamic perspective evolved with emphasis on psychoanalytic concepts originating with Freud and his followers. On the other hand, the behavioral perspective was more influenced by the conditioning theorists, classical as well as operant. Although there have been recent efforts to integrate the two perspectives by way of social learning theory,[7,8,22] many mental health professionals continue to receive training which emphasizes one perspective to the exclusion of the other. This adherence to a particular model influences the approach clinicians take in assessing patients. Clinicians who are from the psychodynamic school tend to use traditional assessment procedures (e.g., psychological testing and diagnostic interview), whereas those from the behavioral school tend to rely on methods such as behavioral analysis and psychophysiological assessment.

---

* Dr. Hall is a former psychologist at North Florida Evaluation and Treatment Center. He is presently Director, Department of Corrections, 1311 Winewood Boulevard, Tallahassee, Florida 32301.

A strict adherence to one theoretical approach to the exclusion of others is limiting. We advocate a comprehensive model that utilizes aspects of both theoretical models. This viewpoint may be seen by some as controversial since the advocates for a purist approach would argue that the psychodynamic and learning theory approaches are diametric opposites in terms of philosophy and underlying assumptions. We argue here, however, that both approaches yield patient information that may be important for treatment. Moreover, data gathered through one approach often complement those obtained through the other, thereby enhancing our understanding of the patient. In order that the reader can better appreciate our position, the discussion now turns to arguments against the exclusive use of either the psychodynamic or the behavioral approach.

ARGUMENTS AGAINST THE EXCLUSIVE USE OF THE PSYCHODYNAMIC MODEL

The last 10 years have witnessed a decline in the use of traditional assessment procedures (e.g., psychodynamic and projective tests flowing from psychoanalytic theory) and an increasing use of behavioral assessment procedures (e.g., behavioral interview, Multiphasic Sex Inventory,[26] Abel's Pedophilic Cognition Scale,[1] and physiological assessment of sexual arousal). This trend seems to be associated primarily with two factors. The first and perhaps most significant factor is the rising popularity of various behavioral* treatment strategies among leading clinicians and researchers (e.g., Abel, Laws, Quinsey, and Barlow) who treat and study sexual disorders and sex offenders. Moreover, interest in more traditional treatment approaches (e.g., psychodynamic and interpersonal) has declined as the popularity of behavioral methods (e.g., relapse prevention, rational emotive therapy, verbal satiation, masturbatory satiation, and olfactory aversion) has increased. This definite shift in preference for the use of behavioral treatment methods gives rise to a preference for behavioral versus traditional assessment as well. This is because behavioral treatment approaches are intrinsically related to behavioral assessment, that is, identification of specific behaviors needing change as well as the antecedents and consequences that control those behaviors.[15] Thus,

---

* As used here, this term includes cognitive-behavioral notions.

behavioral assessment is an essential precursor to behavioral treatment.

The clinician can readily use the results of a behavioral assessment (form, duration, magnitude, and frequency of specific behaviors; antecedents and consequences of those behaviors) in developing a behavioral treatment plan. For example, the form and intensity of a patient's deviant sexual arousal revealed through physiological assessment (penile plethysmography) would be invaluable in planning a behavioral treatment program designed to reduce the deviant sexual arousal.

In contrast, the clinician who uses traditional assessment (e.g., traits, feelings, conflicts, personality features, diagnosis) would likely find that the results are too general to be of much use in behavioral treatment. Moreover, since behavioral assessment is generally an ongoing process, the results from it are often useful in evaluating the effectiveness of treatment.

The second factor that has contributed to a declining use of traditional assessment procedures with sex offenders is the apparent failure of traditional psychological tests to distinguish sex offenders from other types of offenders or to differentiate among types of sex offenders. Notwithstanding serious methodological problems[19] with most of the relevant studies, the Minnesota Multiphasic Personality Inventory (MMPI),[12] for example, has shown little ability to differentiate pedophiles and rapists from men who have committed nonsexual crimes;[16,27,30] or to differentiate between rapists and pedophiles.[6,18] Projective procedures such as the Rorschach,[32] Draw-A-Person Test,[36] and Thematic Apperception Test[25] have not fared much better in differentiating rapists and pedophiles.[28,34,38]

Although the above research findings are fairly convincing, they must be considered tentative at best, given the limitations noted by Levin and Stava,[19] who argue that the MMPI (the test used most frequently in the referenced studies) is a measure of psychopathology rather than personality, and hence may not be the most appropriate test for differentiating sex offenders. The California Psychological Inventory[9] and the Millon Clinical Multiaxial Inventory (MCMI),[24] tests that clearly measure personality traits, may prove to be more effective, especially if they are used in combination with other methods (i.e., a multivariate approach). It has been noted on the basis of clinical observation that child molesters often score very high on the MCMI on subscales 1, 2, and/or 3 (schizoid, avoidant, and dependent) and low on scales 5 and 6 (narcissistic and antisocial). In contrast, rapists often score high on scales 5 and/or 6 and low on scales 1, 2, and/or 3. These relations are currently being studied more formally and the results will be reported in a subsequent article.[11]

Levin and Stava[19] point out further that in many of the studies little attention was devoted to the criminal history of the subjects, making it difficult to conclude that the current offense was representative of past behavior. For example, consider a question that often arises in the case of an offender who is convicted of rape and who also has an extensive history of child molestation (although there has been no actual conviction): Should he be considered a rapist or a child molester? From another angle consider the case of an offender who has an extensive history of nonsexual crimes and one or two occasions of child molestation: Should he be viewed as a child molester?

There is a more basic reason to use caution when accepting those findings that emphasize that traditional tests do not differentiate between "types" of sex offenders. Distinctions are made between clinical and criminal or legal entities. A clinical entity or syndrome is a group of symptoms that occur together and constitute a recognizable condition, whereas a criminal or legal entity is an act that is forbidden by law. Criminal entities are defined more in terms of social deviance. Thus, many acts are socially or morally deviant and are considered criminal solely on the basis of the rule of law.

Clinical entities, in contrast, are less tied to moral sanctions and are defined in terms of covarying symptoms. While a criminal or legal entity may simultaneously exist both apart from and as part of a clinical condition, the two entities remain independent. In other words, the illegal act only comprises part of the clinical syndrome and can never be considered synonymous with the total syndrome.

For instance, while adult criminal behavior is often associated with the clinical condition of Antisocial Personality Disorder, the presence of such behavior is not sufficient to warrant the diagnosis of Antisocial Personality Disorder.[5] Similarly, "isolated sexual acts with children do not necessarily warrant the diagnosis of Pedophilia"[5] (p. 285).

Terms such as *sex offender, mentally disordered sex offender, rapist, child molester,* and *incest offender* are considered legal rather than clinical terms. They are assigned solely on the basis of commission of a specific act prohibited by law. As such, these terms most often do not represent true clinical conditions with covarying symptoms.

Since most of the samples used in the above-referenced research were also defined solely in terms of the commission of criminal acts, those samples were probably not reflective of true clinical entities. It is quite possible that the apparent "failure" of traditional tests to differentiate such groups says more about the legitimacy of the groups than it does about the legitimacy of the tests. Hall, Maiuro, Vitaliano, and Proctor[10] concluded that the failure of the MMPI to differentiate between sex offenders on the basis of offense variables may be evidence that such variables are of "criminological" rather than "psychological" relevance.

ARGUMENTS AGAINST THE EXCLUSIVE USE OF THE BEHAVIORAL MODEL

For clinicians working with sex offenders, the current trend to rely almost exclusively on behavioral assessment is misguided. Several lines of reasoning can be offered to support this contention. First, behavioral assessment, with its emphasis on the analysis of very specific behaviors, encourages the clinician to focus exclusively on deviant sexual behavior or behavior thought to be closely associated with it. Because other important conditions of a nonsexual nature may be overlooked (e.g., Organic Brain Syndrome, Mental Retardation, Personality Disorders, Mood Disorders, and Psychoactive Substance-Induced Disorders), this practice can be problematic. It is important to identify these conditions regardless of whether they are believed to be closely related to the patient's deviant sexual behavior. Such conditions have clinical legitimacy and should be addressed at some point in treatment. If significant nonsexual disorders are present and the treating clinician or program specializes only in the treatment of psychosexual disorders, then concomitant referrals should be made to other programs. It is possible that at times some nonsexual conditions (e.g., severe depression, psychosis, or organic brain syndrome) may need to take precedence in treatment.

Furthermore, traditional assessment procedures may be preferable or at least complementary to behavioral assessment in some cases. Consider, for example, the patient who is too shy, embarrassed, or anxious to participate fully in direct interview, but who may provide relevant information indirectly by means of psychological tests. In this regard, Meichenbaum,[21] a well-known proponent of the cognitive-behavioral approach, has noted that the Thematic Apperception Test[25] (a widely used projective psychological test) may be useful in assessing a patient's cognitive behavior in specific situations.

Similarly, the early stages of some clinical conditions (e.g., depression or psychosis) may be identified through traditional psychological testing, whereas they remain hidden during direct interview. This phenomenon is particularly relevant with patients who are well-defended and/or who are reluctant to admit to personal problems. Also, patient responses on single items of several tests (e.g., Minnesota Multiphasic Personality Inventory[12] and Incomplete Sentences Blank[33]), often referred to as "critical items," can suggest important areas of inquiry for the clinical interview.

ARGUMENTS FOR A COMPREHENSIVE MODEL

Moreover, it seems clinically prudent to conduct a thorough assessment of a patient before, or at least early on in, the treatment process, even if the clinician has decided a priori to use a particular treatment approach. The data obtained from the comprehensive assessment can be used to rule out nonsexual conditions that might demand primacy in treatment, to prioritize treatment efforts, and to enhance the clinician's understanding of the broader context in which the presenting problems occur.

Comprehensive assessment may and perhaps should include behavioral assessment. However, since by definition it involves identification of clinical syndromes (i.e., diagnosis), it *must* include traditional assessment.

Although certain procedures (e.g., personality and intellectual tests) are associated exclusively with traditional versus behavioral assessment, it is not the specific procedure itself that differentiates the two methods of evaluation. Indeed, the clinical interview is a common procedure in both methods. Moreover, all of the procedures employed in both methods are quite similar in that they all sample the patient's behavior.

The essential difference between the two methods lies in the purpose to which the clinician directs the evaluation. In the case of behavioral assessment, the clinician samples the patient's behavior in order to identify parameters of specific behaviors and the antecedents and consequences that help to maintain those behaviors, whereas the clinician utilizing the traditional assessment method samples the patient's behavior in order to identify characteristics (e.g., feelings, conflicts, defense mechanisms, self-concept) that may be associated with a particular presenting problem.

Thus, the former method is less inferential and is more limited in its focus than the latter.

It is the broader focus and purpose of the traditional assessment method that is the sine qua non of comprehensive assessment. Through this method one can more readily obtain not only a description of a particular presenting problem, but also the larger clinical picture, which serves as the background for the presenting problem. Thus, comprehensive assessment or evaluation refers to the *process of identifying specific behavior problems/mental conditions (syndromes) and determining the context in which they manifest themselves.* This definition is essentially synonymous with the definition of diagnosis given in the *Diagnostic and Statistical Manual of Mental Disorders* (DSM-III-R).[5]

Comprehensive assessment requires not only that specific sexually deviant behaviors be assessed, but also that such behaviors and other existing clinical conditions (which are noted on Axis I of DSM-III-R) be evaluated in the broader context of the patient's personality or behavioral style (Axis II). It is also important to examine medical or physical conditions (Axis III) and current social/environmental stressors (Axis IV) that may be contributing factors. Personality traits and, when they exist, personality disorders (Axis II) become important in so far as they form the background out of which clinical syndromes (Axis I) such as Pedophilia manifest themselves.[23] The assumption is that the particular personality disorder on which the Axis I syndrome is superimposed will affect the manifestation of that syndrome.

For example, Pedophilia that presents in a patient with Narcissistic Personality Disorder may be expressed differently from Pedophilia that presents in a patient with Avoidant Personality Disorder. Given the narcissist's lack of empathy, grandiose sense of self-importance, feelings of entitlement, and interpersonal exploitativeness, his manifestation of Pedophilia is likely to be quite pervasive and enduring, involving many different victims and greater potential for physical aggression. Manifestation of Pedophilia in the avoidant person—who in contrast to the narcissist more often shows the capacity for empathy, feels timid and uncomfortable in most social situations, and avoids activities that involve significant interpersonal contacts—is likely to be limited to a few victims whom he knows fairly well and to whom he may offer affection and care in order to avoid rejection.

More important, the patient whose Pedophilia is embedded within the context of Narcissistic Personality Disorder is likely to have different treatment needs than the patient whose Pedophilia is ingrained within the context of Avoidant Personality Disorder. The "avoidant pedophile" and the "narcissistic pedophile" are both likely to be very resistant to initiating treatment. The former is resistant because he fears new situations and the humiliation he expects to experience in the encounter. The latter is resistant because treatment is experienced as humiliating to his grandiose sense of superiority. The "avoidant pedophile," however, is likely to be painfully aware of his deficits and therefore often motivated for treatment, particularly if he feels accepted by the therapist. In contrast, the "narcissistic pedophile" may often lack motivation for treatment because he does not think he has "real" problems, certainly none for which he might need help. Thus, the issue of motivation will perhaps need to be addressed very early in the treatment of the "narcissistic pedophile." Indeed, motivation may need to be given primacy. Otherwise, the clinician runs the risk of losing the patient, particularly in outpatient settings.

When possible, behavioral assessment procedures should be used in conjunction with traditional procedures. Behavioral assessment procedures will not only help to provide a thorough analysis of the problem sexual behavior, but also aid in the formulation of a diagnosis. A patient's pattern of sexual arousal, as revealed through penile plethysmography, will help to define the parameters of deviant and nondeviant sexual arousal, which in turn will aid differential diagnosis.

DIAGNOSIS

As stated above, the term *diagnosis* refers to the process of identifying disorders and the context in which they occur. The term also refers to the classification nomenclature used to denote the outcome of the diagnostic (assessment) process. Thus, one uses "diagnostic" labels to summarize the findings of an assessment and to classify conditions observed into "distinct" categories.

DSM Conceptions: Historical Review

The first edition of the American Psychiatric Association's *Diagnostic and Statistical Manual of Mental Disorders* (DSM-I)[2] grouped Pedophilia as one of several "sexual deviations." The sexual deviations in turn were classified as one of several types of "sociopathic personalities." Sociopathic personalities were described as persons who "are ill primarily in terms of society and of conformity with the prevailing cultural milieu, and not only in terms of personal discomfort and relations with other individuals . . ." (p. 38). Finally, sexual deviations were described as follows:

This diagnosis is reserved for deviant sexuality which is not symptomatic of more extensive syndromes, such as schizophrenic and obsessional reactions. The term includes most of the cases formerly classed as "psychopathic personality with pathologic sexuality." The diagnosis will specify the type of the pathologic behavior, such as homosexuality, transvestism, pedophilia, fetishism and sexual sadism (including rape sexual assault, mutilation). (p. 38)

The second edition of the DSM, DSM-II,[3] continued to group Pedophilia as one of several types of "sexual deviations." However, "sexual deviations" were no longer grouped as a type of sociopathic personality. Instead, they were grouped under the category of "nonpsychotic mental disorders." Like its predecessor, DSM-II did not provide explicit criteria for the diagnosis of Pedophilia. However, the "sexual deviations category," of which Pedophilia was a subtype, was described as follows:

This category is for individuals whose sexual interests are directed primarily toward objects other than people of the opposite sex, toward sexual acts not usually associated with coitus, or toward coitus performed under bizarre circumstances as in necrophilia, pedophilia, sexual sadism, and fetishism. Even though many find their practices distasteful, they remain unable to substitute normal sexual behavior for them. This diagnosis is not appropriate for individuals who perform deviant sexual acts because normal sexual objects are not available to them. (p. 44)

DSM-III[4] departed significantly from its predecessors. It discontinued the use of the term "sexual deviation," replacing it with the term "paraphilias." This new term is less ambiguous because it emphasizes that the deviation ("para") refers to that to which the person is attracted ("philia"). The "paraphilias" are grouped as one of three major subtypes of "psychosexual disorders," itself a major category not subgrouped. In the DSM-III, Pedophilia is described as follows:

The essential feature is the act or fantasy of engaging in sexual activity with prepubertal children as a repeatedly preferred or exclusive method of achieving sexual excitement. The difference in age between the adult with this disorder and the prepubertal child is arbitrarily set at ten years or more. For late adolescents with the disorder, no precise age difference is specified; and clinical judgement must be used, the sexual maturity of the child as well as the age difference being taken into account. . . . Isolated sexual acts with children do not warrant the diagnosis of Pedophilia. (p. 271)

Thus, DSM-III, unlike its two predecessors, defined Pedophilia more in terms of psychological features than deviant behavior. Hence, the emphasis was on "repeatedly preferred fantasy or sexual activity." Moreover, fairly explicit diagnostic criteria for Pedophilia were provided for the first time in the DSM-III.

The revision of DSM-III, DSM-III-R,[5] provides even more explicit criteria. However, the diagnostic criteria were made more inclusive by dropping the requirement that the sexual activity had to be *repeatedly* preferred or that the sexual activity had to be the exclusive method of achieving sexual excitement. The DSM-III-R definition for Pedophilia states the following:

The essential feature of this disorder is recurrent, intense, sexual urges and sexually arousing fantasies, of at least six months duration, involving sexual activity with a prepubescent child. The person has acted on these urges, or is markedly distressed by them. The age of the child is generally 13 or younger. The age of the person is arbitrarily set at age 16 years or older and at least 5 years older than the child. For late adolescents with the disorder, no precise age difference is specified, and clinical judgment must be used; both the sexual maturity of the child and the age difference must be taken into account. . . . Do not include a late adolescent involved in an ongoing sexual relationship with a 12 or 13-year-old. . . . Isolated sexual acts with children do not necessarily warrant the diagnosis of Pedophilia. (p. 284)

Thus, while the fantasies or urges need not be the "repeatedly preferred" means of achieving sexual excitement, the requirement that they be "recurrent or intense" maintains the emphasis on psychological manifestations. Moreover, DSM-III-R provided for differentiation in three areas within the subcategory of Pedophilia. First, the clinician should specify whether the disorder involves primarily children of the same sex, opposite sex, or both. Second, he or she has to specify whether the person's sexual activity is limited to relatives (incest) or includes children outside his family. Finally, the clinician must specify whether the person is attracted only to children (exclusive type) or is also sexually attracted to adults as well (nonexclusive type).

Limitations of the DSM Nomenclature

Several criticisms of the DSM classification of Pedophilia can be made. Some of these comments most certainly apply to other classification systems. First, considerable specific information is inevitably lost when labels are used. At best, the use of a label ensures only that the patient possesses certain characteristics that are assumed to be prototypic of the condition labeled. Thus, patients will almost always show characteristics that are not associated with the diagnostic label assigned to them. Furthermore, two persons with the DSM-III-R label (diagnosis) of Pedophilia will share certain characteristics, but will also differ in other important aspects. Second, the category of Pedophilia is primarily descriptive; it simply *names* but does not *explain* the condition or disorder. Even when etiological factors are implied, these are associational rather than causative. For example, DSM-III-R notes that many persons with Pedophilia have also been victims of sexual abuse in childhood. Although the two circumstances seem to be related, it cannot be assumed that one causes the other.

Third, the DSM category of Pedophilia is not entirely distinct from other paraphilias or from other disorders. For example, considerable overlap exists between Pedophilia and Exhibitionism to the extent that it may be difficult to make differential diagnosis in some cases. Consider the case in which a man primarily exposes himself to prepubescent children and occasionally fondles the children. Is he suffering from Exhibitionism or Pedophilia or both? Furthermore, are we to assume that one who shows all manifestations of the syndrome for only five months is essentially free of Pedophilia? The criterion of six months is obviously arbitrary.

Strengths of the DSM Nomenclature

Despite the above criticisms, the DSM classification system has several laudable features. First, the system attempts to classify disorders that people may be experiencing rather than the people themselves. As noted previously, this approach results in a more precise and potentially valid system. Second, the DSM provides fairly explicit criteria for each disorder. These specifications enhance interrater reliability, on which validity is so dependent.

Third, the DSM system is subject to periodic review and modification designed to improve precision, distinctiveness, and reliability of the categories. One only needs to consider the incremental improvements reflected in the several editions of the DSM to appreciate this third asset.

Perhaps the most significant strength of the DSM classification system is its multiaxial evaluative feature. Each person is evaluated on each of five axes: clinical syndromes such as Pedophilia (Axis I); developmental and personality disorders (Axis II); physical disorders (Axis III); severity of psychosocial stressors (Axis IV); and global assessment of functioning (Axis V). This multiaxial approach to evaluation and diagnosis ensures that the clinician will develop a comprehensive clinical picture of the patient rather than focus on a single presenting problem. Furthermore, it permits the clinician to take account of social and environmental factors that may be affecting the manifestation of the presenting problem.

There is little doubt that the DSM diagnostic nomenclature has much to recommend it to clinicians who assess sex offenders. Moreover, it is the official system available at this time and should be used routinely as part of any assessment of sex offenders. This consideration does not preclude simultaneous use of other classification systems, particularly when they may facilitate treatment planning. Even when the DSM system is not considered particularly useful for treatment purposes, it should still be used to evaluate the offender. In this way the clinician can be assured that the language of his or her assessment will be understood by most other clinicians. Further, routine use of the system for diagnostic purposes will provide data that can be used to improve classification of sex offenders, and thereby facilitate research.

The suggestion that the DSM classification system should be used routinely in the assessment of sex offenders should not be taken to mean that every sex offender is diagnosable as having a psychosexual disorder. It is possible that many offenders will not meet the full criteria for the pedophilic syndrome, even though they have engaged in a pedophilic act. A particular behavior such as sexual abuse of a child is not synonymous with the classification of Pedophilia. The clinician should avoid assigning the diagnosis of Pedophilia unless the patient clearly meets the stated criteria. Otherwise, the utility of the nomenclature will eventually be undermined.

The failure to find a diagnosis of Pedophilia should not necessarily preclude treatment of the sex offender. For example, the offender may have certain skill deficits and/or cognitions that predispose him to engage in sexually deviant behavior. These may be legitimately addressed in treatment, regardless of whether the offender meets the full criteria for Pedophilia.

THE COMPREHENSIVE ASSESSMENT

The evaluation and diagnosis of child molesters is begun by gathering information about the individual's past or present medical and psychiatric history, past or present legal charges, as well as a variety of other information. The evaluation proceeds with an extensive clinical interview by a clinician, a full range of psychological testing when appropriate, and a clinical laboratory assessment, if available, of the individual's response to sexually explicit deviant and nondeviant stimuli (penile plethysmography). At the end of the evaluation, a determination should be made as to whether the individual has a psychosexual and/or other mental disorder, and if so, whether the patient can benefit from treatment.

Clinical Interview

The clinical interview is the clinician's principal diagnostic tool for the acquisition of complex data on which to base the final assessment. The clinical history provides the clinician with a longitudinal view of the personal development of the child molester.

When interviewing the child molester, the clinician should be aware of several considerations. Child molesters are usually highly sensitive about their deviancy. Even when not intentionally deceitful, the child molester may deny the existence of deviant sexual activity in an unconscious effort to rationalize the activity, hoping that others will believe that there is no problem associated with his sexuality. The fact that he may be a child molester could for him be so frightening and distressing as to make him incapable of admitting it. Additionally, if he is aware that he is a child abuser, he probably expects rejection and disapproval whenever the matter is discussed. The clinician may have to probe, challenge, and confront the individual to get the essential information. Care must be taken because bold confrontation may destroy rapport. Unfortunately, however, there is sometimes little other choice. Nevertheless, the clinician should realize that in many instances he or she will not be able to obtain a fully accurate assessment of the patient's deviancy during the formal evaluation process. Almost invariably, the patient reveals additional information about his sexual deviancy over the course of treatment. The clinician should, where possible, and always after informed consent is obtained, gather information from other sources such as significant others, depositions, arrest reports, attorneys, and documents from educational, mental health, military, vocational, social service, and criminal justice agencies. Evidence that contradicts the child molester's statements should be presented to him quite frankly. The general themes from reports of others may be discussed with him, although it is seldom appropriate or necessary to go into specific detail. When the sources of information and details reported are in conflict, as is commonly the case, objectivity is extremely important. Clinical acumen and judgment are necessary in order to determine the relevance, reliability, and validity of the information.

The evaluation process of the alleged child molester, which relies heavily on the clinical interview, is discussed in Chapter 10. Briefly, a general psychological evaluation with specific inquiry into the sexual area is essential. Detailed information pertaining to the child molester's sexual offenses and his current situation should be attained. Sexual history should include evaluation of the educational/learning experience, sexual abuse, paraphilic experiences, and sexual dysfunctions. Otherwise the interview proceeds like a routine diagnostic evaluation as performed for other mental disorders.

Psychological Testing

It could be argued that comprehensive assessment can be done exclusively through clinical interview and need not involve formal psychological testing. However, testing has its advantages in terms of providing a relatively "objective" standard of comparison, producing results that are often quantifiable and therefore useful for research purposes, and bringing a different method to the assessment process. One can have more confidence in the validity of the results to the extent that similar findings are obtained through different methods.

Both traditional psychological tests and newer behavioral or cognitive-behavioral inventories provide a quantitative means for comparison of child molesters with the normal population and, in the case of those standardized on a population with a known paraphilia, a comparison with sexually deviant populations.

Traditional psychological tests. In most traditionally oriented clinical settings, the utility of a psychological test battery containing a variety of measures is generally acknowledged. The need for a battery of tests arises not only because of the limited validity of single tests, but also because different instruments detect different aspects and levels of patient functioning. The Minnesota Multiphasic Personality Inventory (MMPI),[12] for example, is more useful as a measure of general psychopathology than as a measure of general personality style. To assess general personality style, the Millon Clinical Multiaxial Inventory (MCMI)[24] would be a better choice than the MMPI. Likewise, neither the MMPI nor the MCMI provides specific information about a patient's interpersonal behaviors (e.g., assertiveness, aggressiveness, shyness, self-confidence, and disregard for the rights of others). These perhaps can be more effectively assessed with the Interpersonal Behavior Survey (IBS)[20] or other self-report inventories. Because the relationship between tests reflects the person's multilevel system of functioning, a broad-based multidimensional assessment program is needed for child molesters. In many traditionally oriented clinics, "projective" procedures such as the Rorschach Test,[32] Thematic Apperception Test,[25] or Draw-A-Person Test,[36] are commonly combined with "objective" tests such as the MMPI, MCMI, IBS, or the Clinical Analysis Questionnaire.[17] Here again, this use of multiple instruments helps one to develop a comprehensive clinical picture of the patient's level of functioning and psychopathology.

Behavioral measurements. Behaviorally oriented laboratories generally use several types of behavioral measurements when assessing sex offenders. These would include instruments that record the variety of sexual experiences, both normal and pathological, as well as sexual beliefs, attitudes, and orientation. The procedures usually include penile plethysmography, which measures the individual's sexual arousal to a variety of stimuli, both deviant and nondeviant.

PSYCHOLOGICAL ASSESSMENT
BATTERY UTILIZED AT NFETC

In order to maximize validity and to facilitate comparison between patients for research purposes, the evaluating psychologist uses the following assessment battery when possible:

1. *Clinical interview.* This interview includes a mental status examination, psychosocial history and a detailed psychosexual

history of the patient. The psychosexual history includes detailed questioning about nondeviant (i.e., with consenting peers) and deviant sexual encounters. Particular attention is paid to deviant sexual behavior, including: (1) the age of the victim; (2) the social relationship between the patient and the victim; (3) the nature, frequency, and persistence of the sexual activity; (4) the frequency and nature of fantasies that precede or accompany the deviant behavior or that accompany masturbation; and (5) the distinguishing characteristics of the victims.

2. *Wide Range Achievement Test-Revised Reading Subtest.*[14] This test is used to obtain an estimate of the person's reading level in order to aid with test selection and to assess the resident's need for help in processing written materials used in the treatment program.

3. *Wechsler Adult Intelligence Scale-Revised (WAIS-R).*[37] Unless the patient has a history of academic failure, deficient intelligence, or other evidence of possible cognitive impairment, the psychologist begins by administering the Silverstein two-subtest (vocabulary and block design) abbreviated WAIS-R.[35] If this initial testing yields a score below the Low Average range or reveals significant discrepancy between the two subtest scores, then the full WAIS-R is administered.

4. *Personality testing with the Minnesota Multiphasic Personality Inventory,*[12] *Millon Clinical Multiaxial Inventory,*[24] *Draw-A-Person Test,*[36] *and Incomplete Sentences Blank.*[33] Additional testing may be done with the Rorschach[32] and/or Thematic Apperception Test[25] when indicated, such as in cases when the patient lacks sufficient reading ability to complete objective tests, or when the results of the standard battery yield inconsistent results.

5. *Interpersonal Behavior Survey*[20] *and the Personality Research Form-E.*[13] These two instruments are used to assess more directly specific traits and interpersonal behaviors that can only be inferred from the standard personality tests. These include such things as general assertiveness, general aggressiveness, dominance, endurance, and autonomy. In addition, these two instruments are more conducive to measuring change in the patient's interpersonal behavior over time than are the standard personality tests.

While the above procedures comprise assessment, in most cases additional testing may be done, depending on the results obtained from the standard battery. Further testing most often involves neuropsychological screening procedures that are administered to help determine functional abilities when the question of brain dysfunction has been raised.

CASE EXAMPLE DEMONSTRATING THE
USE OF TRADITIONAL ASSESSMENT

The following case is presented in order to show how data from traditional assessment procedures are integrated with behavioral assessment data to develop a comprehensive clinical picture of the patient. The behavioral data included the form, the frequency, and the duration of fantasy, as well as the actual sexual behavior involving children. This information was obtained through an interview. The traditional assessment procedures included: the Wide Range Achievement Reading Test-Revised (WRAT-R);[14] Wechsler Adult Intelligence Scale-Revised (WAIS-R);[37] Minnesota Multiphasic Personality Inventory (MMPI);[12] Millon Clinical Multiaxial Inventory (MCMI);[24] Draw-A-Person Test (DAP);[36] Bender Gestalt Test;[29] Rey Complex Figure Test;[31] and the clinical interview.

Demographic and Historical Data

The patient was a married, white male in his thirties who was serving two concurrent prison sentences (less than 10 years each) for the crimes of Lewd and Lascivious Conduct and Lewd Conduct in the Presence of a Child. The crimes occurred when the patient fondled a 13-year-old girl, and, on a different occasion, forced a seven-year-old female child to masturbate him. Both victims were friends of the patient's daughters and the patient was well acquainted with the victims' parents. Both victims were spending the night at the patient's home at the time they were molested.

The patient was a high-school graduate and a veteran of the Marine Corps who had worked sporadically as a laborer. He had been married twice and had fathered nine children, most of whom he had not had contact with for several years. He had a history of prior arrests, convictions, and incarcerations for various crimes, including Driving While Intoxicated, Breaking and Entering, Failure to Pay Child Support, Unemployment Fraud, and Violation of Probation.

The history also included heavy abuse of alcohol, after which he often became violent. The violence took the form of wife beating, tearing up the home, and on one occasion, breaking the windows of his car. The medical history included bleeding ulcers (age 21), and a concussion (age 25). In addition, he attempted suicide (age 23) by driving his car into a guard rail at a high rate of speed after his first wife threatened to leave him. Shortly after this suicide attempt, his wife did leave, and the patient then experienced a "nervous breakdown." He was voluntarily hospitalized for 30 days, during which time he apparently received antidepressant medication and psychotherapy.

Behavioral Assessment Data

The first sexual encounter occurred at age 12 when the patient fondled an eight-year-old girl after convincing her to go somewhere alone with him. This pattern of talking young girls into going off with him and then fondling them continued until age 18 when he entered the Marine Corps. He reportedly dated girls his age throughout high school, but did not have intercourse until age 19 when he became involved with a prostitute while overseas. The fondling of young girls (ages seven to 13) was reportedly stopped temporarily over an 11-year period from age 18 to 29, although he continued to engage in sexual fantasy involving young girls during this period. The deviant behavior resumed for unknown reasons, always taking the form of molesting the female friends of his children. The patient reportedly never molested his own children, although he had continued to have sexual fantasies involving his 10-year-old stepdaughter from his current marriage. These fantasies occurred on the average of one to two times daily, lasted for about 10 minutes, and involved imagery of touching and intercourse with the child. He masturbated to the fantasies at least once a week.

Intellectual Data

The WAIS-R revealed Average intellectual functioning as indicated by Verbal, Performance, and Full Scale IQ scores of 111, 86, and 99 respectively. The discrepancy between Verbal and Performance IQ and the pattern of performance on the several subtests suggested clear deficits in the ability to perform tasks that require visual perception, visual motor coordination and speed, or visual motor construction (e.g., copying or drawing figures). These same deficits were also evident in the patient's performance on the Bender Gestalt Test[29] and the Rey Complex Figure Test,[31] both of which were administered because of the Verbal-Performance IQ discrepancy.

Personality Test Data

Collectively, the testing and interview impressions were consistent in revealing pervasive impulsivity, intolerance for delay or frustration, easy boredom, and deficient planning and problem-solving ability. These features were accompanied by rebellious and revengeful attitudes, and relatively low regard for obligations, routines, or others. Interpersonally, the patient appeared distrustful and hypersensitive to criticism. Testing also suggested difficulty experiencing tender emotions and limited skill in taking the role of others. Finally, he seemed to experience periodically mild to moderate depression over repeated failures and over his inability to maintain satisfying and stable intimate relationships.

Overall Clinical Formulation

This appears to be a case of Pedophilia, nonexclusive type (attracted to female children and adults), involving fantasy and sexual behavior with nonfamily members primarily, but with active fantasy and suspected involvement with family members as well. The patient is not currently depressed, but probably experiences mild to moderate bouts of depression, especially in response to interpersonal disappointments. The history of parental loss in the early years may be associated with the depressive features. The Pedophilia is accompanied by chronic alcohol dependence. Both of these disorders occur in the context of a longstanding personality disorder with narcissistic and antisocial features. The narcissistic and antisocial features combine to yield a guarded prognosis. This is because such persons typically experience little or no anxiety. Without sufficient anxiety, the patient will find it very difficult to maintain motivation. Even when the clinician is able to sustain motivation through external means, the patient may work only hard enough to avoid some negative consequence. Furthermore, the narcissistic-antisocial personality has impaired capacity to form and maintain close relationships. Unfortunately, this deficit also applies to the "therapeutic" relationship, which no doubt accounts for much of the positive gains made in therapy across various techniques and approaches. As if his impaired capacity to form close relationships is not enough of an obstacle to treatment, the narcissistic-antisocial personality also tends to be very mistrustful and resentful toward authority. This mistrust and resentment is likely to be expressed through resistance and outright noncompliance with treatment.

Notwithstanding the poor prognosis, the patient appears amenable for treatment on the basis of his average intelligence, lack of severe personality disturbance, and manifestation of Psychosexual Disorder. Moreover, he seems interested in treatment, although one suspects that his motivation is primarily external. In order to maximize the effects of treatment, some effort should be devoted toward increasing internal sources of motivation. While the therapist is likely to have some difficulty establishing a working relationship with the patient, the inpatient setting permits more intensity with which the clinician might be able to work past the patient's resistance. In this particular case, it might be helpful for the clinician to consider establishing substantial rapport before making aggressive confrontations. In addition, the clinician should be prepared for inevitable resistance and power plays so as to resist the temptation to be pulled into power struggles with the patient. Although the patient has a tough exterior, underneath he is quite easily hurt and threatened. Very strong confrontation and criticism is likely to bolster his defensive armor, especially if this occurs early in the treatment process.

Treatment should also address the depressive features, the patient's pervasive impulsivity, deficient problem-solving ability, poor empathic ability, and limited skill in the appropriate expression of anger. Finally, deviant sexual arousal should be reduced, perhaps through masturbatory satiation and/or olfactory aversion.

SUMMARY

Comprehensive assessment and diagnosis of the child molester is necessary in order for the clinician to develop and implement a viable treatment plan. Without thorough assessment prior to the initiation of treatment, one cannot be reasonably certain that the treatments are consistent with the client's needs.

A thorough assessment provides an accurate description of the form, duration, intensity, and frequency of problematic sexual behaviors. It also identifies the presence of other (nonsexual) psychological problems, whether or not these are believed to be associated with the client's problematic sexual behaviors. Of equal importance, the comprehensive assessment identifies the broader personal and social context within which problem behaviors (sexual and nonsexual) manifest themselves.

The objective of comprehensive assessment of the child molester—description of sexual and nonsexual psychological problems and the personal/social context in which these problems are manifested—can be accomplished most reliably through use of traditional and behavioral assessment procedures. In combination, these two approaches can yield a much more complete clinical picture than what can be obtained through use of either approach alone.

Furthermore, assessment of child molesters should when possible, result in the assignment of a diagnosis from the *Diagnostic and Statistical Manual of Mental Disorders* (DSM). This is not to suggest that every person who engages in inappropriate sexual behavior with children is diagnosable as suffering from a Psychosexual Disorder (paraphilias and sexual dysfunctions) as defined by the DSM. Nor is it suggested that psychological treatment should be contingent upon the finding of a Psychosexual Disorder. In fact, many sex offenders in need of intervention to reduce their risk to the community will not meet the full criteria for Psychosexual Disorder as specified in the DSM. Routine diagnosis of the child molester, whether or not it confirms the presence of a Psychosexual Disorder, will, however, facilitate future empirical study of this client group as well as the relative effectiveness of treatments provided to them.

REFERENCES

1. Abel, G. G., Becker, J. V., Cunningham-Rathner, J., Rouleau, J. L., Kaplan, M., & Reich, J. (1984). *The Treatment of Child Molesters.* Atlanta, GA: Behavioral Medicine Laboratory, Emory University.
2. American Psychiatric Association (1952). *Diagnostic and Statistical Manual of Mental Disorders (DSM-I).* Washington, D.C.: American Psychiatric Association.
3. American Psychiatric Association (1968). *Diagnostic and Statistical Manual of Mental Disorders, Second Edition (DSM-II).* Washington, D.C.: American Psychiatric Association.
4. American Psychiatric Association (1980). *Diagnostic and Statistical Manual of Mental Disorders, Third Edition (DSM-III).* Washington, D.C.: American Psychiatric Association.
5. American Psychiatric Association (1987). *Diagnostic and Statistical Manual of Mental Disorders, Third Edition, Revised (DSM-III-R).* Washington, D.C.: American Psychiatric Association.
6. Anderson, W. P., Kunce, J. T., & Rich, B. (1979). Sex offenders: Three personality types. *Journal of Clinical Psychology, 35,* 671.
7. Bandura, A. (1977). *Social Learning Theory.* Englewood Cliffs, NJ: Prentice-Hall.
8. Dollard, J., & Miller, N. E. (1950). *Personality and Psychotherapy: An Analysis in Terms of Learning, Thinking and Culture.* New York: McGraw-Hill.
9. Gough, H. G. (1956). *California Psychological Inventory.* Palo Alto: Consulting Psychologists Press.
10. Hall, G. C. N., Maiuro, R. D., Vitaliano, P. P., & Procter, W. C. (1986). The utility of the MMPI with men who have sexually assaulted children. *Journal of Consulting & Clinical Psychology, 54,* 493.
11. Hall, R. L., & Jenkins-Hall, K. D. (1987). MCMI profiles of child molesters versus rapists (Research in Progress). The authors can be

contacted at the Center for Prevention of Child Molestation, University of South Florida, 13301 N. Bruce B. Downs Blvd., Tampa, FL 33612.

12. Hathaway, S. R., & McKinley, J. C. (1967). *Minnesota Multiphasic Personality Inventory*. Minneapolis: University of Minnesota Press.

13. Jackson, D. N. (1984). *Personality Research Form Manual*. Port Huron, MI: Research Psychologist Press.

14. Jastak, S., & Wilkinson, G. S. (1984). *The Wide Range Achievement Test-Revised*. Wilmington, DC: Jastak Associates.

15. Kanfer, F. H., & Phillips, J. S. (1970). *Learning Foundations of Behavior Therapy*. New York: Wiley.

16. Karacan, I., Williams, R. L., Guerrero, M. W., Scales, P. J., Thornby, J. I., & Hursch, C. J. (1974). Nocturnal penile tumescence and sleep of convicted rapists and other prisoners. *Archives of Sexual Behavior. 3*, 19.

17. Krug, S. E. (1980). *Clinical Analysis Questionnaire Manual*. Champaign, IL: Institute for Personality and Ability Testing.

18. Langevin, R., Paitich, D., Freeman, R., Mann, K., & Handy, L. (1978). Personality characteristics and sexual anomalies in males. *Canadian Journal of Behavioral Science, 10,* 222.

19. Levin, S. M., & Stava, L. (1987). Personality characteristics of sex offenders: A review. *Archives of Sexual Behavior, 16,* 57.

20. Mauger, P. A., & Adkinson, D. R. (1980). *Interpersonal Behavior Survey Manual*. Los Angeles: Western Psychological Services.

21. Meichenbaum, D. H. (1976). A cognitive-behavior modification approach to assessment. In M. Hersen, & A. S. Bellack (Eds.), *Behavioral Assessment: A Practical Handbook*. New York: Pergamon.

22. Millon, T. (1981). *Disorders of Personality: DSM-III: Axis II*. New York: John Wiley and Sons.

23. Millon, T. (1987). Personality disorders and their assessment with the Millon inventories (Training workshop conducted in Dallas, Texas, June, 1987).

24. Millon, T., Green, C. J., & Meagher, R. B. (1982). *Millon Clinical Multiaxial Inventory*. Minneapolis: National Computer Systems.

25. Murray, H. A. (1943). *Thematic Apperception Test Manual*. Cambridge: Harvard University Press.

26. Nichols, H. R., & Molinder, I. (1984). *Multiphasic Sex Inventory Manual*. Tacoma, WA: Nichols and Molinder.

27. Panton, J. H. (1958). MMPI configurations among crime classification groups. *Journal of Clinical Psychology, 14,* 305.

28. Pascal, G. R., & Herzberg, F. L. (1952). The detection of deviant sexual practice from performance on the Rorschach. *Journal of Projective Techniques, 16,* 366.

29. Pascal, G. R., & Suttell, B. J. (1951). *Bender Gestalt Test Manual*. New York: Grune & Stratton.

30. Quinsey, V. L., Arnold, L. S., & Pruesse, M. G. (1980). MMPI profiles of men referred for a pretrial psychiatric assessment as a function of offense type. *Journal of Clinical Psychology, 36,* 410.

31. Rey, A. (1970). *Complex Figure Test*. Berwyn, PA: Swets North America, Inc.

32. Rorschach, H. (1954). *Psychodiagnostic Plates*. New York: Grune & Stratton.

33. Rotter, J. B. (1950). *Incomplete Sentences Blank.* New York: The Psychological Corporation.
34. Scott, R. L. (1982). Analysis of the need systems of twenty male rapists. *Psychological Reports, 51,* 1119.
35. Silverstein, A. B. (1982). Two- and four-subtest short forms of the Wechsler Adult Intelligence Scale-Revised. *Journal of Consulting & Clinical Psychology, 50,* 415.
36. Urban, W. H. (1963). *The Draw-A-Person Manual.* Los Angeles: Western Psychological Services.
37. Wechsler, D. (1981). *Wechsler Adult Intelligence Scale–Revised.* Cleveland, OH: The Psychological Corporation.
38. Wysocki, A. C., & Wysocki, B. A. (1977). Human figure drawings of sex offenders. *Journal of Clinical Psychology, 33,* 278.

CHAPTER 5

Treatment and Management

The primary goal of the treatment of the child molester is to control the deviant behavior patterns, impulses, and preoccupations that impel the sexual exploitation of children. These characteristics must either be internally or externally inhibited to reduce the risk of repeated offenses. However, it is common for clinicians to meet some deeply rooted and complex resistances to treatment from sex offenders. Langevin and Lang point out that clinicians cannot change the child molester's preference for children.[37] The pedophile may be reluctant to give up the ego-syntonic behavior that prompts child victimization because the actual act is linked with the molester's sexual identity, and, as such, is valued by the offender. When asked in a study by Frederic, very few pedophiles indicated that they wanted to lose their erotic attraction to children.[24]

As mentioned earlier, Krafft-Ebing despaired at how difficult and tiring it often seems to treat child molesters and that treatment is more often than not a waste of time. He concluded that the most effective treatment measure is to keep the potential child molester away from children. Interestingly, society currently adheres to this form of ostracism by incarcerating known sex offenders. However, incarceration, at best, is an incomplete, temporary solution, since most imprisoned sex abusers are released into the community. For clinicians who treat sex offenders, the objective must therefore be not only to effect changes in the external living environment, but also to alter the internal psychological predisposition of the offender.

In this chapter, four treatment approaches will be discussed: (1) organic, (2) psychotherapeutic, (3) behavioral, and (4) psychosocial. Although all approaches should be considered as possible avenues of treatment, ultimately the clinician must integrate the identified needs of the child molester with the available resources.

ORGANIC INTERVENTIONS

As noted in Chapter 3, the androgen testosterone, formed by the interstitial cells of the testes, is the most important hormone in the maintenance of and the determining factor in male sexual behavior.[12,32] Not only does this hormone promote the production of sperm, but it also causes the development of secondary sexual characteristics and instigates the male sex drive.

There are two organic treatments that reduce a child molester's sexual interest by lowering the testosterone level: surgical castration and antiandrogen therapy.

Castration

Throughout history surgical castration, or the removal of the testes, has been practiced on sex offenders as both a preventive intervention and as a retribution for deviant sexual behavior. Castration results in the complete shutdown of androgen production from the testes, which produces 95% of the body's total testosterone; the remaining 5% is secreted from the adrenal cortex of the adrenal gland.

Although serious criticisms regarding the methodology employed to determine relapse rates have been raised,[33] recidivism rates of 1.1% to 16.8% following castration have been reported.[10,12,54] In a review of castration as a treatment for sex offenders, Bradford[12] concludes: "There is no doubt that castration, even allowing the largest margin for methodological difficulties, has a massive effect on sexual recidivism in the post-castration state" (p. 368). Yet, regardless of the efficacy of the treatment, the many ethical considerations involved with this irreversible procedure make castration an unacceptable treatment modality.

For further analysis of surgical castration as a treatment approach for sex offenders, the reader may consult Freund's work on therapeutic sex-drive reduction,[25] Bradford's distillation on organic treatments for the male sexual offender,[12] Berlin's biomedical report on sex offenders,[9] Heim and Hursch's review and critique of recent European medical literature regarding castration for sex offenders,[33] and Stürup's "Castration: The Total Treatment."[54]

Hormonal Treatment

If deviant sexual arousal or undesirable sexual behavior is determined at least to some extent by sex drive, which is androgen-dependent in most males, then the aberrant urges and behavior may be brought under better control by interfering with the hormonal mechanisms. At the present time there are two medications called *antiandrogens* that are being used to regulate unwanted sexual behavior. Medroxyprogesterone acetate (MPA) and cyproterone acetate (CPA) are antiandrogenic compounds that inhibit the action of androgens (i.e., testosterone). In contrast to the surgical removal of the gonads, antiandrogens provide a reversible means to lower male sexual hormones, and, therefore, sex drive. In this case, the strength of arousal is reduced only temporarily, and the sex drive (including any uncorrected aberrant arousal patterns) returns when the drug is discontinued.

Recent studies and case reports support that the use of MPA and CPA suppresses libido and overt sexual behavior in sex offenders.[4,5,10,13,19,26,57] The results of more than 20 years of studies in the United States, Canada, and Europe have shown that sex offenders who are treated with antiandrogen hormones, usually in addition to ongoing counseling, have been able to self-regulate their sexual behavior. For the child molester there is said to be a decreased erotic "turn on" to children. When used with an individual who is motivated to govern his sexual behavior, these medications may work successfully.

The outcome studies evaluating the effectiveness of MPA have determined that the drug is quite effective during treatment, but relapses occur frequently following discontinuation of the treatment.[30] When examining the literature on the effectiveness of CPA, the recidivism rates of sex offenders ranged from 54%–100% prior to treatment, and fell to 0% with treatment.[12]

Medroxyprogesterone Acetate (MPA)

Depo-Provera is a long-acting form of medroxyprogesterone. Although it is unknown how Depo-Provera exactly functions, it is thought that the drug suppresses the release of testosterone from the testes through its effect on the brain and the pituitary gland's secretion of LH. The ultimate effect of Depo-Provera is a reduction of the level of testosterone in the blood stream. Typically, when an adult male is given oral MPA or Depo-Provera, the blood level of testosterone is lowered to that of a normal prepubertal boy. Because testosterone not only affects sex drive but also contributes to the general energy drive of the male, individuals taking Depo-Provera can expect to be less energetic and aggressive.

The Johns Hopkins' group conducted the longest series of studies evaluating the effectiveness of MPA. They followed 20 adult paraphilic sex offenders who were treated with MPA for periods ranging from three months to five years, nine months (the median is two years, five months).[10,46] At one year, and again at 13 years, these subjects and their families and/or social agencies were interviewed. In this study, "relapse" is defined as reinstitutionalization or assignment to probation, so the actual recidivism rate may have actually been higher than the data indicate. According to the results, three (15%) of the 20 men relapsed while they were taking MPA. Alcohol was clearly implicated in one of the relapse cases. At the 13-year follow-up, it was determined that 65% of these 20 offenders had relapsed after discontinuing treatment. In general, the tendency toward relapse was associated with failure to comply with the therapy, with drug or alcohol intake, and with lack of peer-bondedness to a significant other.

A study by Gagne[26] reported on 48 sex offenders who were treated with MPA, both while in the hospital and after discharge. As outpatients, they were evaluated weekly and had their testosterone levels monitored monthly for 12 months. Forty offenders (83%) were relapse-free during treatment for a period ranging from one-to-three years. One patient terminated because of phlebitis, and seven offenders who had antisocial personalities returned to deviant sexual behavior. Although the results are promising, the research design, based on self-report, may devalue the study's reliability.

Numerous other side effects from MPA have been cited. Those resulting from these medications are reproduced in Table 5.1 from Hucker.[34] However, the effects of Depo-Provera are reversed by stopping medication, and within one-to-three weeks after cessation, sexual arousal (whether deviant or nondeviant), penile erection, and the ability to ejaculate begin to return. The erotic stimulus, whether one is attracted to adults or children, remains unchanged.

While Depo-Provera is available in the United States, it has not received the Federal Food and Drug Administration's (FDA) official labeling approval for use in treating sex offenders. However, once approved for marketing, the FDA does not limit how physicians must use a drug.[22] According to the FDA, such unapproved or

Table 5.1
Reported Effects and Side Effects of
Medroxyprogesterone Acetate (Provera)

| ↓ Frequency and intensity of sexual thoughts/erections/ejaculations |
| ↓ Ejaculatory volume |
| ↓ Sperm count (↑ abnormal forms) |
| Hypogonadism |
| ↑ Appetite and weight gain |
| ↑ Fatigue |
| Mild depression, lethargy, nervousness, restlessness |
| Insomnia; headaches; nightmares |
| Hot and cold flashes |
| Loss of body hair |
| Gastro-intestinal upsets; nausea |
| Leg cramps; hyperglycemia; dyspnea |
| Irregular gallbladder function |
| Diverticulitis |
| Aggravation of migraine |
| Hypertension; phlebitis |
| Breast tumors (in beagle dogs) |

From "Management of Anomalous Sexual Behavior with Drugs," by Stephen J. Hucker. *Modern Medicine of Canada, 40,* 1985. Reprinted by permission.

unlabeled applications may be appropriate and rational in certain circumstances and may, in fact, reflect approaches to drug therapy already extensively reported in the literature.[22] The use of Depo-Provera for the management of such anomalous sexual behavior as child molestation appears to fall into this category.[56]

Protocol for Using MPA

Before beginning treatment, the child molester should be given a general physical and neurological examination. Often, consultation with an internist or endocrinologist is advised. A laboratory examination, including a full blood count, liver functioning tests, serum testosterone level, FSH level, LH level, glucose, and electrolytes are recommended.

As in all major treatments requiring informed consent, the patient should then be counseled by the physician and given sufficient information concerning the risks and benefits of the drug therapy.[56] The purpose of the medication, its expected effects, and its undesired side effects should be discussed with the patient. Only those individuals who voluntarily accept the drug therapy should be medicated. Table 5.2 (see pp. 78 and 79) shows the consent form used by The Johns Hopkins Hospital Sexual Disorders Clinic.

The dosage level for Depo-Provera must be tailored for the specific patient. Intramuscular (IM) injections of Depo-Provera range from 100–800 mg every seven days. According to the Johns Hopkins group, the typical IM weekly maintenance dose for sex offenders is 500 mg.[11] Hucker[34] reports that a dose of 200–400 mg IM every seven-to-ten days is usually required. The oral dose can begin with 100–200 milligrams, once daily. Although some patients seem to need as much as 400 mg, Hucker notes that such a large dose is generally undesirable. Because there is no tolerance buildup to MPA, during the course of treatment most patients do not require a progressively increasing dosage. However, some patients apparently develop psychological dependence on the medication and prefer to continue indefinitely on a low maintenance dosage of Depo-Provera.

Hormonal measures of testosterone, LH, and FSH should be monitored periodically. Hucker[34] recommends monthly monitoring while the drug is being given, and he maintains that the level should be regulated at prepubertal level. However, he notes that the patient's subjective report is a better gauge to dosage, provided that the offender is a reliable historian. In addition to Hucker's precautions, Freund[25] recommends not only periodically assessing plasma testosterone levels, but also evaluating nocturnal penile tumescence and giving physical checkups to minimize general health hazards.

The Johns Hopkins group[11] reports that in some cases there is a long-lasting remission associated with Depo-Provera treatment. In these cases the patient reports that he is no longer compelled to commit sexual offenses. However, if while tapering off on the medication an offender should feel increased urges toward sexual molesting behavior, the dosage should then be increased to a sufficient level to control the tendency.

Despite the ongoing disagreement about how sex offenders must be treated, there should be the awareness that there are three components—thoughts, feelings, and behavior—that must be given attention and possible redirection. While some theorists say that the ideal goal of the treatment process is to modify the child molester's thought patterns, since these deviant thoughts result in pleasurable fantasies that trigger deviant sexual arousal, others would argue that rather than to try changing the offender's deviant thoughts and fantasies, the aim is to modify the molester's ability to act upon them. These modifications can be achieved either through behavioral or chemical means or both.

Supporters of Depo-Provera propose that through the use of chemical means a sex offender's arousal patterns can be kept at such a sufficiently low level that the molester will not respond to his urges. Further, they suggest that it may be possible to titrate the drug so that the child molester loses his arousal toward children but maintains his attraction toward adults, if, of course, the offender originally felt attraction toward both children and age-appropriate adults.

The literature indicates that it may be easier to control or inhibit arousal patterns toward deviant stimuli (i.e., children) than it is to generate arousal patterns toward more age-appropriate stimuli.[39] Because the medications do nothing to replace deviant sexual interest following discontinuation of the drug therapy, the offenders are highly vulnerable to relapse. However, the period under medication provides the child molester with the opportunity to develop appropriate sexual conduct through additional forms of treatment—such as behavior therapy, psychotherapy, or psychosocial education. Thus, it is recommended that such treatments be carried out concurrently.

Cyproterone Acetate (CPA)

Cyproterone acetate (CPA), a progesterone derivative, is an antiandrogen agent that is not currently available in the United States, and, therefore, will only be mentioned briefly here. According to Cooper,[18] CPA became available in Europe during the early 1970s. It is noted to provide a very considerable reduction in sex drive in 80% of the cases when a daily dosage of 100 mg is administered orally.[40] In 20% of the cases, however, only 20 mg daily is needed to achieve a comparable effect. It has also been observed that most individuals who are treated with CPA respond after about one week of treatment. Generally, the patient notices a reduction of sexual appetite and ability to achieve an erection.

In a study assessing the side effects of CPA, Laschet and Laschet[41] reported on the use of CPA for the treatment of 300 men, including a follow-up period of up to eight years. These investigators indicate that the drug was well tolerated by the liver. They observed, however, that during the second-to-sixth week of treatment, such side effects as increased fatigue, the need for more sleep, increased appetite, and mild depression were reported, and that in about one-fifth of the group some gynecomastia was observed after approximately six months of treatment.

Table 5.2
Consent Form of
The Johns Hopkins Hospital Sexual Disorders Clinic
for Use of Depo-Provera

NAME _____

THE JOHNS HOPKINS HOSPITAL
SEXUAL DISORDERS CLINIC   HISTORY # _____

DATE _____

I agree to take medroxyprogesterone acetate (Depo-Provera) in order to try to help reduce the intensity of my sexual urges so that I can better control them. I will also attend regular counseling sessions if requested to do so. Because this medication has only been available for this purpose for a few years I agree to have periodic blood tests and recordings of my weight and blood pressure taken. The amount of blood needed will be about three test tubes full once every six months. I understand that this is being done to help monitor for possible side effects, and to document the effects of treatment upon my hormone levels.

All medications do have side effects which are the unwanted effects that sometimes occur in addition to the planned therapeutic effects. The most common side effects of treament with Depo-Provera include weight gain and increased blood pressure. If your blood pressure becomes too high we may need to treat you with additional medications to lower it. Less common side effects are nightmares, cold sweats and hot flashes. Temporary sexual impotence is also possible. Muscle cramps and a tendency to become easily fatigued have also been reported. You should check with us before taking any other medications. Depo-Provera lowers the sperm count. Therefore, you will likely be unable to father a child while receiving this treatment. However, Depo-Provera should *not* be considered a guaranteed method of birth control.

Depo-Provera is a hormone which is similar to those contained in birth control pills. Therefore, the risk of developing blood clots may exist. Depo-Provera has also been found to increase the frequency of malignant breast tumors (breast cancer) in female beagle dogs, and of uterine cancer in female monkeys. There have been no reports of this drug causing cancer in men.

Other side effects not listed above may also occur in some patients. If you notice any other side effects be sure to notify us. You may phone Dr. Fred Berlin . . . for advice should any suspected side effects occur. During the course of your treatment here we may do additional periodic blood tests to make certain the medication is acting properly and not causing medical problems.

Depo-Provera is usually given once a week by means of two injections, one in each side of your hind end, or if you prefer, one in each arm.

If you sign this form, this will indicate that you are willing to receive the type of treatment outlined here. Your doctors will also explain to you other kinds of treatments that are available to you. You should ask any questions you have about this form of treatment or alternative forms of treatment. You may ask questions in the future if you do not understand something that is being done.

The records from your treatment here will be kept confidential, as is the policy with all medical records in this hospital. If your treatment here involves the use of a drug which is under the jurisdiction of the Food and Drug Administration

(FDA), FDA government officials may look at relevant parts of your medical records as part of their job to review new drugs, or new uses of approved drugs. Depo-Provera has not been approved by the FDA at this time for use as a "sexual appetite suppressant," although the FDA has deemed it to be effective for human use for other purposes. It is, however, permissible for your doctor to prescribe this medication for you through this clinic with your consent.

If you want to talk to anyone about your treatment here because you think you have not been treated fairly or because you think you have been in some way injured you should call Fred S. Berlin, M.D., Ph.D. at . . ., or you may contact the Office of Public Relations here at the Johns Hopkins Hospital.

If, in spite of our recommendations, you do not wish to receive Depo-Provera treatment through this facility, you are permitted to refuse such treatment. Even if you are in this treatment program as a condition of probation, you are still not obligated to take Depo-Provera. If you are receiving counseling here as a condition of probation and you fail to adhere to your agreed-upon appointment schedule, we will notify your Probation Officer that you have been noncompliant. We will not, however, report to your Probation Officer information you tell us as part of the normal doctor–patient privileged relationship. If we felt that in the absence of this form of medication treatment you would very likely not succeed in controlling your sexual behaviors appropriately, we would tell you so. If you decide not to accept Depo-Provera treatment here for your sexual disorder, you would still have the same quality of medical care available to you at Johns Hopkins Hospital for any medical or psychiatric difficulty which you might have, or which might develop in the future. Some patients in our clinic have conditions which do not require Depo-Provera treatment.

If you are agreeable to receiving treatment here with Depo-Provera in the manner outlined above, please sign your name below.

_____   _____
PATIENT'S SIGNATURE   DATE

_____   _____
SIGNATURE OF PARENT OR GUARDIAN   DATE
              (where applicable)

_____   _____
WITNESS TO ABOVE SIGNATURE(S)   DATE

_____   _____
SIGNATURE OF ATTENDING PHYSICIAN   DATE

Note: The protocol outlined above is intended to provide you with treatment for your sexual disorder. From time to time patients receiving treatment through our clinic may be asked to participate in research. If you are asked to participate in research, you will be provided with a separate consent form to be signed agreeing to participate in that particular investigation.

Reprinted by permission of The Johns Hopkins Hospital Sexual Disorders Clinic.

In addition to the above study, Cooper[18] studied nine subjects manifesting deviant hypersexuality who participated in a 20-week outpatient program using the trial drug CPA. By comparing his group to those who used either a placebo or received no drug treatment, Cooper interpreted his results as indicating that CPA had a highly significant effect in reducing male sexual drive and associated sexual arousal. He also noted that the clinical effects were paralleled by approximately a 30% reduction of plasma testosterone levels. The clinical and endocrine changes were completely reversible within a month's period following discontinuation of the drug. For further information about the antiandrogen CPA, readers should consult the publications by Cooper and Laschet and Laschet cited above.

Psychopharmacological Agents

Sexual drive reduction using more standard psychopharmacology has been described.[3,12,55] Abel and his group[3] recommend the addition of minor tranquilizers and/or antipsychotic medication (e.g., Trilafon or Prolixin) when lack of control of deviant impulses is imminent and nonresponsive to behavioral strategies. Another group[55] makes use of a common side effect of phenothiazine antipsychotics—secondary impotence—and prescribes Mellaril as a form of external, albeit temporary, control. Antipsychotic medications are commonly used for all types of aggression; however, sedative side effects are probably the mechanism of action rather than antipsychotic properties.[58] In a similar manner, sexual drive may not be reduced, but rather, side effects (e.g., impotence, bradykinesia) are probably operative.

Although standard psychopharmacological agents may not consistently alter a child molester's aberrant sexual arousal, these drugs may be used to control other forms of psychopathology such as thought disorders or affective disturbances. For example, antipsychotic medications may be indicated when the child molester displays schizophrenia. Major mood disorders may require lithium therapy or antidepressant medication.

In practice, the clinician may be in a difficult position if the child molester who is being treated is overtly psychotic. Under these circumstances, the physician should assess the degree of behavior controls to determine the patient's need for structure and assistance. Inpatient treatment may be necessary. For instance, if the patient is expressing a schizophrenic disorder and is obsessing about molesting children, the clinician may find it safer to hospitalize the patient for the sake of undergoing antipsychotic treatment rather than to risk carrying out the treatment process on an outpatient basis. Even if it is determined that a schizophrenic patient is capable of outpatient treatment, the practitioner would probably need to alter the more aggressive therapeutic style of intervention by relating to the patient in a less probing and more supportive manner.

During some part of the treatment process it is not uncommon for the child molester to become sufficiently depressed that anti-depressant medication may be indicated. This reaction is especially true for those child sexual abusers who feel plagued with sexual obsessions, causing them to devalue themselves and spurring low levels of self-esteem.

PSYCHOTHERAPY

Unlike organic intervention, the psychotherapeutic approach is based on the belief that the urge to molest children cannot be changed without also modifying the individual's intrapsychic and interpersonal conflicts. By emphasizing the interpersonal relationship between the clinician and the patient, psychotherapeutic communication is used to achieve the following: (1) to alleviate any underlying emotional disturbance or conflict; (2) to reverse or modify maladaptive patterns of deviant behavior; and (3) to encourage growth and personality development.

Individual Psychotherapy

Prior to the 1960s individual psychotherapy, or psychoanalysis, was the sole psychotherapeutic treatment for child molesters. As discussed in Chapter 2, the underlying theories of psychodynamic therapy perceived the child-molesting behavior as a symptom of a complex set of character problems stemming from the molester's early childhood experiences with his parents or other close relatives.[38] This theoretical model hypothesizes that the child molester underwent a significant trauma (or traumas) in childhood that overwhelmed him during a fragile stage of development, causing considerable psychological conflict. The subsequent repression of the feelings associated with the pathological experience (e.g., extreme sadness, loneliness, inadequacy, anxiety, and so on) is then unconsciously acted out in adult life, in the form of child-molesting behavior, as an attempt to relieve the psychic discomfort. In this manner, the sex offender's molestation of children is symptomatic of internal emotional conflicts.

According to psychodynamic theory, if treatment is to be successful, the child molester must gain insight and resolve the causative intrapsychic conflict(s), reexperience the affect of the previously repressed traumatic event(s), supplant early life experiences with growth from a corrective emotional experience, and become aware of the situations in his present adult life that trigger association with the earlier trauma(s). Thus, instead of bypassing the unpleasant memory, the molester is able to tolerate the painful associations without the necessity of engaging in child-molesting behavior. In short, he developed better controls over his deviant sexual acting out through introspection and personal awareness.[31]

In the past, research on the efficacy of various forms of psychotherapy yielded little in the way of conclusive findings.[30] This is partly because of methodological problems, some of which include: the lack of standardization of diagnoses; vague or incomplete measures of outcome (often based on recidivism rates); and inadequate monitoring of therapists' techniques for consistency in treatment. The crux of the problem is that it is a difficult task to systematically decode what goes on between a patient and a therapist—a relationship involving a multitude of dynamic and uniquely complex interpersonal interactions. Some therapists are convinced that psychotherapy should not be the treatment of choice and believe that its effectiveness is far outweighed by the great investment of time that it requires.

Despite the inherent limitations in assessing the value of the psychotherapeutic approach in treating child molesters and the paucity of material on individual psychotherapy with child molesters, we believe that psychotherapy is useful in the treatment of some, but probably not all, child molesters. There have been a few cases reported of individual psychotherapy with positive outcomes.[17] For this reason, even without verifiable research evidence, we believe that psychotherapy remains a valuable technique when augmented by other methods.

Group Psychotherapy

Like individual psychotherapy, group therapy has been poorly evaluated in general. Outcome studies[30] are mixed and ambivalent. However, group therapy is often considered to be more cost- and time-effective than individual therapy. Treatment is usually offered in groups of four to as many as 30 patients. During group sessions, the members examine old concepts and new ways of dealing with other persons. Generally, the esprit de corps that develops with others who share the same problem (i.e., child-molesting behavior) is a strong and effective agent for provoking meaningful introspection within each of the participants. The rationalizations, denials, and weak excuses given by one participant are usually attacked quite vigorously by the other group members, but typically the rebukes are balanced by sympathetic and supportive understanding. Because the therapy not only involves intellectual examination but also relies on the use of personal relationships within the group dynamics, patients often accept very pointed criticism from other sex offenders that they would not tolerate coming from a clinician.

The therapist running the session should assure the group that the meetings are goal-directed by initially centering discussions around common problems that members have had with sexuality and aggression, as these relate to child sexual abuse. Therefore, early in the course of treatment it is routine for the therapist to take an active role in the sessions. Gradually, the clinician should become a less dominant figure in the group process as group members start working more collectively, and it then becomes the therapist's primary function to maintain an adequate focus and structure to ensure treatment objectives. Obviously, group therapy is not designed for individuals who are unable to talk rationally, are severely impaired cognitively, are mute, or show overtly psychotic thinking.

According to Langevin and Lang,[37] there are several guidelines to follow when psychologically treating child molesters. Before therapy can be effective, the molester must admit his sexual preferences and the extent of his actual involvement with children; he must see the child as victim, and not as a consenting partner; and he must overcome rationalizations about his own motives for sexual involvement with children. Like all psychotherapeutic intervention strategies, implicit in these guidelines are the molester's willingness and ability to recognize the need for change in his own behavior.

The Family Systems Approach

A variety of other forms of psychotherapy, including family therapy, conjoint therapy, marital counseling, and others, fall into the broader category of the family systems approach. In general, these techniques have been applied more often to the incestuous child molester (although they are not solely delegated to incest cases). According to Lanyon,[38] the family systems approach is the most widely recommended and utilized treatment method in incest cases.

Some clinicians view incest as a symptom of family, rather than strictly individual, dysfunction. In this approach, treatment includes the family as a target of change. Both the husband and the wife are helped to accept individual as well as mutual responsibility for achieving family stability. Treatment usually involves a combination of individual psychotherapy for each family member as well as couples therapy. Later, family therapy, group therapy, and self-help support groups may be utilized.

The Child Sexual Abuse Treatment Program (CSATP) of Santa Clara County, California, started in 1971 by Henry Giarretto, is perhaps the most well-known program of this type.[29] The CSATP is comprised of three elements. The first consists of integrated interventions from the professional law enforcement, criminal justice, and human service agencies. Self-help groups such as Parents United, Daughters and Sons United, and Adults Molested as Children make up the second component, and a group of trained professionals make up the third element.

In 1982, Giarretto[28] reported that the CSATP has provided therapy to over 4,000 children and their families, with a total of 14,000 individuals being served. Over 90% of the children avoided foster or institutional placement and remained with their mothers and siblings. Father-offenders were given "no contact" orders and were asked to leave the home. After long-term therapy, father-offenders were returned to their homes only if they were deemed both physically and psychologically safe from molesting their children. Among those father-offenders who completed treatment, there was a reported recidivism rate of less than 1%.

Other clinicians strongly believe that incest should not be viewed as a family problem. To them the father, as the offending parent, is the primary, if not the exclusive source, of the family pathology, and the other members should not be blamed for the father's destructive acting out behavior. These clinicians may employ family, as well as individual, therapy, but place the emphasis on role responsibility which views the father as offender and the other members as victims. Clinicians with this perspective argue that this approach keeps the offender from denying his responsibility for his incestuous behavior and thus encourages him to bring about constructive changes in his belief systems and his behaviors.

Cognitive Therapy

Cognitive therapy focuses on the child molester's distorted thinking patterns. Since it is characteristic of child molesters to attempt to justify their abusive acts,[2] the sex offender often develops a set of highly individualized beliefs which rationalize the molesting behavior on the basis of false assumptions, misperceptions, and self-serving interpretations.

Cognitive therapy assumes that these cognitive distortions lead to sexual acting-out behavior and that the way to change the behavior is to change the distorted thinking patterns. The clinician and the patient focus on the here and now, using both their own interaction and what is currently happening in the life of the molester as material for discussion. During treatment sessions, the therapist explains and discusses examples of distorted thinking, and also uses role playing during critical situations. Because the emphasis is placed on the sex offender's attempts to correct distorted thought patterns, a daily record of activities and aberrant thoughts may be kept. The sessions should focus on specifically targeted goals and on developing skills to monitor the cognitive distortions that the patient can later use after therapy has ended.[3]

BEHAVIORAL APPROACHES

Behavioral therapies emphasize the patient's current functioning, a data-based approach to specific treatment interventions, and the use of measurable changes in cognitive, affective, physiological, or interpersonal behavior to assess treatment progress. Many behavioral approaches have shown promise in clinical and research settings for some offenders.

The assumption of behavioral therapies is that child-molesting behaviors are learned and reinforced by the environment. For instance, a shy, awkward teenage boy who is frightened to ask girls to dance at a party is so anxious and socially inept that when he finally does approach a girl to ask her to dance, his own self-conscious behavior discourages the would-be dance partner. After several similar rebuffs, his shoulders may physically hunch and his head droop as evidence of his inability to relate to age-mate peers. With sufficient reinforcement, the pattern becomes fixed. As the teenager's sexual drive increases he may look for youngsters as possible sexual outlets because he notices that he is much more competent and less anxious with young children. In this case, sexual interactions with children are felt to be a pleasant and rewarding experience to the awkward adolescent child molester.

The focus of behavioral approaches in treating child molesters is twofold: (1) to decrease the strength of deviant sexual arousal toward age-inappropriate partners, and (2) to increase sexual arousal toward age-appropriate partners.

Decreasing age-inappropriate arousal. The procedures used to reduce inappropriate sexual arousal include: aversive techniques; covert sensitization; masturbatory satiation technique; shame therapy; biofeedback; and others.

Kelly[35] reviewed 32 behavioral studies that represent the implementation of more than 20 different procedures aimed at developing more appropriate sexual activity in pedophiles. He found that 78% of the reported studies used some form of aversive conditioning. The medium for aversion can take many forms, including electric shock, foul odors, chemically induced nausea, as well as imagined distress. Aversion techniques commonly involve the pairing of "noxious" stimuli with arousal to externally produced deviant cues (i.e., slides, tapes, pornography).

The most common form of aversion currently in use is covert sensitization, in which the patient's self-induced negative fantasies (the aversive stimulus) are paired with a deviant sexual fantasy. Covert sensitization[3] is based on the belief that child-molesting behaviors are usually the product of a lengthy chain of events involving fantasy and other pre-assault behaviors. In therapy the molester is helped to recognize and then to verbalize the sequential fantasy elements of his paraphilic arousal; at the point of intense arousal, he learns to switch to the highly aversive consequence(s) of his molestation (e.g., ostracism by the family, infection with AIDS, a prison term, and so on). Subsequently, it is expected that the child molester will recognize the antecedent thoughts and actions of his arousal pattern and be able to turn off his sexual urges toward children by substituting the erotic fantasies with aversive, inhibiting thoughts. An advantage of covert sensitization is that it employs a self-regulating method, needs no equipment, and requires little intervention by a therapist beyond the initial instruction in monitoring its proper use.

The masturbatory satiation technique[3,44] is an aversion method that requires the molester to masturbate to ejaculation while verbalizing nondeviant sexual thoughts and then to continue to masturbate following ejaculation (or satiation) for a prolonged, refractory period (see Chapter 3) while verbalizing deviant sexual fantasies. Because masturbating well beyond the point of orgasm ceases to be stimulating and can even be painful, the aversion is one of satiation. Abel[1] regards masturbatory satiation as the single most effective treatment available (see Chapter 7).

In another aversion technique, shame therapy, the molester is required to act out his sexual abuse of a child while being watched and "shamed" by his therapist and/or group members and/or spouse and/or others.[30] The rationale behind this approach is that the situation of being shamed will provoke enough anxiety within the molester that appropriate sexual behavior will become paired with relief from the noxious situation (or stimulus).

Forms of biofeedback are also used to suppress deviant sexual arousal.[42,51] One technique involves using the voluntary suppression of arousal to deviant stimuli as a result of the feedback from cues generated either internally or externally. This procedure involves giving a signal to the child molester when his penile response to an arousing stimulus (e.g., slides of children) exceeds a certain point. Combined with aversion therapy, a signaled punishment paradigm can be instigated. Quinsey, Chaplan, and Carrigan[51] compared the efficacy of biofeedback alone with that of biofeedback with aversion, in which the pedophile received an electrical shock whenever he experienced erection while viewing slides of children. The results favored the signaled punishment plus biofeedback over biofeedback alone. Five out of six subjects who received a combination of signaled punishment and biofeedback improved significantly, whereas only four out of 12 who received biofeedback alone improved.

The above behavioral methods are among the most promising methods now being used to reduce the strength of deviant sexual arousal and preference. They have the advantage that their effects can be demonstrated objectively when combined with the penile plethysmograph, a device which can register the phallometric measures of a patient's erections during exposure to descriptions of a variety of deviant and nondeviant sexual acts. Quinsey and Marshall,[50] as well as Grossman,[30] presented critical reviews of the available behavioral literature on procedures for reducing inappropriate sexual arousal. In general, it has been noted that there are few systematic, large-scale studies of these techniques.[49] More controlled research with appropriate follow-up and controls is needed. However, a number of case studies and preliminary investigations suggest that behavioral therapies are clinically useful.

Increasing age-appropriate sexual arousal. The behavioral forms of treatment used to condition arousal to age-appropriate partners include masturbatory conditioning and fading, systematic desensitization, aversion relief, and social skills retraining.

Masturbatory conditioning, or orgasmic reconditioning, is a technique which stipulates that the molester masturbate during his favorite deviant fantasy, but that he switch to nondeviant age-appropriate fantasy at the moment of orgasm.[14,23,36] This pairing of pleasurable stimuli (i.e., masturbation) to appropriate cues can be imagined or externally produced (e.g., through slides or tapes). A study by Brownell, Hayes, and Barlow[14] determined that this method increased the arousal to nondeviant stimuli but did not change the pattern of deviant sexual arousal. Thus, they concluded that the two patterns may be independent.

Some molesters reported that they had difficulty switching between fantasies at the point of orgasm. This obstacle led to the suggestion that other shaping devices be used. The fading technique[7] requires that the subject view stimulus slides that are superimposed with inappropriate sexual objects. The inappropriate stimuli are clearly perceptible at first, but gradually fade as the appropriate slides become more visible. For example, the projected image of a young male slowly transforms or fades into a more age-appropriate subject. Hence, there is a progressive shift of arousal cues away from "deviant" to "normal" stimuli.

Two current techniques generally not associated with the treatment of child molesters are worth mentioning. Systematic desensitization,[6] frequently used to treat psychosexual dysfunction, has also been attempted with child molesters to decrease the anxiety associated with nondeviant sexual behaviors. This procedure involves a reduction and/or elimination of anxiety related to nondeviant sexual behavior with age-appropriate peers by training the subject to relax while a hierarchy of stimuli, from lesser to greater strength, is progressively presented. The second technique, aversion relief, involves the pairing of a stimulus with relief from a noxious or unpleasant stimulus. In 1973, Barlow[6] commented that although this technique had been widely utilized in an attempt to increase heterosexual responsiveness, he noted that there is no evidence that aversion relief increases heterosexual responsiveness nor that it decreases heterosexual anxiety. Similarly, at this juncture there is no clear experimental evidence proving that systematic desensitization increases appropriate sexual behavior in child molesters.

Behavioral Treatment Overview

Although research has not strongly supported the efficacy of shame therapy or biofeedback in reducing sexual arousal to inappropriate stimuli, masturbatory satiation, covert sensitization, aversion therapy, and a combination of these have had an impressive success record in a number of studies. There is evidence that these techniques continue to be effective in reducing deviant sexual behavior following treatment when booster sessions are provided. Among the techniques that attempt to increase appropriate sexual behavior (i.e., orgasmic reconditioning, other fantasy modifications, exposure to explicit appropriate sexual stimuli, fading techniques, and systematic desensitization with aversion therapy) are the most successful.[30]

In the present decade comprehensive behavioral treatment packages[3,45,52] are in vogue. Briefly, the strategy is to assess the strengths and weaknesses of the offender and to administer treatment only in the deficit areas. These multidimensional approaches often combine aversive and positive paradigms, including interventions designed to decrease heightened sexual arousal to children, and procedures to increase preference capacity for age-appropriate partners. Early reviews[20] are optimistic about these comprehensive behavioral models, but further evaluation and scrutiny is needed.

Abel and colleagues investigated the relative effectiveness of six treatment modalities of an outpatient program. The 87 voluntary sex offenders in this study were treated using the Abel group's treatment manual.[3] Of the six treatment elements that the manual describes, the first two components, covert sensitization and satiation, are designed to assist the molester in decreasing his sexual arousal toward young children. According to the manual, satiation therapy attempts to reduce arousal by boring the patient with his own deviant sexual fantasies, whereas covert sensitization teaches the patient to disrupt fantasies of young children by replacing them with aversive images. Sex education and cognitive restructuring make up the next two elements of the manual. Cognitive restructuring is defined as an attempt to modify the faulty attitudes or beliefs regarding child molestation by gaining feedback from others regarding the molester's cognitive distortions. Sex education is used to increase a molester's basic sexual knowledge and to provide solutions to problems that can develop during sexual interactions with age-appropriate partners. The final two elements in Abel et al.'s manual are social skills training and assertiveness skills training. Specific social skill techniques are created to help the child molester interact more effectively with adults in such situations as carrying out an initial conversation, maintaining the flow of the conversation, and other social contact with adult partners. As part of the assertiveness skills training module, the manual encourages that child molesters be trained to express their feelings and thoughts.

Abel's group determined that the most effective sequence of the six treatment modalities in the manual were covert sensitization and satiation, followed by social skills, assertiveness training, cognitive restructuring, and sex education. They state that the optimal group size was 14 and note that less than seven hours per patient of the therapist's time was required. The stated success rate after six-to-12 months was 97.2%. In other words, only 2.8% continued to molest children.

In a study conducted by Maletzky,[43] 100 sex offenders (38 homosexual pedophiles and 62 exhibitionists) were followed by 36 months of treatment. Treatment consisted of one session per week for 24 weeks followed by booster sessions every three months for four years. Self-report, penile plethysmography, and interviews with significant others were used to assess outcome. The results indicated not only significant decreases in self-report deviant behavior, but also in penile responses to paraphilic stimuli.

George and Marlatt[27] have prepared a treatment manual for relapse prevention with sex offenders. This method involves six group therapy sessions followed by 52 weekly individual follow-up sessions. The technique requires that the molester be motivated and that he cultivates a self-controlled regime; thus, the offender must take responsibility for his own treatment. Such aspects as self-monitoring, developing coping skills, improving social interaction, and creating constructive lifestyle habits are dimensions used to promote adaptive functioning, self-efficacy, and decreased recidivism.

One approach designed specifically to develop coping skills is a form of cognitive behavioral therapy called stress inoculation. The treatment involves developing adaptive skills and then exposing the molester to manageable doses of nonoverwhelming stressors that evoke his defenses. The strategy is to prevent the occurrence of maladaptive anger, to regulate anger when it does occur, and to use the performance skills needed to manage the provocation.[48]

Behavioral therapies appear promising, but have their own inherent weaknesses. Behaviorists often downplay the development of adaptive functioning and sexual and affectional drives. Interpersonal, familial, psychosocial, and general system issues are often not addressed. We believe that the clinician should not restrict himself exclusively to behavioral modalities. A variety of therapeutic approaches to increase coping skills and lessen the likelihood for relapse should be employed.

PSYCHOSOCIAL EDUCATION

Psychosocial strategies can be initiated either before or after molestation. Such approaches as equipping children with the knowledge and skills to protect themselves and educating the public on the problem of child molestation are strategies that are implemented as primary preventive measures (i.e., before molestation occurs). An outline amplifying the rationale behind such a primary prevention approach is reproduced in Table 5.3.

Primary Prevention

In 1985 the National Committee for the Prevention of Child Abuse sponsored a working conference,[15,16] which reviewed the current

Table 5.3
The Rationale for a Prevention Approach to Child Molesting

1. Child sexual abuse is a very complex problem requiring multiple prevention strategies.
2. Knowledge about sexual abuse and its prevention is quite imperfect, suggesting that a strategy for prevention cannot be based entirely on empirical findings.
3. There is no profile of the sexual abuser. Therefore, preventive efforts cannot be restricted to individuals who are thought to be high-risk sexual abusers.
4. Sexual abuse does not begin when one turns 21 or enters adulthood. Preventive efforts should be directed at adolescents and even younger children.
5. Sexual abuse is not strictly an issue of power but involves sexual ideas, beliefs, misconceptions, and preferences. Prevention efforts should address these issues.
6. Sexual abuse exists, in part, because of the values and messages that are transmitted to everyone in this country through the media. Strongly voiced taboos in our society, saying it is not okay to molest kids, are lacking.
7. Sexual abuse exists, in part, because children do not know how to resist abuse.
8. Sexual abuse exists, in part, because children are sometimes in non-protected environments.
9. Sexual abuse is a problem that is so deeply embedded in our societal values; there is no single law and no single profession that can handle this problem.
10. Public understanding of the problem of sexual abuse and public support for preventive programs are essential.

From "Preventing Adults from Becoming Sexual Molesters," by A. Cohn. *Child Abuse & Neglect, 10*, 560. Copyright 1986, Pergaman Journals, Ltd. Reprinted by permission.

knowledge about why adults sexually abuse children and developed reasonable and comprehensive strategies aimed at preventing potential molesters from abusing children. More than 15 members with varying backgrounds and expertise in particular areas regarding child sexual abuse participated. The result of this conference was an annotated listing of child sexual abuse preventive approaches based on the best knowledge and experiences available. One conclusion drawn at the conference was the following[16]:

> Given the complexities of sexual abuse, an approach to prevention must be multifaceted, directed at a variety of population groups in a variety of ways. A truly comprehensive approach would include helping potential victims from becoming victims *and* treating actual perpetrators to stop abusing. However, the clear focus of preventive activities should be on keeping potential perpetrators from ever becoming perpetrators in the first place. (p. 15)

Educating the general public about the magnitude and seriousness of the problem of child molestation, as well as counteracting misconceptions regarding sexual abuse, could be the focus of a media blitz. Why not develop a campaign targeted at actual or potential child molesters which informs individuals about the following information?—that sexual abuse is a crime; that children get hurt from sexual abuse; that children are incapable of acting as consenting sexual partners; that the abuse is chronic unless helped; that there is help available; and that there is a number to call to get help and what that number is. Smith[53] has authored a provocative pamphlet for potential molesters entitled, "You Don't Have to Molest That Child," which addresses these issues.

Educators, clinicians, parents, and others should establish additional programs that teach children how to protect themselves from sexual abuse by learning to "say no" and to stress that sexual abuse is not their fault, that it is important to reach out for help, and that help is available. Video programs aimed at youngsters are appropriate and of value and already exist.[47] Education for parents and children is also encouraged.[15,16] Flynn[21] offers a guide to parent-child education. Since adolescents are a high-risk group of potential child molesters, primary preventive efforts should focus on this group.

In order to help break the child molestation cycle, intensive treatment for offenders and for victims and widespread training for helping professionals are recommended. Legal reforms should assure that current laws are enforced as consistently and judiciously as possible and that children are not revictimized because of the failure of the criminal justice process. Improved organization on the community, state, national, and international level is needed to combine the resources of the private sector with government entities. Central resource centers should be created to provide training and technical assistance in information exchange and dissemination, not unlike the cocaine hotline or the missing children's network that have proliferated recently.

Beyond diagnosis and treatment, the public rely on clinicians for guidance and protection. Each year in the United States hundreds of thousands of children are sexually molested. The traumatic experience often has far-reaching experiential, psychological, and symbolic significance for the victim. Adults who suffered from childhood sexual abuse may be more likely to become molesters themselves than are those who have not experienced sexual abuse.[16] Therefore, therapeutic emphasis should be placed on those actions that will aid in preventing these and other high-risk individuals from offending.

Clearly, known sexual offenders—in or out of the judicial system—are at increased risk for recurrence of sexual assault. After all, future behavior is best predicted by past behavior. We encourage direct counseling, treatment, and management of known molesters. Children, adolescents, and retarded persons who think about or engage in sexual activity with children are another high-risk group. Aggressive intervention should be available. Victims paradoxically also comprise a high-risk group. The clinician must always be alert to the possibility that victims are ignored, neglected, and untreated. Unfortunately, often the cycle is left to repeat itself with some of the former victims becoming abusers.

Rehabilitation

After-the-molestation intervention consists of teaching known offenders the life management skills that they lack which will allow them to function interpersonally, to cope more adaptively, and to stop their abusive behavior. Several of the elements in the Abel group's manual[3] (social skills training, assertiveness training, and sex education) would probably better fall in the category of rehabilitation training, rather than in the classification of behavioral therapy approaches.

In general, psychosocial educational intervention strategies lend themselves to learning activity packaging or modular components similar to those described in the behavioral treatment section. As in behavioral treatment packages, psychosocial educational measures commonly include pre- and post-instruction assessment to evaluate competence in particular areas. Thus, it is sometimes difficult to determine whether the module is behavioral or psychosocial in orientation.

The psychosocial rehabilitation of an identified child molester contains several components.[31] A basic program in human sexuality is indicated for those child molesters who have limited or erroneous sexual knowledge. Sex education focuses on myths about sex and answers questions and concerns on aspects of reproduction, sexual roles, gender identity, variations in sexual behavior, values, and attitudes. Role playing, assertiveness training, anger modulation, social skills training, and similar techniques are directed toward improving the offender's interpersonal communication, self-control, and ability to empathize. Alcohol dependence is highly prevalent among child molesters, and alcohol abuse is a common concomitant of sexual abuse. Therefore, alcohol and drug rehabilitation becomes an essential psychosocial issue.

Since many child molesters were themselves physically, sexually, or emotionally victimized as youngsters,[8] these offenders are helped to understand the impact of their past traumas on current attitudes, values, fantasies, and behavior. Understanding the aftereffects of sexual assault from the victim's perspective helps the offender to more fully comprehend and empathize with the victim.

The effectiveness of this approach is largely untested, however. Yet, as a form of treatment it has several advantages: the goals of treatment are identified and carried through in an organized, structured fashion; and because each component is time-limited, this approach is particularly suited for offenders with low endurance who need instant gratification.

CLOSING WORDS

Although the existing knowledge used to treat child molesters is imperfect, the fact remains that child sexual abuse is an enormous social problem. Clinicians need to become familiar with intervention strategies to help patients control their deviant behaviors, impulses, and preoccupations. Many of the above treatment modalities appear promising, but have not been systematically tested over an adequate period of time to determine the efficacy or permanence of their effects. Until systematic research confirms the effectiveness of attempts to change molesters' sexual preferences for children, clinicians must be satisfied with helping these people manage their deviant and socially unacceptable urges. Because of the limited treatment outcome data, extended follow-up aftercare of each child molester or potential sex abuser is highly advocated.

REFERENCES

1. Abel, G. G. (1986). M. D.: Sex offenders need treatment, not punishment. *American Medical News*, October 10, 21.
2. Abel, G. G., Becker, J. V., & Cunningham-Rathner, J. (1984). Complications, consent and cognitions in sex between children and adults. *International Journal of Law and Psychiatry, 7*, 89.
3. Abel, G. G., Becker, J. V., Cunningham-Rathner, J., Rouleau, J. L., Kaplan, M., & Reich, J. (1984). *The Treatment Manual: The Treatment of Child Molesters*. Atlanta: Emory University.
4. Bancroft, J. (1977). Hormones and sexual behaviour. *Psychological Medicine, 7*, 553.
5. Bancroft, J., Tennent, G., Loucas, K., & Cass, J. (1974). The control of deviant sexual behaviour by drugs: 1. Behavioural changes following Oestrogens and Anti-Androgens. *British Journal of Psychiatry, 125*, 310.
6. Barlow, D. H. (1973). Increasing heterosexual responsiveness in the treatment of sexual deviation: A review of the clinical and experimental evidence. *Behavior Therapy, 4*, 655.
7. Barlow, D. H., & Agras, W. S. (1973). Fading to increase heterosexual responsiveness in homosexuals. *Journal of Applied Behavior Analysis, 6*, 355.
8. Barnard, G. W., Fuller, A. K., & Robbins, L. (1988). Child molesters. In J. Howells (Ed.), *Modern Perspectives in Psycho-Social Pathology*. New York: Brunner/Mazel.
9. Berlin, F. S. (1982). Sex offenders: A biomedical perspective and a status report on biomedical treatment. In J. G. Greer & I. R. Stuart (Eds.), *The Sexual Aggressor: Current Perspectives on Treatment*. New York: Van Nostrand Reinhold Company.
10. Berlin, F. S., & Meinecke, C. F. (1981). Treatment of sex offenders with antiandrogenic medication: Conceptualization, review of treatment modalities, and preliminary findings. *American Journal of Psychiatry, 138*, 601.
11. Berlin, F. S., Money, J., Falck, A., Stein, M., Rider, M., & Dean, S. (1986). Antiandrogenic and counseling treatment of sex offenders. Paper presented at Sexual Disorders Clinic, Johns Hopkins University, Baltimore, MD.
12. Bradford, J. M. W. (1985). Organic treatments for the male sexual offender. *Behavioral Sciences & the Law, 3*, 355.
13. Bradford, J. M. W., & Pawlak, A. (1987). Sadistic homosexual pedophilia: Treatment with cyproterone acetate: A single case study. *Canadian Journal of Psychiatry, 32*, 22.

14. Brownell, K. D., Hayes, S. C., & Barlow, D. H. (1977). Patterns of appropriate and deviant sexual arousal: The behavioral treatment of multiple sexual deviations. *Journal of Consulting & Clinical Psychology, 45,* 1144.

15. Cohn, A. (1986). Preventing adults from becoming sexual molesters. *Child Abuse & Neglect, 10,* 559.

16. Cohn, A., Finkelhor, D., & Holmes, C. (1985). Preventing adults from becoming child sexual molesters. Working Paper Number 25. Chicago, IL: National Committee for the Prevention of Child Abuse.

17. Conn, J. H. (1949). Brief psychotherapy of the sex offender: A report of a liaison service between a court and a private psychiatrist. *Clinical Psychopathology, 10,* 347.

18. Cooper, A. J. (1981). A placebo-controlled trial of the antiandrogen cyproterone acetate in deviant hypersexuality. *Comprehensive Psychiatry, 22,* 458.

19. Cordoba, O. A., & Chapel, J. L. (1983). Medroxyprogesterone acetate antiandrogen treatment of hypersexuality in a pedophiliac sex offender. *American Journal of Psychiatry, 140,* 1036.

20. Earls, C. M., & Quinsey, V. L. (1985). What is to be done? Future research on the assessment and behavioral treatment of sex offenders. *Behavioral Sciences & the Law, 3,* 341.

21. Flynn, E. M. (1987). Preventing and diagnosing sexual abuse in children. *Nurse Practitioner, 12,* 47.

22. Food and Drug Administration (1982). Use of approved drugs for unlabeled indications. *FDA Drug Bulletin, 12,* 4.

23. Foote, W. E., & Laws, D. R. (1981). A daily alternation procedure for orgasmic reconditioning with a pedophile. *Journal of Behavior Therapy & Experimental Psychiatry, 12,* 267.

24. Frederic, B. (1975). An enquiry among a group of pedophiles. *Journal of Sex Research, 11,* 242.

25. Freund, K. (1980). Therapeutic sex drive reduction. *Acta Psychiatrica Scandinavica (Suppl. 287), 62,* 5.

26. Gagne, P. (1981). Treatment of sex offenders with medroxyprogesterone acetate. *American Journal of Psychiatry, 138,* 644.

27. George, W. H., & Marlatt, G. A. (1986). *Relapse Prevention with Sexual Offenders: A Treatment Manual.* NIMH Grant No. 1 RO1 MH42035, "Prevention of Relapse in Sex Offenders," D. R. Laws, Ph.D., Principal Investigator.

28. Giarretto, H. (1982). A comprehensive child sexual abuse treatment program. *Child Abuse & Neglect, 6,* 263.

29. Giarretto, H. (1982). *Integrated Treatment of Child Sexual Abuse: A Treatment and Training Manual.* Palo Alto, CA: Science & Behavior Books.

30. Grossman, L. S. (1985). Research directions in the evaluation and treatment of sex offenders: An analysis. *Behavioral Sciences & the Law, 3,* 421.

31. Groth, A. N., Hobson, W. F., & Gary, T. S. (1982). The child molester: Clinical observations. In J. Conte & D. A. Shore (Eds.), *Social Work and Child Sexual Abuse.* New York: Haworth.

32. Guyton, A. C. (1986). *Textbook of Medical Physiology.* Philadelphia: Saunders.

33. Heim, N., & Hursch, C. J. (1979). Castration for sex offenders: Treatment or punishment? A review and critique of recent European literature. *Archives of Sexual Behavior, 8,* 281.

34. Hucker, S. J. (1985). Management of anomalous sexual behavior with drugs. *Modern Medicine of Canada, 40.*

35. Kelly, R. J. (1982). Behavioral reorientation of pedophiliacs: Can it be done? *Clinical Psychology Review, 2,* 387.

36. Kremsdorf, R. B., Holmen, M. L., & Laws, D. R. (1980). Orgasmic conditioning without deviant imagery: A case report with a pedophile. *Behaviour Research & Therapy, 18,* 203.

37. Langevin, R., & Lang R. A. (1985). Psychological treatment of pedophiles. *Behavioral Sciences & the Law, 3,* 403.

38. Lanyon, R. I. (1986). Theory and treatment in child molestation. *Journal of Consulting & Clinical Psychology, 54.* 176.

39. Laschet, U. (1973). Antiandrogen in the treatment of sex offenders: Mode of action and therapeutic outcome. In J. Zubin, & J. Money, (Eds.), *Contemporary Sexual Behavior: Critical Issues in the 1970's.* Baltimore: Johns Hopkins University Press.

40. Laschet, U., & Laschet, L. (1969). Three years clinical results with cyproterone-acetate in the inhibiting regulation of male sexuality. *Acta Endocrinology Supplement, 138,* 103.

41. Laschet, U., & Laschet, L. (1975). Antiandrogens in the treatment of sexual deviations of men. *Journal of Steroid Biochemistry, 6,* 821.

42. Laws, D. R. (1980). Treatment of bisexual pedophilia by a biofeedback-assisted self-control procedure. *Behaviour Research and Therapy, 18,* 207.

43. Maletzky, B. M. (1980). Assisted covert sensitization. In D. J. Cox, & R. J. Daitzman, (Eds.), *Exhibitionism: Description, Assessment, and Treatment.* New York: Garland.

44. Marshall, W. L. (1979). Satiation therapy: A procedure for reducing deviant sexual arousal. *Journal of Applied Behavior Analysis, 2,* 93.

45. Marshall, W. L., Earls, C. M., Segal, Z., & Darke, J. L. (1983). A behavioral program for the assessment and treatment of sexual aggressors. In K. L. Craig, & R. McMahon, (Eds.), *Advances in Clinical Behavior Therapy.* New York: Brunner/Mazel.

46. Money, J., & Bennett, R. G. (1981). Postadolescent paraphilic sex offenders: Antiandrogenic and counseling therapy follow-up. *International Journal of Mental Health, 10,* 122.

47. Muller, D. J., Shaw, D. F., & Towner, M. (1987). Preventing child abuse: An evaluation of two video programmes. *Health Visitor, 60,* 15.

48. Novaco, R. W. (1986). *Stress Inoculation for Anger and Impulse Control: A Treatment Manual.* Prepared as part of NIMH Grant No. 1 RO1 MH42035, "Prevention of Relapse in Sex Offenders," D. R. Laws, Ph.D., Principal Investigator.

49. Quinsey, V. L. (1983). Prediction of recidivism and the evaluation of treatment programs for sex offenders. In S. Simon-Jones, (Ed.), *Sexual Aggression and the Law.* Criminology Research Centre, Simon Fraser University, Burnaby, British Columbia.

50. Quinsey, V. L., & Marshall, W. L. (1983). Procedures for reducing inappropriate sexual arousal: An evaluation review. In J. G. Greer &

I. R. Stuart (Eds.), *The Sexual Aggressor: Current Perspectives on Treatment.* New York: Van Nostrand.

51. Quinsey, V. L., Chaplin, T. C., & Carrigan, W. F. (1980). Biofeedback and signalled punishment in the modification of inappropriate sexual age preferences. *Behavior Therapy, 11,* 567.

52. Quinsey, V. L., Chaplin, T. C., Maguire, A. M., & Upfold, D. (1988). The behavioral treatment of rapists and child molesters. In E. K. Morris, & C. J. Brackman, (Eds.), *Behavioral Approaches to Crime and Delinquency: Application, Research, and Theory.* New York: Plenum.

53. Smith, T. A. (1987). *You Don't Have to Molest That Child.* Chicago: National Committee for Prevention of Child Abuse.

54. Stürup, G. K. (1972). Castration: The total treatment. In H. L. P. Resnik, & M. E. Wolfgang, (Eds.), *Sexual Behaviors: Social, Clinical and Legal Aspects.* Boston: Little, Brown.

55. Travin, S., Bluestone, H., Coleman, E., Cullen, K., & Melella, J. (1985). Pedophilia: An update on theory and practice. *Psychiatric Quarterly, 57,* 89.

56. Wettstein, R. M. (1987). Legal aspects of neuropsychiatry. In R. E. Hales, & S. C. Yudofsky, (Eds.), *The American Psychiatric Press Textbook of Neuropsychiatry.* Washington, D.C.: American Psychiatric Press.

57. Wincze, J. P., Bansal, S., & Malamud, M. (1986). Effects of medroxyprogesterone acetate on subjective arousal, arousal to erotic stimulation, and nocturnal penile tumescence in male sex offenders. *Archives of Sexual Behavior, 15,* 293.

58. Yudofsky, S. C., Silver, J. M., & Schneider, S. E. (1987). Pharmacologic treatment of aggression. *Psychiatric Annals, 17,* 397.

II. A MODEL RESIDENTIAL EVALUATION AND TREATMENT PROGRAM FOR SEX OFFENDERS

CHAPTER 6

A Computerized Residential Assessment Program for Sex Offenders

INTRODUCTION

The program for mentally disordered sex offenders of the North Florida Evaluation and Treatment Center (NFETC) has been in existence for over 10 years. NFETC is a Florida Department of Health Rehabilitative Services (HRS) forensic institution located east of Gainesville, Florida. The 216-bed facility, serving only male patients, includes a 63-bed residential treatment program for men who have been convicted of sexual offenses and were sentenced. While in prison, they volunteered to participate in the treatment program at NFETC. As volunteers, they can elect to leave the program and return to prison at any time.

During the past decade several hundred sex offenders have been evaluated and treated at the facility. In April 1984, the Governor's Task Force on Sex Offenders and Their Victims for the State of Florida recommended that a research and evaluation effort be instituted at the Center that would not be disruptive to the ongoing treatment program.

In Chapter 4 we discussed the need for a comprehensive assessment, including both traditional psychological tests and a more behavioral approach. Prior to 1985, the Sex Offender Treatment Unit lacked this comprehensive approach, emphasizing a more

Portions of this chapter have been published previously in the *Bulletin of the American Academy of Psychiatry and Law*, 15(4), 339–347, 1987. The authors wish to express their appreciation to the Editor for permission to use the material.

traditional type of assessment. After a review of the literature and discussion of the problem with some leading investigators in the field of sex offender treatment, it was decided to expand the assessment procedure at NFETC to include the behavioral approach previously lacking.

PURPOSE AND GOALS

When we first conceptualized an assessment laboratory for the NFETC Sex Offender Treatment Unit, the laboratory was conceived to meet both treatment and research goals, emphasizing the following four aims:

1. To define the nature and extent of the individual's sexual deviancy, ideally during the first weeks of his treatment.
2. To obtain comprehensive, uniform data on each incoming resident that will provide the basis for diagnostic assessment and treatment planning.
3. To repeat the testing to assess the resident's progress during treatment.
4. To gather follow-up data to assess the impact of treatment on the resident.

Additionally, we wanted a database for research purposes; specifically, we wanted to study differential changes in the residents resulting from the treatment program and to examine the psychosocial development of the overt pedophilia.

As the reader can well imagine, translating these lofty goals into a practical assessment program that would serve both clinical as well as research purposes represented a herculean task. Based on our past experience, we knew that it was difficult to enlist the cooperation of clinicians to obtain data from the patient in a uniform and consistent manner. The clinicians resisted the imposition of structured interview instruments, preferring the greater autonomy allowed in the free form interview. For research purposes, however, the laissez-faire approach to the interview resulted in missing data, a severe handicap to thorough analyses. Yet our effort to urge clinicians to collect patient data that had little or no significance to their clinical duties was met with extreme resistance. Therefore, our task was to develop a program that would blend the clinical and research world together through some common avenue that would meet the needs of both.

At this point, the possibility of using the computer technology to replace the clinician as the primary data collector and to administer interactively the psychological and behavioral assessment instruments was explored. We turned to the literature to review the research in the area of computer-assisted psychological assessment.

The following section reviews our findings and the process of selecting the psychological tests.

History of Computer-Assisted Testing

Computer-assisted psychological assessment has been operational for about 25 years. Fowler,[9] in a review of its history and development, stated that psychometricians were among the first faculty members to make use of computers when they began to be established on university campuses in the mid-1950s, although the post-World War II enthusiasm for psychological assessment had begun to wane by the late 1950s. The establishment of Community Mental Health Center systems led to a resurgence in the demand for psychological testing. The Minnesota Multiphasic Personality Inventory (MMPI) was a natural choice for experimentation in the area of computerized interpretation. Marks and Seeman's[23] handbook, published in 1963, was the first large-scale application of the actuarial method to clinical prediction. This work, together with other "actuarial cookbooks" for the MMPI, paved the way for MMPI administration and evaluation by computer technology. The first such program became operational in the Mayo Clinic in Rochester, Minnesota, in the early 1960s. Shortly thereafter, three other computer-based test interpretation systems (CPTI) appeared; perhaps the best known was that developed by Fowler.[8] Fowler's system was made commercially available by Roche in 1965 and was the first national MMPI mail-in CBTI service for psychologists and psychiatrists.

The first direct computer interview was performed in 1966 at the University of Wisconsin. By the 1970s, developments in computer technology had made it possible to administer items on the screen of a computer terminal and to permit the subject to respond on the keyboard. At this point, MMPIs could be administered in relatively remote locations and subjected to on-line testing and interpretation.

However, a major breakthrough in the use of computer technology occurred in 1971 when Johnson and Williams[16] developed computer programs to administer, score, and interpret several psychometric and social history instruments at the VA Hospital in Salt Lake City, Utah. By 1973 they had established a computer-based psychiatric unit (PAU) in the hospital. Johnson and Williams' test battery included an MMPI, an intelligence test, a social history and problem checklist, a depression inventory, and a structured mental status examination conducted by an interviewer and recorded at the terminal. Several studies[19,20] comparing the PAU with the traditional approach at the hospital were reported. The results of these studies suggested that the PAU assessments were superior and more internally consistent in such parameters as diagnostic accuracy, decision making, patient and staff acceptance, and cost efficiency as compared with traditional methods; and additionally, the system provided reports in half the time.

Along with the growing availability of a wide variety of computerized psychological testing within various mental health disciplines, there has been a predictable outbreak of territorial disputes. Much of the benefit of computer interviews is derived from their inherent structure and specificity. For example, in 1973 Weitzel, Morgan, and Guyden[32] compared free-form and structured checklist examination reports on 49 patients for 15 mental status items. The study found the tendency for the examiners to omit items on the free-form method surprisingly high. In contrast to human-administered interviews, computer interviews never forget to ask a question, and, given the same pattern of responses by a patient, the computer will always ask the same question in the same way. Thus, computer interviews are 100% reliable. Additionally, they have the potential to make the patient feel less uncomfortable or embarrassed, especially when such sensitive information as thoughts of suicide, sexual difficulties, or other more compromising psychological problems are being covered.

Several studies have helped to confirm the preference for computerized as opposed to human-administered testing. Greist and Klein[11] showed that volunteer subjects were significantly more likely to reveal their sexual problems to the computer than to a psychiatric interviewer, even when administered by an interviewer of the same sex. To judge from the studies reported to date, patients do not seem to feel ill-used by computer-administered testing. In 1983 White[33] found that 80% of a sample of college students preferred taking the MMPI by computer while none preferred pencil-and-paper administration. Further, Johnson and Williams[17] reported that 46% of subjects said that they were more truthful when responding to the computer than to the clinician. Overall, they reported that patients participating in their PAU program felt strongly favorable to computerized testing.

Although some clinicians claim that computer interviews are impersonal and, therefore, inhumane, this concern is voiced much more frequently by the professionals than by their patients. Other criticisms of computerized interviews include the difficulty in handling anything other than structured verbal information and the relative inability of the computer to tailor the wording of questions. To some degree these objections have been met by the technique of "branching," in which the answer to a single critical question can determine which series of questions the individual will be exposed to next.

Validity and Other Considerations

In a review of validity studies, Moreland[26] concluded that most of the research supports the validity of computerized testing as compared to testing administered and interpreted by mental health professionals. He felt that the evaluation of validity in this burgeoning area of computerized psychological testing to be sufficiently important that he developed 14 desirable characteristics for such studies in the future.

Further, after analyzing some of the recent advances, suggestions for future directions for which the versatility and flexibility of computerized personality assessment can be improved were reviewed by Butcher, Keller, and Bacon.[6] They emphasized that computer administration of standard tests offers a potential savings in testing time, a reduction of examinee mistakes, and an increase in the number of valid protocols, since the computerized procedure forces the examinee to answer all the questions. However, it cannot be assumed that computer-administered versions of personality instruments are parallel forms to the paper-and-pencil versions. Factors such as test instructions, difficulty of response requirements, and the computer's response latency may all possibly interact with personality or psychopathological states of the examinees and make particular error patterns more likely.

Hofer and Green[13] addressed some of these issues from a somewhat different perspective. They pointed out that irrelevant or extraneous factors, incidental to the computerized administration, may adversely affect test performance so that people would not receive the same score if tested by computer that they would receive if they had been tested conventionally. People accustomed to working with computers might have an advantage taking computerized tests, particularly if the procedures were complicated. Unfamiliarity with computers is probably correlated with ethnicity, gender, age, and socioeconomic status. A nonequivalence resulting from unfamiliarity might appear statistically as poor performance by many groups. Further differences between a pencil-and-paper test and computer administration include the need to push a button once a response has been given, thus preventing the possibility of changing one's reply later and leading to frustration in some test takers. Despite these considerations, Hofer and Green concluded that the computer presentation is probably psychometrically superior since the first answer given is probably most likely to be truly representative of what the patient feels at that time. The inability to retrace one's steps and change responses may still lead to differences between the administration of conventional, as opposed to computerized, testing.

In addition to the above considerations, test performance is particularly vulnerable to surroundings. This element is especially true when dealing with something as unfamiliar as a computer. Issues which would avoid extraneous factors that may affect response include the following: the need for a comfortable, quiet room; adequate rest periods; a clean computer display with adequate resolution; absence of glare; clear response devices; and short and uniform time delays between items. A more cautious approach was taken by Matarazzo,[24] who in a recent article expressed concern over the possibility of misuse of the readily available computerized testing systems and questioned the credibility of current validity tests.

Psychological Tests and Behavioral Instruments

In the process of selecting the psychological tests, we consulted with directors of laboratories engaged in research with the sex offender and reviewed the sex offender assessment literature.[4,17,18,22,24] We were unable to secure permission from several of the publishers to write the software to test interactively at the computer, so we had to substitute other tests. There were three tests, however, for which we could not find adequate substitutes: the Interpersonal Behavior Survey, the Wide Range Achievement Test, and the Shipley Institute of Living Scale. These tests are given in the paper-and-pencil form. The technician scores them by hand and enters the data into the computer.

Because we needed short tests that would provide good estimates of the resident's intelligence and reading level, we selected the

Shipley Institute of Living Scale,[12,29] from which we derived an estimated verbal intelligence quotient, and the Wide Range Achievement Test,[15] which provided an estimate of grade reading level. We included two measures of general personality. The Personality Research Form-E[14] gives 20 different personality measures that are of relevance in understanding a population of sex offenders. The Interpersonal Behavior Survey[25] measures the presence of aggressive and assertive behaviors and assesses their effects on interpersonal interactions. Since so many of our sex offender population report problems with alcohol, we included the Michigan Alcoholism Screening Test,[28] an instrument devised to detect alcoholism.

Several inventories were included that document the resident's sexual attitudes, beliefs, and experiences. The Clarke Sex History Questionnaire[21] is an instrument that investigates sexual experiences through the life span. It requires detailed responses of the nature, frequency, and diversity of sexual activity. Cognitive distortions related to pedophilia are detected by the Abel Pedophilia Cognition Scale.[2] The Burt Scales[5] measure cognitive acceptance of interpersonal violence and rape myth, sex role stereotyping, sex role satisfaction, adversarial sexual beliefs, and sexual conservatism. Abel and Becker's Sexual Interest Cardsort[1] measures the degree of sexual arousal or repulsion to scenarios describing the variants of sexual behavior. The Multiphasic Sex Inventory,[27] a test that has proven to have real value in further delineating the resident's deviant sexual interests and behavior, assesses a wide range of psychosocial characteristics. It has a child molest scale, a rape scale, an exhibitionism scale, an atypical sexual outlet scale, a sexual dysfunction scale, and a sex knowledge scale.

Modified Keyboard

In pretesting these computerized tests, we saw the need for a simplified keyboard. We made up double-key covers with the question responses, *true, false, yes, no* and the numbers 1 through 10. We blanked out all the other keys on the keyboard. Since our program allows the resident to go backward to previous questions and change his answers, we made key covers that read *forward* and *backward*. We also included a key cover that read *stop*, which allows the resident to stop the testing procedure at any point and to pick up at a later time. And, finally, arrow keys were added to indicate the manner in which the cursor is moved around on the screen. We found this simplified keyboard to be nonthreatening to the user. We "locked" the other keys, that is, made them nonusable, so there is very little the resident could do to disrupt the testing procedure through improper response at the keyboard.

Computer-Assisted Psychosocial Assessment (CAPSA)

In addition to these psychological tests, we developed a computer-assisted psychosocial assessment program (CAPSA) which each resident takes interactively at the computer following his battery of psychological tests. CAPSA provides a comprehensive database of the subject's psychosocial history. The CAPSA is based on the psychiatric tradition of taking a detailed longitudinal history from the resident. The concept behind such a history is that problems manifested by the resident are rooted in his background. If we can understand these origins it makes it easier to bring changes in his current maladaptive behaviors.

We have worked from a model emphasizing that each resident has his origin in a family that gives him his own unique genetic loading and provides a unique social setting in which to learn and to identify with his parents. We obtain information about the biological as well as psychological parents. We attempt to determine if any parent has had psychiatric problems or difficulties with the law or has been a substance abuser. Specifically, we are looking for origins of violence in the individual and are seeking to determine if there has been physical or emotional abuse within the family of origin. More specifically, since we are dealing with sex offenders, we wish to determine if the resident has been sexually abused as a child. If so, we seek to know by whom, over what period of time, and what types of abuse were experienced.

Because our aim for the CAPSA is to pinpoint problems the resident has that will need to be addressed in depth by clinical therapists, we have focused on the characterological development of the resident. We have included many of the variables that researchers have indicated as being significant in the prediction of violence. Starting with the resident's childhood, we look at problems in adjusting to family, peer, and authority figures. We track his behavior and types of adjustment in school to determine if he has learning disabilities or conduct disorders that will handicap and impede his learning. We follow him as he leaves his home environment and enters adulthood by tracking his problems adjusting to marriage, employment, and military service. We examine his sexual history in great depth to see the types of sexual experiences he has had from early childhood through adolescence into adulthood. Finally, we seek to determine his gender of orientation and his satisfaction with his sexual performance, as well as any types of problems he may have had.

The CAPSA is not meant to replace the clinician, but rather to give the clinician a substantial amount of information prior to the time of the clinical interview. In addition to the social and characterological factors, we focus on the resident's medical background. We attempt to learn if he has had major types of illness or trauma that would have sequelae and might influence his adjustment within the treatment program. In addition to the medical factors, we also focus on his psychiatric history to determine if he has had significant emotional impairment in the past. If so, we obtain the age of onset and the type of therapeutic approaches that have been necessary to intervene. We seek to determine if he has made suicidal attempts in the past, and, if so, when he made his last attempt, so that the staff can be alert to the potential of suicidal risk within the treatment program. Since so many of the residents give a history of substance abuse, we take a detailed review of alcohol and other substance abuse. In the process we seek to determine what types of social impairment may have come about as a result of abusive behavior and the types of therapeutic programs, if any, that the resident has encountered.

Because all of the residents have come to the treatment program from the criminal justice system, we take a detailed criminal history from them, documenting both juvenile and adult arrests, the types of crimes for which they have been charged, and the outcomes of their encounter with the criminal justice system.

As we previously mentioned, CAPSA has been designed to supplement and augment the skills of clinicians. Because the CAPSA is based on self-serving subjective statements made by the resident, not unlike the clinical history obtained by clinical psychiatrists, psychologists, and social workers, the CAPSA has a built-in redundancy factor that will assist the clinician in being aware of some of the inconsistencies that may emerge in a history; but its main strength lies in looking at repetitive patterns of behavior shown by the resident.

While it is not designed specifically to give a DSM-III Axis I diagnosis, CAPSA provides sufficient information so that the clinician is made aware of major problem areas underlying an Axis I diagnosis. However, it has all of the elements necessary to determine if the resident meets the criteria for an Axis II diagnosis. If the resident meets only some of the criteria of an Axis II diagnosis, it prints out the item loadings on the Personality Disorder criteria.

The CAPSA takes a more detailed history than most clinicians are inclined to do. Furthermore, it has a built-in logic that branches into detail only in the areas where the resident has a positive history. Using the CAPSA report, the clinician can inquire from the resident about significant factors alluded to but not covered in detail. The clinician may also confront the resident with contradictions or inconsistencies. When used in this manner, some of the residents have clarified historical accounts or have admitted lying as they interacted with the computer.

CAPSA provides the clinician with a comprehensive report from which to determine the clinical problems needing to be addressed in the treatment program. It also establishes a base point for evaluating behavior changes resulting from therapeutic approaches. Further, because it contains many items that have been shown to have significance in the study of sex offenders, CAPSA has great potential for research purposes. We expect that it will contribute significantly to our understanding of sex offenders. Since CAPSA was developed to have application for general psychiatry as well as the sex offender, we expect it to have research applicability with the general psychiatric population as well.

PHYSIOLOGICAL TESTS

The physiological portion of our assessment program is comprised of a penile plethysmograph. The computerized penile plethysmograph by Technicraft measures the sexual arousal experienced by the resident in response to specific stimuli. During this test, the resident sits in a private, sound-attenuated room with a mercury strain gauge fitted on the shaft of his penis. The computer runs the projector or the tape recorder, records the baseline level, measures the percentage of full erection and the length of time the erection is maintained, converts from analog to digital data, determines when detumescence has occurred, and then presents the next stimulus.

At the present time we have the capability of using slides that were obtained from another research laboratory and audiotapes. We have three slides each in nine different categories: consenting heterosexual sex; consenting homosexual sex; prepubertal females; prepubertal males; prepubertal female interacting with adult male; prepubertal male interacting with adult male; pubertal male and female interacting; violence without nudity; and violence with nudity.[10] The audiotapes that we developed are based on the Tanner[30] developmental stages (I-V) for males and females. The audiotapes also include the continuum of consensual sex, threat of violence, violence with sex, and violence without sex.

The plethysmograph reports have had significant value insofar as some residents who deny their paraphilias in the psychological testing admit to them when confronted with these data. However, the plethysmograph data, while extremely valuable, are not "foolproof," since some individuals have the ability to suppress physiological responses to the stimuli.

PROCEDURE FOR TESTING

Each resident is tested in the first week following his admission to NFETC. During the several days delegated to the laboratory assessment, the resident is kept relatively isolated from the other residents in the sex offender unit. We instituted this procedure to control the passing of information from longer-term residents about the nature of the assessment and the "proper" ways to respond.

THE COMPUTERIZED REPORT AND STAFF CONFERENCE

The 25–30-page report consists of the CAPSA narrative, the psychological and behavioral test results, and the plethysmograph printout of the individual's response to audio or visual stimuli. The report format contains a wealth of information, but it is presented in a style that facilitates integration and interpretation by the experienced psychiatrist or psychologist.

At the conclusion of the second week, the psychiatrist reviews the assessment laboratory's report with members of the multidisciplinary team in a staffing on the new resident. In order to enhance objectivity and reduce bias, the psychiatrist summarizes and interprets the computerized report prior to interviewing the resident. Other members of the clinical team then give additional data or impressions from observations and interactions with the resident. The resident is then brought into the staff conference and is interviewed by the psychiatrist to clarify ambiguous or conflicting information in the computerized assessment. It has been our experience that this clarification–elicitation–confrontation procedure has been quite useful. In such a complex undertaking as this, some data may appear to be contradictory. Reviewing this information with the resident may aid in determining whether he has misunderstood or lied about certain issues.

In order to give an overview of the assessment report, a brief precis of a report on an incoming child molester in the sex offender treatment unit at NFETC follows.

Identifying Information

S. N. is a 36-year-old white, married male who was evaluated in the psychosocial assessment laboratory on December 20, 1987, the day he was admitted to NFETC.

The Official Record of Legal Charges

S. N. had been arrested and charged with two counts of lewd and lascivious behavior with a child under 16 years of age. He pleaded no contest, was found guilty, and was sentenced to two concurrent sentences of five years with five years of probation to follow. His sentence expires on December 1989.

The Official Report of Circumstances Surrounding the Crimes

Approximately 20 months prior to the time of admission to NFETC, S. N. is said to have entered the bedroom of his 12-year-old stepdaughter. He is said to have held her down, covered her mouth to keep her from screaming, and had vaginal intercourse. Approximately two weeks later, he is reported to have had his stepdaughter touch his penis and again to have had vaginal intercourse with her. The victim reported the two incidents to her teacher who notified police and officials with Health Rehabilitative Services. Subsequently, S. N. was arrested and placed in jail.

Legal History

He was never arrested as a juvenile and was first arrested and charged for a crime at the age of 18 years. Including the present offense, he has been arrested two times as an adult. The only arrest for a sexual crime is the present arrest.

Past History

S. N. was born on September 1, 1954. He has one full sibling. His parents were married at the time of his birth but separated when he was five years old. He was raised at times by his biological mother and at other times by his father. Both parents are alive at the present time. He described his father as being an unintelligent, dishonest person and acknowledged that he felt ashamed of his father. Although he felt there were some positive aspects of his relationship with his father, they were outweighed by the negative features. He denied any identification with his father. He reported that his father had neglected him or was unavailable during his childhood. There is no history of his father being mentally ill, of having abused alcohol, or of having a criminal record. There is no history of the father having shown abusive behavior toward the resident.

The resident also thought his mother was an unintelligent and dishonest person. Overall, he described the relationship with his mother as a negative one and did not find any aspect of their relationship pleasing. He often argued with his mother and reported that the punishment he received from her was harsh and cruel. She had a bad temper and directed it toward him. Although he said his mother did not have a psychiatric history, he himself considered her to be mentally ill. The resident said his mother was not a heavy drinker, but she did become violent when drinking alcohol. She had no criminal history. He reported that his mother "wore the pants in the family."

Developmental History

As S. N. was growing up he believed he was treated worse by his parents than his brothers or sisters were. He had few friends and felt inferior to others. He had a poor sense of self-esteem and because he wished he could have been more muscular, more athletic, and stronger, he expressed having negative feelings about his body image. While he considered himself to be more masculine than feminine in appearance, he thought he was more feminine than masculine in personality.

Educational History

S. N. thought that he had not performed to the best of his abilities in school. He reported that he failed two grades. He graduated from high school and later took some college courses while in prison. He was considered to be a hyperactive child in school. He never took medication for hyperactivity and his hyper behavior caused problems with his adjustment and in getting along with teachers and classmates. He considered himself to be disciplined harshly by teachers for hyperactivity as well as for smoking and drinking alcohol. He denied that he ever skipped school.

Military History

He served two years in the armed forces. While he had discipline problems during his tour of duty, he received an honorable discharge.

Employment History

He has had many jobs that lasted for only a short period of time, but stayed at one job for nine years. He frequently was absent from work and on numerous occasions quit his job without having another one lined up. He has been fired because of arguments with his employer, disagreements with his co-workers, and for abuse of alcohol and poor job performance.

Sexual History

S. N. reached puberty at the age of 12 years. He had intercourse for the first time at age 15 and on a regular basis from the age of 18 years. As a child he was punished for sexual activity. He received his sex education from school chums after he reached puberty. As a child he was sexually abused three times: the first occurred at age four and the last at age eight years. He claimed to have been abused by his mother, a male relative, and another male.

Although not charged with sex offenses other than the present offense of his stepdaughter, he reported having molested girls under the age of 11 on eight occasions and girls ages 11 to 18 on three occasions. Since he has been an adult, he has had urges and excitement about forcing sex. He acknowledged that there have been four incidents where he forced sex. He reported that he preferred female sexual partners. On occasion he has had difficulty getting and keeping an erection. Sometimes he has had premature ejaculation.

Marital History

He has been married three times and presently is in a marriage that has lasted seven years. This marriage sometimes has been stressful because of problems with in-laws and children, but overall he considers it to have been satisfactory. He denied he ever beat his wife or forced sex on her. He has had extramarital affairs.

Parenting History

He has two children. Overall he does not consider his relationship with them to be a pleasing one. While he did not punish them harshly and never punished them with a strap, switch, or cane, he considered himself to have been cruel to his children. He acknowledged having sexually abused his stepdaughter.

Medical History

Physical health. On the whole he rated his physical health as good. In his lifetime he has been hospitalized on three occasions for surgical procedures. During the 12 months prior to his evaluation he has seen a physician once. He reported no serious medical illnesses and specifically denied having fits, convulsions, seizures, or venereal disease.

Mental health. While he reported that he had experienced emotional problems as a child, he has not had any treatment. Although the exact nature of his problems are not known and he denied having experienced a severe mood disorder with mania or depression, in his lifetime he has attempted suicide on two occasions. The last attempt occurred about four years ago in an overdose attempt. He denied having experienced any form of hallucinations.

Alcohol and Drug History

He first began to drink alcohol when he was 10 and reported that by the age of 12 he was drinking heavily on a regular basis. While he reported that his use of alcohol has caused problems with school, employers, the law, and his family, he denied he was a problem drinker. This is in spite of the fact that he was arrested for DWI, lost a job as a result of his drinking, and has committed an act of violence while using alcohol. He reported never having blackouts, DTs, or any treatment for alcohol abuse. He denied that he ever used any street drugs.

Psychological and Behavioral Test Results

While S. N. reported that he had finished high school, his approximate reading level as tested on the Wide Range Achievement Test (WRAT) is the end of the sixth grade.

His Personality Research Form-E (PRF-E) test scores were judged as being valid. Results from the PRF-E suggest that while he is a very impulsive person he does not engage in risk-taking behavior if personal safety is involved. He is seen as a timid individual who does not express his opinions readily, who likes his environment to be without change, and who does not show discontent when he is restricted in his environment. He is a person who does not notice different body sensations, and he does not appear to be intellectually curious. He tends to give up quickly and is not willing to work long hours.

The Interpersonal Behavior Survey (IBS) shows a slight tendency to deny common, but socially undesirable, traits. Although the validity scales are within the acceptable range, this denial tendency should be kept in mind. His overall pattern of results is characterized by an absence of pervasive, aggressive attitudes toward others and a deficiency of assertiveness skills. His pattern is sometimes associated with a passive person who has a naive and unsophisticated perspective of the world. Based on this test result, there is decreased likelihood he would easily display his temper. He is likely to show reluctance in giving praise and to be uncomfortable in receiving compliments. He is also unlikely to stand up for his rights or opinions if they would cause conflict with others. He is likely to have only a few close friendships and will probably avoid social situations. He may show interpersonal anxiety.

The Abel Pedophilic Cognition Scale indicates he does not admit to any of the cognitive beliefs commonly associated with pedophiles.

In the Abel's Sexual Interest Scales there is indication that adult heterosexuality and pedophilia of an incestuous nature with girls are his most arousing interests. These are followed to a slightly lesser degree by an interest in pedophilia of a nonincestuous nature with girls. He reports a very mild arousing state with voyeurism of adult females. He reports other forms of sexuality, including sadism, masochism, pedophilia with boys, and adult homosexuality, to be repulsive to him.

On the Clarke Sexual History Questionnaire he admitted having had intercourse with a number of different adult females and a small number of pubescent females including his stepdaughter. His Z scores in relationship to a total sample as well as to a deviant and heterosexual consensual sample indicate he is elevated in the hebephilic (pubescent) frequency. His only other elevation of his Clarke scores in comparison with other samples is in regard to frequency of group sex.

The Multiphasic Sex Inventory (MSI) indicates that he has a moderately elevated child molest score directed toward girls. He has a mildly elevated score on the rape scale. He is judged to be open about his sexual deviance toward children but to have suppressed his deviant interest toward rape. On the MSI he indicates he is highly motivated to receive treatment.

On the Michigan Alcohol Status Test (MAST) his low score, in spite of his admitted problems with alcohol abuse, brings cause for suspicion that he was not admitting his difficulty with alcohol. His truthfulness on this measure is suspect.

The plethysmographic response to the audiotapes indicates that, although he claimed on the Abel Sexual Interest Cardsort to have found an equal interest in adult females and pedophilia with girls, he finds consenting sex with a female at Tanner Stage 3 (approximate mean age 12.25 yrs) to be the most arousing, followed by having sex with females at Tanner Stage 1 (prepubertal) and Tanner Stage 3 using threats of violence. He does not show arousal to consenting sex with adult females nor does he show arousal toward males at any developmental stage.

Summary, Opinions, and Recommendations

S. N. is a man who has had relationship problems since childhood. Overall, he felt neglected by his father and unduly dominated and controlled by his mother. He developed a poor self-concept as a child. This low self-esteem continued into adulthood. His interpersonal problems were not only with his family but also with his peers and teachers in school, which led to problems adjusting academically. Since these interpersonal problems extended into the military, employment, and marital experiences, he had discipline problems in the military, difficulty keeping jobs, and has been married four times. As a child he was sexually abused on several occasions and as an adult he has sexually abused his stepdaughter as well as other female children. He has a history of abusing alcohol, so it has caused him problems with employers, family, and the law. His low self-esteem has shown itself with two suicide attempts. His personality assessment is marked by his impulsivity with low dominance and low endurance, coupled with low aggressiveness and low assertiveness. His MSI scales and his penile response on the plethysmograph confirm his sexual interest and penile arousal to female children.

It is my opinion that he meets the criteria on Axis I for Pedophilia as well as Alcohol Abuse. Data from the CAPSA indicate that on Axis II he has criteria for a Mixed Personality Disorder with traits of Antisocial, Avoidant, Sadistic, and Self-defeating Personality Disorder.

While he expresses strong motivation to change and to receive treatment, he may be handicapped by his dislike for new and different experiences, together with his tendency to give up quickly in problem solving.

It is thought that he may have denied and repressed his aggressive tendencies so that his overall level of assertiveness is low. It is recommended that he be given the opportunity to participate in the assertiveness training module early in the course of treatment so he may tap this energy and be able to use it constructively later in the course of treatment.

DISCUSSION AND FUTURE DEVELOPMENTS

The laboratory is fully functional and is currently running smoothly. As we suspected, the rapidity with which the initial evaluation can be performed greatly expedites the development of a personalized treatment plan and initiation of treatment. In our next phase we will retest subjects at 12 months and again prior to discharge. In this way we can begin to determine how, if at all, the residents change with the treatment program further described in Chapter 7.

Although we have no concrete evidence at present, it would seem that unless all deviant sexual arousal choices can be addressed in treatment, rather than merely the one for which the individual is convicted, the likelihood of recidivism will be increased. Abel et al.[3] found that 70% of their 24 cases showed paraphilic arousal not reported during the initial clinical interview. While we have not yet analyzed our data, our clinical impression is that our population of sex offenders will confirm this finding. Many of these offenders report a variety of paraphilic behaviors from which no legal charges have resulted. Thus, the idea of a "pure" rapist, child molester, sadist, voyeur, or exhibitionist may indeed be more rare than was previously thought.

Although penile tumescence measurements may be inconclusive in one-third of admitting and two-thirds of nonadmitting pedophiles, they do remain the most reliable indication we have of sexual preference and lend themselves to correlation with information obtained in the sexual history and questionnaire.

It is hoped that future data gathered by the laboratories will throw further light on the childhood and adolescence characteristics of child molesters and other sex offenders. These data should enable us to continue our investigation in this important and little understood area.[31] Although our psychological consultants feel that we have "a good mix" for our psychological and behavioral tests, in the future we will certainly add, omit, or in other ways change the existing protocol as experience is gained. From our immediate perspective, benefits in terms of rapid comprehensive diagnosis and objective measurement of the progress of treatment are deemed to be invaluable to the sex offender program at NFETC.

REFERENCES

1. Abel, G. G., & Becker, J. V. (1985). *Sexual Interest Cardsort*. Atlanta, GA: Behavioral Medicine Laboratory, Emory University.
2. Abel, G. G., Becker, J. V., Cunningham-Rathner, J., Rouleau, J. L., Kaplan, M., & Reich, J. (1984). *The Treatment of Child Molesters*. Atlanta, GA: Behavioral Medicine Laboratory, Emory University.
3. Abel, G. G., Mittelman, M. S., & Becker, J. V. (1985). Sexual offenders: Results of assessment and recommendations for treatment. In M. H. Ben-Aron, S. J. Hucker, & C. D. Webster (Eds.), *Clinical Criminology: Current Concepts*. Toronto: M & M Graphics.
4. Barlow, D. H. (1977). Assessment of sexual behavior. In A. R. Ciminero, K. S. Calhoun, & H. E. Adams (Eds.), *Handbook of Behavioral Assessment*. New York: Wiley.
5. Burt, M. R. (1980). Cultural myths and supports for rape. *Journal of Personality & Social Psychology, 38,* 217.
6. Butcher, J. N., Keller, L. S., & Bacon, S. F. (1985). Current developments and future directions in computerized personality assessment. *Journal of Consulting & Clinical Psychiatry, 53,* 803.
7. Erdman, H. P., Klein, M. H., & Greist, J. H. (1985). Direct patient computer interviewing. *Journal of Consulting & Clinical Psychology, 53,* 760.
8. Fowler, R. D. (1964, September). Computer processing and reporting of personality test data. Paper presented at the meeting of the American Psychological Association, Los Angeles, CA.
9. Fowler, R. D. (1985). Landmarks in computer-assisted psychological assessment. *Journal of Consulting & Clinical Psychology, 53,* 748.
10. Fuller, A. K., Barnard, G. W., Robbins, L., & Spears, H. (1988). Sexual maturity as a criterion for classification of phallometric stimulus slides. *Archives of Sexual Behavior, 17,* 271.
11. Greist, J. H., & Klein, M. H. (1980). Computer programs for patients, clinicians and researchers in psychiatry. In J. B. Sidowski, J. H. Johnson, & T. A. Williams (Eds.), *Technology in Mental Health Care Delivery Systems*. Norwood, NJ: Ablex.
12. Heinemann, A. W., Harper, R. G., Friedman, L. C., & Whitney, J. (1985). The relative utility of the Shipley-Hartford Scale: Prediction of Wais-R IQ. *Journal of Clinical Psychology, 41,* 547.
13. Hofer, P. J., & Green, B. F. (1985). The challenge of competence and creativity in computerized psychological testing. *Journal of Consulting & Clinical Psychology, 53,* 826.

14. Jackson, D. N. (1984). *Personality Research Form Manual*. Port Huron, MI: Research Psychologist Press.
15. Jastak, S., & Wilkinson, G. S. (1984). *The Wide Range Achievement Test-Revised*. Wilmington, DE: Jastak Associates.
16. Johnson, J. H., & Williams, T. A. (1975). The use of on-line computer technology in a mental health admitting system. *American Psychologist, 30*, 388.
17. Johnson, J. H., & Williams, T. A. (1980). Using on-line computer technology in a mental health admitting system. In J. B. Sidowski, J. H. Johnson, & T. A. Williams (Eds.), *Technology in Mental Health Care Delivery Systems*. Norwood, NJ: Ablex.
18. Johnson, J. H., & Johnson, J. N. (1981). Psychological considerations related to the development of computerized testing stations. *Behavior Research Methods and Instrumentation, 13*, 421.
19. Klinger, D. E., Miller, D. A., Johnson, J. H. & Williams, T. A. (1976). Strategies in the evaluation of an on-line computer-assisted unit for intake assessment of mental health patients. *Behavior Research Methods and Instrumentation, 8*, 95.
20. Klinger, D. E., Miller, D. A., Johnson, J. H., & Williams, T. A. (1977). Process evaluation of an on-line computer-assisted unit for intake assessment of mental health patients. *Behavior Research Methods and Instrumentation, 9*, 110.
21. Langevin, R., Handy, L., Paitich, D., & Russon, A. (1985). Appendix A: A new version of the Clarke Sex History Questionnaire for Males. In R. Langevin (Ed.), *Erotic Preference, Gender Identity, and Aggression in Men: New Research Studies*. Hillsdale, NJ: Erlbaum.
22. Laws, D. R., & Osborn, C. A. (1983). How to build and operate a behavioral laboratory to evaluate and treat sexual deviance. In J. G. Greer & I. R. Stuart (Eds.), *The Sexual Aggressor: Current Perspectives on Treatment*. New York: Van Nostrand Reinhold.
23. Marks, P. A., & Seeman, W. (1963). *The Actuarial Description of Abnormal Personality: An Atlas for Use with the MMPI*. Baltimore: Williams & Wilkins.
24. Matarazzo, J. M. (1983). Computerized psychological testing. *Science, 221*, 323.
25. Mauger, P. A., & Adkinson, D. R. (1980). *Interpersonal Behavior Survey (IBS) Manual*. Los Angeles, CA: Western Psychological Services.
26. Moreland, K. L. (1985). Validation of computer-based interpretations: Problems and aspects. *Journal of Consulting & Clinical Psychology, 53*, 816.
27. Nichols, H. R., & Molinder, I. (1984). *Multiphasic Sex Inventory Manual*. Tacoma, WA: Nichols and Molinder.
28. Selzer, M. L. (1971). The Michigan Alcoholism Screening Test: The quest for a new diagnostic instrument. *American Journal of Psychiatry, 127*, 1653.
29. Shipley, W. C. (1939). *Shipley-Institute of Living Scale for Measuring Intellectual Impairment: Manual of Directions and Scoring Key*. Hartford, CT: The Institute of Living.
30. Tanner, J. M. (1978). *Foetus Into Man: Physical Growth from Conception to Maturity*. Cambridge, MA: Harvard University Press.
31. Tingle, D., Barnard, G. W., Robbins, L., Newman, G. & Hutchinson, D. (1986). Childhood and adolescent characteristics of pedophiles and rapists. *International Journal of Law & Psychiatry, 9*, 108.

32. Weitzel, W. D., Morgan, D. W., & Guyden, T. E. (1973). Toward a more efficient mental status examination. *Archives of General Psychiatry, 28,* 215.
33. White, D. M. (1983). An assessment of the comparability of a computer administration and standard administration of the MMPI. Unpublished Master's Thesis, University of Alabama.

CHAPTER 7
A Residential Treatment Program for Sex Offenders

This chapter describes treatment of mentally disordered sex offenders (MDSO) in the MDSO unit of the North Florida Evaluation and Treatment Center (NFETC). In order to diversify and strengthen the treatment program, over a year ago the staff at NFETC initiated more intensive and innovative treatment techniques for sex offenders including behavioral, psychotherapeutic, and psychosocial modalities.

SELECTION PROCESS

The sex offender unit at NFETC is a treatment program for men who have been convicted of a sexual offense and sentenced to a prison term. The MDSO population is comprised of child molesters, incest offenders, exhibitionists, and rapists who volunteer for treatment and pass screening by a prison psychologist and a professional staff member of the Sex Offender Treatment Unit. Final selection into the treatment program is determined at the end of an eight-week clinical evaluation period.

The following criteria are used in the screening process for accepting sex offenders into the program: (1) there must be evidence of a psychosexual disorder; (2) the inmate must volunteer for treatment; and (3) the inmate must accept responsibility for the crime. Inmates are automatically excluded from MDSO treatment if they present one of the following characteristics: (1) have a sentence in excess of 15 years or less than 18 months; (2) show significant evidence of a major mental illness (e.g., psychosis); (3) have murdered their victim(s); (4) are actively appealing their conviction or sentence; or (5) have significant medical problems which may be exacerbated by the stress of the treatment program.

Inmates selected for the MDSO program are placed on a waiting list and provided information on the two state programs, one located in south Florida and the other located in north Florida. The professional staff consider the location of family and community support systems in making their recommendation for placement.

The residents assigned to NFETC are transferred directly from the Department of Corrections (DOC) for an eight-week period of orientation and clinical evaluation to determine their abilities and the strength of their desires to engage in meaningful change. If, at the end of this eight-week period, the staff believes that a resident is motivated toward treatment and is capable of altering his deviant behavior, he is accepted into the treatment phase of the program. Because the program is entirely voluntary and not court-ordered, the residents can change their minds, elect to leave the program, and return to prison at any time.

THE STAFF AND FACILITIES

The sixty-three bed MDSO unit is situated in three medium-security, electronically controlled individual treatment buildings. Two buildings house 18 men in a two-pod floor plan and one houses 27 men in a three-pod floor plan, with nine individual rooms per pod. Each pod has a common area for group or recreational activities which is monitored visually and audibly by a single building control room.

The administrator of NFETC is aided by an assistant administrator who is in charge of the medical clinic and the psychology unit and a staff attorney who acts as a legal advisor (see Table 7.1). The administrative staff of the sex offender unit consists of the following: a unit director (TS), who is responsible for the administration and clinical management of the entire treatment program and who acts as co-director of the psychosexual assessment laboratory; an assistant director, who administers the intake and advanced resident programs; and the unit treatment rehabilitation supervisor, who oversees the unit rehabilitation supervisors and rehabilitation specialists. The treatment staff is comprised of

Table 7.1
North Florida Evaluation and Treatment Center
Sex Offender Unit: Table of Organization

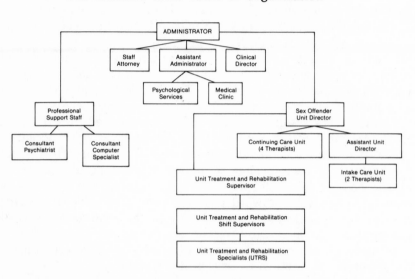

six therapists, 12 unit treatment rehabilitation shift supervisors, and 30 unit treatment rehabilitation specialists.

In addition to the sex offender unit treatment staff, the professional support staff consists of the following: a unit psychiatrist, who has clinical responsibility for the residents; a clinical psychologist, who submits a comprehensive psychological report on each incoming resident and recommends treatment approaches; a consulting psychiatrist (G.B.), who is co-director of the psychosexual assessment laboratory; and a consulting computer specialist (L.R.), who develops the computer programs and supervises data handling within the laboratory.

The Medical Clinic has a primary physician who examines each incoming resident and gives routine medical treatment, a health coordinator nurse, and a dentist.

Each therapist (Master's level training) is a case manager for a pod of nine sex offenders. The therapist develops treatment plans for the residents in his or her assigned pod, conducts group therapy sessions, runs the modular programs, writes progress notes and clinical summaries, and makes staffing recommendations regarding the resident's ongoing status within the program. The therapist discusses the residents' behavior and progress with the unit psychiatrist and the unit director on the weekly rounds. Although shift supervisors may restrict the resident's mobility, the therapist has the power to raise the resident's movement status, that is, give the resident an increased measure of autonomy in his movement around the campus.

Each building has a treatment rehabilitation shift supervisor who maintains staff coverage 24 hours a day. The supervisors are responsible for building security. In addition, they provide supervision and paraprofessional-level counseling to the residents. These staff personnel are trained in basic counseling skills, as well as crisis intervention and cardiopulmonary resuscitation.

The unit treatment rehabilitation specialists (UTRS, Bachelor's level training) are paraprofessional staff who have the clinical responsibility of tracking the residents' compliance with treatment plans and progress through the treatment modules. They record each resident's rule violations within the center and can recommend altering the resident's movement downward, that is, remove a degree of autonomy in his campus movements when a rule or rules are broken.

Treatment progress is monitored weekly during clinical rounds conducted by the unit director, the unit psychiatrist, the therapists, the UTRS, and the nurse.

TREATMENT GOALS

In her recent book, *Retraining Adult Sex Offenders: Methods and Models*, Knopp[12] describes six comprehensive treatment goals for the current sex offender discipline:

1. Each sex offender needs a complete, individualized assessment and treatment plan; effective initial and ongoing assessment are prerequisites for successful treatment.
2. Each sex offender needs to (a) accept responsibility for the offense(s) in which he was involved and (b) have an understanding of the sequence of thoughts, feelings, events, circumstances, and arousal stimuli that make up the "offense syndrome" that precedes his involvement in sexually aggressive behaviors.
3. Each sex offender needs to learn how to (a) intervene in or break into his offense pattern at its very first sign and (b) call upon the appropriate methods, tools or procedures he has learned, in order to suppress, control, manage, and stop the behavior.

4. Each sex offender needs to engage in a re-education and resocialization process in order to (a) replace antisocial thoughts and behaviors with prosocial ones, (b) acquire a positive self-concept and new attitudes and expectations for himself, and (c) learn new social and sexual skills to help cultivate positive, satisfying, pleasurable, and non-threatening relationships with others.

5. Each residential sex offender needs a prolonged period during his treatment when he can begin to test safely his newly acquired insights and control mechanisms, in the community, without the risk of affronting or harming members of the wider community.

6. Each sex offender needs (a) a post-treatment support, peer or "rap" group and (b) continual postrelease access to therapeutic treatment so he can maintain permanently a safe lifestyle. (pp. 28–29)

The modular inpatient sex offender treatment program at NFETC, described below, is predicated on Knopp's laudable goals and strives to implement them. However, goals 5 and 6, which refer to the monitoring of the sex offender upon release into the community, are beyond the confines of the state-mandated program at the present time. Plans are underway to provide for the follow-up monitoring that is so necessary to resettling and maintaining the former sex offender in the community.

PHILOSOPHY AND MODALITIES OF TREATMENT

The basic philosophy underlying the comprehensive treatment program offered at NFETC is that sex offenders develop their deviant behavior through multiple and diverse ways and consequently require a variety of treatment approaches to alter this aberrant behavior.

The treatment process is conceptualized as being directed at four different areas requiring change: characterological, sexual behavior, general behavior, and physical and mental wellness (see Table 7.2). The resident is provided the opportunity to undergo change in each area during the course of treatment. He may gain insight into his character structure in order to reduce his maladaptive behavior; modify his deviant sexual arousal patterns and learn ways to adopt more acceptable and healthy sexual behaviors; learn the coping skills that will enable him to handle life's stresses; and promote his personal health and well-being.

A wide variety of therapeutic techniques are offered. For instance, in order for a resident to gain insight into his character structure, an analytic process utilizing intensive group therapy is required. Role playing of traumatic events may be part of the group therapy process, while changing sexual behavior may be accomplished through behavior modification techniques. Learning to control anger or learning a more assertive approach may require a combination of behavior modification and role-playing techniques. In addition to these other strategies, increasing the resident's self-esteem may be aided through physical conditioning and learning stress management or educational skills.

ORIENTATION AND EVALUATION PHASE

During the first eight weeks following admission to the program, the staff evaluate the offender's amenability for treatment and clarify his specific treatment needs. This clinical evaluation process is comprised of a computerized psychosexual assessment, along with staff observations of the resident's behavior and analysis of his attitudes and motivations toward treatment. During this time the expectations and regulations are conveyed to the resident. The staff determines to what degree he can be open and honest and whether he is willing to look at himself and his behavioral patterns.

Group Therapy

The new resident attends group therapy, a therapeutic approach which continues throughout his treatment. These sessions are facilitated by his therapist twice weekly for approximately two-and-a-half hours each session. During these group meetings, residents are required to present detailed descriptions about their offenses. Each resident role plays his most significant sex offense in front of the rest of the group.

Lifeline

Another major component of the orientation module is the lifeline, a life history outline that the resident writes and presents to the pod therapy group. In the lifeline, the resident tracks his social and sexual development, highlighting important events in his developmental history. This life history is an important tool to help the resident better understand the significant events that have had an impact on his life. For many men it is the first time in their

Table 7.2

Sex Offender Treatment Modules at North Florida Evaluation and Treatment Center

Areas of Change			
Characterological	Sexual Behavior	General Behavior	Physical/Mental Well-Being
Purpose			
Gain insight into character structure with goal of lessening maladaptive behavior	Modify deviant sexual arousal patterns and facilitate his ability to adopt more acceptable and healthy sexual behaviors	Teach social skills, methods of coping, and mastery of life stresses	Increase self-esteem, physical well-being, and level of knowledge
Modules			
Experiential	*Behavioral*	*Skills Acquisition*	*Health/Education*
Interpersonally Oriented Groups	Masturbatory Satiation	Cognitive Restructuring	Personal Health Project

| Modules (cont'd) | | | |
Experiential	Behavioral	Skills Acquisition	Health/Education
Peer Facilitated Groups	Covert Sensitization	Communication Skills/Assertiveness Training	General Education
Role Playing		Social Skills	Sex Education
Sensitivity Training		Relapse Prevention	Occupational Education
Traumatic Events		Substance Abuse	Art Therapy
		Stress Inoculation/Anger Management	Body Work/Meditation
		Family Visits/Family Therapy	

lives that they have reminisced on past experiences. They often remember key traumatic or significant events that had been repressed or simply forgotten.

The lifeline also creates an opportunity for the resident to receive feedback from his peers and therapist regarding not only the resident's past life events but his cognitive distortions of those events.

The resident revises and expands his lifeline throughout his treatment program. As he gains access to memories which he has previously repressed, suppressed, or denied, he is expected to document them. From this lifeline comes the material for traumatic events work.

Crime Description

The sex offender's inclination to minimize, rationalize, and lie about his sex-offending behavior is challenged directly by the detailed crime description each new resident is required to write during his first six weeks of treatment. He presents the detailed description of his offense within the treatment group and is open to challenge about any statements that he makes which would tend to place responsibility for the offense on his victim or other innocents. The therapists watch for blame-placing statements such as those beginning with "Just" or "No, except for."

Frequently, the offender's first crime description fails to assign responsibility for the offense to himself, and it may leave out highly significant details about the offense as documented in the victim's testimony, in the arrest report, or by witnesses. After feedback from his pod and treatment groups, the resident rewrites his crime description until it is totally accepted by his group and his therapist. Once approved, it is the offender's responsibility to reenact the offense. He is evaluated based on his ability to portray the offense honestly without minimization or subterfuge.

Criminal Thinking Errors Class

Based on the work of Yochelson and Samenow,[20] the resident is taught to recognize his own criminal thinking patterns. With advanced residents in the treatment program as instructors, the module uses reading, discussion, and structured homework assignments to make residents more aware of their patterns of distorted thinking and disturbed behavior.

More specifically, the module focuses on specific, common components of criminal thinking (e.g., victim stance, lack of empathy or trust, opportunism), the effects these have on criminal behavior, and successful strategies for changing these patterns of thoughts and behaviors. A link is made between criminal thinking and sexual exploration. We believe that completing this component assists the residents in maintaining the motivation to complete the more challenging components of the treatment program.

Body Work/Meditation

The body work/meditation component[4,9] is a brief module included within the orientation module for new residents. Through practice, the residents learn relaxation techniques[2] that they can employ to effectively cope with stress when they leave the Center. Within the treatment unit, relaxation also has a very valuable function as a management tool. By engaging the residents in relaxing behaviors at least twice a day, it serves to control acting-out behavior.

The meditation component of the module has been adapted from the Clinically Standardized Meditation model developed by Carrington.[3] This model, similar to Transcendental Meditation, is a relatively unstructured mantra meditation. Sessions last from 10–20 minutes twice a day. Sitting in a comfortable position, the resident simply repeats his chosen mantra for the designated period of time.

The body-work component of the module is based primarily on yoga postures, breathing, and stretches. The residents are taught a series of postures and breathing exercises, some variation of which they practice twice a day throughout their treatment.[10, 11]

Treatment Selection Conference

At the end of this eight-week clinical evaluation period, the multidisciplinary treatment team holds a staff conference to review the resident's amenability for treatment. The staff seeks to determine if the resident has shown himself to be motivated, and whether he appears able to handle confrontation and to develop a degree of self-understanding. They assess whether he has shown an ability to process his emotional experience without becoming so overwhelmed by his feelings that he loses control to the degree that he becomes self-destructive or destructive toward others. Staff consider and evaluate the resident's compliance with his treatment program assignments, his ability to participate in group therapy, and his ability to get along with peers and staff. The results of psychological testing and portions of the computerized psychophysiological assessment (described in Chapter 6) are also considered in forming the decision to accept or reject him for extended treatment. The resident's therapist writes the summary which is reviewed by the unit director, the clinical director, the psychologist, the staff attorney and the administrator. The administrator then attaches a cover letter and sends it to the Department of Corrections (DOC). At this point the resident is eligible to participate in the regular treatment modules if he has, in fact, been found to be amenable for treatment. If not, he is transferred back to the DOC to complete his sentence.

TREATMENT PHASE

After successfully completing the evaluation phase, the resident is accepted into the treatment program, which may last up to 18 months. Child molesters, incest offenders, rapists, and exhibitionists are grouped together. During treatment each resident is required to successfully complete the experiential, behavioral, skills acquisition, and educational modules. (See Table 7.2. For purposes of simplification, the modules are somewhat arbitrarily grouped under these headings. It should be noted that each module may have properties in common with modules in one of the other classifications.)

1. The *experiential modules* are designed to facilitate characterological understanding and openness to change. In these modules the offender identifies and works through the "psychological blocks" to healthy functioning that may result from early trauma and/or lifelong unhealthy functioning. Experiential components include the cognitive/insight and peer facilitated group therapies, traumatic events modules, role play, and sensitivity training.
2. The *behavioral therapy modules* are designed to alter behaviors associated with the psychosexual disorder. Modules in this class include masturbatory satiation and covert sensitization.
3. The *skills acquisition modules* have been developed to improve the offender's level of psychosocial functioning. These include cognitive restructuring, communication and social skills training, relapse prevention, stress inoculation/anger management, substance abuse management, and family therapy modules.
4. The *health/education modules* include the personal health project, academic courses, sex education, vocational training, art and music therapy, and bodywork/meditation.

Treatment Schedule

The resident is enrolled in three different modules at any given time, each module lasting for a 12-week period. On a typical day, the residents have breakfast and the daily cleanup until 8:45, at which time those residents not involved in the psychiatric rounds have bodywork and meditation until 9:30 a.m. From 9:30 a.m. until noon the residents are in their modules, except for Tuesday and Friday when they are in interpersonally oriented group therapy. For 30 minutes following lunch on Wednesday the residents have a building business meeting and on Thursday they have an open time period. Otherwise they are engaged in their modules until 4:30 p.m. when they again have 30 minutes of body work and meditation. The exception is Friday afternoon when they are given free time from 3 p.m. until the 4:30 p.m. body work/meditation period. Following dinner from 5 p.m.–6 p.m., the residents have 30 minutes of open time.

Their activities continue into the evening hours. From 6:30 p.m. until 8:15 p.m. on Monday night they have lifeline or crime description; on Tuesday they have study hall or resident government; on Wednesday they have feedback or treatment plan review with the UTR; on Thursday they have study hall; and on Friday night they have a pod group. In addition, on Tuesday and Friday evenings at 8:15 p.m. they have triad meetings lasting until 10 p.m.

No scheduled treatment occurs on Saturday and Sunday, when the residents take care of personal matters—that is, wash clothes, write letters, visit with family members, watch TV, work in their gardens, play games, swim, and so forth. On Sunday evening there is a weekly AA meeting. (See Table 7.3 for Daily Schedule.)

Experiential Modules

As noted earlier, child molesters are individuals who carry out sexually inappropriate and socially unacceptable acts with children. If the molester even subtly accepts society's moral code but nevertheless continues his deviant behavior, anxiety, guilt, and remorse often result. As a way to avoid these unpleasant feelings, the molester relies on unconscious defense mechanisms to prevent his experiencing conflict. One of the defense mechanisms that is frequently employed by the child molester is rationalization and the related process of cognitive distortion (see Chapter 3). For instance, a child molester might hold the belief that sexual relations between a child and an adult cause the child no emotional harm.

Table 7.3
Daily Schedule in MDSO Unit at North Florida Evaluation and Treatment Center

Time	MONDAY	TUESDAY	WEDNESDAY	THURSDAY	FRIDAY	SATURDAY	SUNDAY
8:00	DAILY CLEANUP					VISITATION AND FREE TIME	VISITATION AND FREE TIME
:15							
:30							
:45							
9:00			Rounds Bldg. 11	Rounds Bldg. 15			
:15	BODYWORK AND MEDITATION						
:30							
:45	Cognitive Restructuring		Communication	Traumatic Events			
10:00		Pod Groups			Pod Groups		
:15	Relapse Prevention		Behaviorial Sensitivity	New Residents' Module			
:30							
:45	Study Hall		C.T.E.'s	Study Hall			
11:00	Rounds Bldg. 12						
:15							
:30							
:45							
12:00	LUNCH						
:15							
:30							
:45							
1:00	Substance Abuse		Bldg Business Meeting	Open Time		VISITATION AND FREE TIME	VISITATION AND FREE TIME
:15							
:30							
:45							
2:00	Work Program	Relapse Prevention	Role Play Module	Sex Education	Social Skills		
:15							
:30	Study Hall			Stress Anger MGT	Study Hall		
:45							

Table 7.3
Daily Schedule in MDSO Unit at North Florida Evaluation and Treatment Center (continued)

	MONDAY	TUESDAY	WEDNESDAY	THURSDAY	FRIDAY	SATURDAY	SUNDAY
3:00	Art Therapy	RP continued	PM continued	Personal Health Project	Free Time		
:15							
:30							
:45							
4:00							
:15							
:30	BODYWORK AND MEDITATION						
:45							
5:00	DINNER						
:15							
:30							
:45							
6:00	OPEN						
:15							
:30							
:45	Lifeline or Crime Description	Study Hall or Resident Government	Feedback or Treatment Plan Review	Study Hall Psychosexual Disorder Module	Pod Group		
7:00							
:15							
:30							
:45							
8:00	Open	Triad Meeting	Open	Open	Triad Meeting	RAM Contact	A.A. Meeting
:15							
:30							
:45							
9:00							
:15							
:30							
:45							
10:00							

This type of belief system will be identified, labeled, clarified, and challenged repeatedly by the therapist and members of the molester's treatment group during the course of therapy. In this section some of the experiential means that are used at NFETC to change not only cognitive distortions but also other defensive and characterological patterns of the child molesters are reviewed. These experiential techniques include interpersonally oriented and peer-facilitated groups, role playing, sensitivity training, and traumatic events.

Interpersonally oriented groups. As the resident enters the cognitive/insight group therapy, he is encouraged to accept responsibility for his child-molesting behavior, that is, to regard himself as a child molester. Group therapy uses a mixture of psychodynamic and learning theory approaches. Many of the residents themselves have been sexually abused as children. For this reason, during the group therapy session the resident has the opportunity to recall traumatic experiences of sexual abuse that he has experienced. Role play is used to reexperience the traumatic events and provide catharsis. Through the support provided by the therapist and his peers, the resident is able to relive the trauma without feeling overwhelmed and is able to perceive it differently. In this manner he is able to master the traumatic event.

The resident is taught to look at the chain of events, including thoughts, feelings, and behaviors that led to his inappropriate sexual behavior with children. At NFETC this self-examination is referred to as "central process" and is synonymous with Knopp's "offense syndrome."[12] In group therapy the offender is repeatedly provided with the opportunity to look at some of the core conflicts that he may have carried from his own childhood which set the stage for his child-molesting behavior.

For example, during his childhood Tom was repeatedly anally molested by his stepfather. He felt overpowered and helpless. Yet, he was terrified of the stepfather and was afraid to tell his mother about the molestation because of his stepfather's threats. He felt ashamed of himself for being unable to stop the molestation and believed that other boys his age would have been more effective in terminating it. Thus, through the series of molestations and the resultant feeling of impotency, there was a gradual shaping of his self-concept. He came to see himself as totally lacking in courage and having no control over his environment. Through a process of repression, many of these childhood events and memories were lost from his conscious awareness.

Later, as Tom became an adult and engaged in child-molesting behavior, he lacked any understanding of the connection between his own sexual abuse and his abusive behavior toward children who were around the same age that he himself was when victimized. It was only during the process of group therapy and the role playing of his offense that he became aware of the connection. He recognized that as the child victim he had felt helpless, whereas as an adult abuser he could control the child as his stepfather had controlled him. Unconsciously he had identified with his aggressor and blotted out the feelings of anxiety and fear associated with being a victim. Reliving those old memories and reexperiencing this anxiety was a painful process, but he gained this awareness and insight with the support of his therapist and group members.

Later Tom learned that his child-molesting behaviors were not caused solely by his history of repetitive sexual abuse, but that many childhood and adult experiences contributed to his development as a child molester. At first he was unable to detect any significant factors. Gradually, however, he saw one or more repetitive patterns taking place prior to his inappropriate behavior with children. One of these patterns was choosing to engage in social roles that placed him in contact with young boys; for instance, he chose to become a boy scout leader. He recognized that when he was rejected or belittled by another person, he would feel badly about himself and increase his alcoholic intake. While intoxicated, he would fantasize about and focus on pleasurable feelings that he had when he was with boys. His self-esteem increased because the boys admired him and looked up to him. Once involved in the fantasies, he felt a strong urge to seek out a boy and have sex with him. In therapy, he learned that this cruising behavior was a part of the chain of events that ultimately led to his molesting behavior.

Initially, Tom talked as though he had no control over his actions; once the thoughts and fantasies came into his awareness he saw it as inevitable that he would act on them. His therapist challenged this belief set and helped him to understand that simply because he had the fantasy, even with lowered inhibitions caused by the alcohol, he did not have to act upon it. Instead, he was helped to look at the destructive effects, both immediate and long-term, that his molestation could have on both himself and his victim. This reevaluation was not an easy thing for him to do because for years he had carried the distorted belief that what he was doing with the child was not harmful but, indeed, was helpful. Over a period of time he let go of his distorted belief as well as the rationalization that he had no power to intervene and stop the process.

Therapy facilitated Tom's self-awareness and insight about himself, and it also gave him specific behavioral skills that he could use to interrupt the repetitive sequence of the offense syndrome that had led to his child-molesting behavior.

Peer-facilitated groups. Although all of the treatment modules currently in use in the program at the treatment center are facilitated by professional and trained paraprofessional staff, the residents themselves engage in numerous resident-facilitated groups and treatment components. Each resident is assigned to a treatment triad comprised of two other residents, one of whom is always an advanced resident. These individuals are on call for each other for feedback and support and as a preliminary sounding board prior to taking an issue to a large group. In this manner, residents are encouraged to process interpersonal conflicts in a group setting to surface underlying cognitive distortions and unhealthy patterns of behavior that may be associated with their present interpersonal conflicts. Frequent observation and confrontation by peers allows for a greater frequency of examination of these distorted cognitive-behavioral processes.

A structured resident government handles many activities formerly handled by staff and minimizes the us-against-them syndrome which maximum security facilities tend to foster. Much of the security and safety needs of the unit are handled by the residents themselves. Residents also provide progress review boards and report on residents' progress to the therapists. Residents nearing the completion of their treatment live in the advanced resident pod and participate as advanced participants and facilitators in group therapy sessions during the orientation module of the new residents. These advanced residents then serve as role models for new residents entering the program and practice their newfound skills prior to returning to the community.

Role-playing module. Role playing of offenses has a long tradition at NFETC. The role-play module helps the offender to accept the extent of his responsibility for the offense as well as to recognize the impact of his offense on himself, his victim, and others. Similar to the Modified Aversive Behavioral Rehearsal Technique developed by the Northwest Treatment Associates in Seattle, Washington,[19] the role-play module at NFETC utilizes videotape. As mentioned earlier, during the course of the 12-week module, each of the nine offenders presents a detailed crime description which is evaluated by peers and co-facilitators. Using another offender to play the opposite role, each participant role plays at least one offense acting as the offender and then role plays the same offense as the victim. Each week the offenders who did not participate are required to watch and then write a reaction paper; in this manner they provide feedback to the resident-roleplayers. The reenactments are reviewed by the offender later in his pod group, after which time he, too, is required to produce a reaction paper to his own experience while he played both offender and victim. Offenders are rarely initially cognizant of the negative impact that their offending behaviors have had on their self-concept and lives. Many offenders report that the reviewing of the videotape of the offense is especially effective in their recognizing the impact of the offense both on their victims and on themselves.

Since role play is a powerful experience in which many raw and often painful emotions are exposed, the group is taxing for offenders and therapists. A debriefing phase is necessary to defuse the emotionally charged focus and to reintegrate the experience into the here and now. Evidence shows that the impact of this module requires more debriefing than any other component of treatment. For this reason, members of the role-play module remain on call for each other after group.

Offenders report that role playing is very effective in decreasing the proclivity toward minimizing, denying, or distorting the memory of their sex-offense behaviors. By exposing the most offensive part of himself, the offender effectively demonstrates his willingness to be open and honest and to attempt to change his lifestyle. This approach is directly antithetical to traditional nonspecialized outpatient programs where the sex-offending behavior is never mentioned, much less dealt with in so revealing a manner. In the traditional nonspecialized programs, the emphasis is often put on generalized coping skills as the patient deals with problems of the here and now. This is in contrast to specialized programs for sex offenders in which attention of the therapist and offender is more focused on or directed to behaviors reflecting sexual pathology or attitudes reinforcing the child-molestation behavior. Without much experience in dealing with sex offenders, the nonspecialized programs often are reluctant to confront sex offenders about negative aspects of molesting behavior. By avoiding these aspects, however, clinicians allow the offender to maintain his belief (cognitive distortion) that his behavior is appropriate. Therapists often find themselves being "conned" by the molester into discussing issues that are only peripheral or tangential to his sex-offending behaviors.

Sensitivity training module. The sensitivity training module was developed for the treatment program by professional staff with specialized training in gestalt therapy, yoga, and bioenergetics. The sensitivity training module at NFETC is based on the belief that sex offenders typically are unable to connect with their own experience, both emotionally and physiologically, and are unable to relate to the experience of others. In order to experience empathy, one must first be aware of one's own feelings. Denial, avoidance of painful emotions, and physiological correlates allow sex offenders to become numb to their own feelings. The very challenging and rewarding experiences provided by the 12-session sensitivity training module give the offender a new reference point; perhaps for the first time in many years, the offender has experiences that are congruent with an integration of body and mind. Each session begins with 15 minutes of individualized, self-directed bodywork which includes yoga postures, stretching, and movement. Gestalt techniques,[13,17,18] including gestalt movement therapy and gestalt art therapy, are interspersed throughout the 12-week rotation. The offender learns to consciously experience muscle tension and muscle relaxation, to recognize the ways in which he blocks his conscious experience of himself, as well as the way he blocks his awareness of others.

Offenders develop dream logs. They also record their reactions to various growth-potential exercises, including "cradling." Cradling is designed to reawaken nurturing memories from their childhood.

This module is offered in the spirit of an enriching experience. It is felt that this approach is particularly effective with offenders who have learned to cope with their hurt by closing off all feelings and by operating primarily by cognitive input, however distorted or maladapted.

Traumatic events module. Since a significant number of sex offenders report serious past traumas, the traumatic events module is designed to help the offender work through past devastating events in order to decrease the cognitive distortions and resultant emotional distress. This approach is accomplished through a series of 12 therapist-facilitated structured experiences. In these sessions the therapist uses modalities of relaxation, hypnosis, and visualization to help the molester reexperience the childhood trauma in a degree that can be tolerated without arousing undue anxiety. In this manner the trauma loses some of its destructive influence and the resident is thus able to cope more effectively than he did as a child.

Behavioral Therapy Modules

Rotations in the treatment program modules have been designed so that each sex offender can begin the modularized treatment program with the behavioral therapy module. Abel and colleagues'[1] study suggests that ordering the behavioral therapy module first would assist the offender in having the motivation and strength to successfully complete the remainder of the program. The behavioral therapy module includes two components: covert sensitization and masturbatory satiation. Both of these modules were adapted from treatment modalities used by Abel[1] in his program in New York.

Masturbatory satiation. Masturbatory satiation is a method of controlling deviant fantasies through depowering the fantasy associated with aversive sensations. Essentially, the technique is a simple one in which the offender, in the privacy of his room, audiotapes two different sets of fantasies, one nondeviant and the other deviant, while masturbating. He fantasizes about a nondeviant sexual experience and masturbates to the point of ejaculation, recording the time that it took for the ejaculation to occur. After waiting two minutes, he then masturbates to a deviant fantasy. As he masturbates, he narrates the fantasy aloud into the tape recorder. The instructions prohibit switching from fantasy to fantasy or going forward or backward in a fantasy. Instead he must focus his concentration on one element of the fantasy to the point of boredom. The purpose of this masturbation to the deviant fantasy during the refractory phase is to create an association between masturbation and the aversive sensation without enjoying the pleasure of ejaculation. He continues this aversive masturbation for a full fifty minutes. The entire session lasts about one hour. The tape is spot-checked by the therapist for compliance. If the offender desires, the therapist and other members of the group will critique the tape as well.

In our experience, continued urges to molest distress incarcerated sex offenders since they have direct evidence from their current incarceration that child molestation has aversive consequences. Thus, many offenders who go through the masturbatory satiation module report an immediate decrease in stress resulting from decreased deviant urges. After completion of this module, offenders at NFETC are much more willing to challenge distorted beliefs condoning child abuse.

Covert sensitization. Covert sensitization has two main goals: to teach the sex offender the concept of "chaining" or "linking" events which lead to the act of child molestation, and to help the offender to develop a method for controlling his own behavior through the use of aversive thoughts. In order for this notion to be understood, the offender must realize that, since he found child molesting to be a pleasurable experience, it was a rewarding or "reinforcing" event for him. If he desires to stop the molesting behavior, he must be willing to give up the sequence of events that are associated with the pleasure that he felt during child molestation. As in other modules, the offender must comprehend the concept of "offense syndrome," that is, the chaining of events that led to the act of child molesting. By "chaining" it is meant that the molester first has thoughts of child molesting; undergoes the cruising behavior in search of a child victim; performs "grooming" behavior in which he seeks acceptance from the child, and, at times, others; tests the waters prior to making physical contact to see if there is acceptance; and finally, if he is accepted by the child, whether through bribes, persuasion, or threats, carries out the child-molesting behavior.

In the covert sensitization module there are four categories of thoughts: neutral thoughts, child-molesting thoughts, aversive thoughts, and pleasurable thoughts associated with consensual sex with an adult partner. The offender is asked to develop detailed fantasies and scenes involving these four categories. With the child-molesting scene he breaks down the sequence in discrete steps, going from thought to cruising to approaching and on to molesting behavior. Using a tape recorder, he tapes fantasies from the different categories of neutral, child molesting, aversive, and consensual sex thoughts. For the aversive scenes he must come up with several different types of unpleasant effects that may occur if he is caught molesting a child. These are highly individualized, but include such things as being verbally rebuked by his family, having his own children harassed by other children when they learn that their father is a child molester, the thought of imprisonment and rape by inmates when they learn that he is a child molester, or contracting the deadly disease AIDS.

The offender is then taught the power of sequencing and interchanging these different scenes. He follows a child-molesting scene with its chain of events, but inserts a selected aversive thought into the chain early enough so that the later stages (i.e., cruising, molesting) do not occur. He is also taught to escape from aversive or unpleasant thoughts by going to thoughts of consensual sex with an adult partner. The offender tapes these scenes in his room and later brings them into the group for spot-checking and discussion of the responses to this learning process.

The potency of this module depends on the proper completion of the tapes. If done correctly, antecedent events which otherwise might trigger fond memories of the ultimate sex offense and the pleasure that it gives to the resident will instead instigate the newly associated aversive memory or other aversive stimuli. This triggering breaks the chain of events leading to the sex offense. The strengths of this treatment modality are (1) its ability to make the sexually abusive behavior less attractive and (2) its capability to act as a technique that can be used by the offender at a later time, should he discover that events in his life are causing him to either fantasize about or have urges to molest children.

Skills Acquisition Modules

Cognitive-restructuring module. The cognitive-restructuring module has been adapted from the work of Lange.[13] There are three primary goals that are accomplished during the 12 sessions of this module:

1. Challenging the irrational beliefs and rationalizations that have been used to justify sex-offending as well as other disturbed behaviors.
2. Increasing the child molester's beliefs that he can control his deviant thoughts and behaviors.
3. Developing increased interpersonal effectiveness through cognitive and behavioral skills training.

The cognitive-restructuring module uses rational-emotive therapy (RET) originally developed by Albert Ellis.[5,6] In RET, the resident looks at process thinking. In other words, he is encouraged to observe and understand how thoughts, feelings, and actions are linked together and how one behavior may significantly influence other behaviors. He is taught that often what happens to us may not be as important as how we perceive and interpret what has happened. The ramification of this perspective means that the way we think about events significantly influences whether we perceive them as pleasurable or painful. The strength of the model relies on the premise that individuals can learn to alter their experience of events by modifying their thoughts and beliefs about those events. In order to make the necessary changes in their thoughts and attitudes the residents segment their experiences into components: the activating event; the thoughts and beliefs about the event; and the molester's feelings about the event.

The series of exercises in this module enable him to look at his cognitive distortions which facilitated and encouraged his child-molesting behavior. At the same time he learns strategies to help eliminate the cognitive distortions or irrational beliefs. For example, a sex offender may have beliefs or thoughts regarding interactions with peer females that cause him to feel uncomfortable (i.e., heterosocial anxiety). In order to avoid these feelings he turns to children for his social and sexual outlets. Exploration of thoughts and beliefs about social anxiety and discomfort with peer females might disclose that the resident believes that women are very powerful, that women enjoy making fools of men, that women are able to control him, and that adult women will make fun of his body or his genitals. The molester learns that these beliefs cause him to be anxious and upset.

The resident is encouraged to challenge these irrational or dysfunctional beliefs and thoughts, and to replace them with more socially acceptable beliefs. Examples of acceptable beliefs would be that women can be very caring and understanding, that particular women might not in any way dislike the individual's body, that women are not necessarily always going to attempt to control or injure him in some way, and so forth. By replacing irrational beliefs and negative thoughts with positive beliefs and constructive thoughts, he can be shown how feelings of relaxation and pleasure result from these positive thoughts. During the module he also looks at cognitive distortions and attempts to change these beliefs. (See Chapter 8 for a case presentation and discussion of a child molester using the theoretical framework of RET.)

Changing entrenched beliefs is difficult. However, this module strives to help the sex offender become a healthy person with a sense of control over his feelings and experience. Neutralizing resistances to change requires repeated clarification, confrontation, and interpretation during his course of treatment. Some find the demands of therapy too threatening and abort treatment. Others find therapy acceptable and are well motivated to use the skills offered.

Communication skills module. The communication skills module currently in use at the treatment center was developed by NFETC professional staff. It focuses on meaningful communication of thoughts and feelings, both verbally and nonverbally, as well as assertiveness training. Research has shown that sex offenders often lack the ability to interact effectively with adults. This social impairment leaves some child molesters frustrated and may in turn lead him to engage in sexual activities with children. Because of his inability to establish meaningful relationships with peers, he more easily rationalizes manipulating children to engage in sex with him.

Beginning with a written and experiential pretest, the communication skills module is comprised of 11 classes: an introduction, a theoretical framework for understanding communication, the steps toward open and effective communication, the communication of genuineness and warmth, self-disclosure, risk taking, confronting, and then four sessions specifically focused on assertiveness training. The module concludes with a posttest.

Social skills module. The social skills module, another skills acquisition treatment component, was developed to specifically teach the offenders, through didactic and experiential sessions, to more effectively interact with adults in a social setting. Sex offenders are taught to pay greater attention to their appearance, to make appropriate eye contact during conversations, and to actively listen to others. These components have been demonstrated in several research studies to be the determinants that cause women to choose continuing to interact with a man in social situations. The social skills module has an experiential pretest and posttest.

Relapse prevention module. The relapse prevention module used at the treatment center has been adapted from one developed for the Florida Mental Health Institute in the treatment of child molesters.[7] The NFETC module lasts for 12 sessions. Relapse prevention is a concept that has received a great deal of support and widespread use recently in treatment programs throughout North America. A relapse is "a violation of a self-imposed rule or set of rules governing the rate or pattern of a selected target behavior"[7] (p. 1). This model has been used extensively with substance abusers, smokers, and dieters. The term *lapse* refers to any single incident of violating the rules which might be a precursor to a relapse. In the case of a child molester, an example of this lapse would be a child molester cruising the streets looking for young male victims to molest after a poorly handled interpersonal interaction with a peer. A lapse would be the preliminary behavior associated with the overt act of child molesting, such as driving around in his car cruising for a victim. A relapse for this individual would be to molest another child. Since fantasizing about sex with children is also directly related to sex offending, fantasy is generally a precursor to sex offending. Thus, deliberate fantasizing is also considered a lapse for the purpose of this module.

During the course of the 12-session module, residents learn more appropriate interpersonal social interaction and develop strategies for healthier lifestyles. Extensive homework assignments and structured review of the resident's participation during each session are employed. The offender is helped to recognize that his sex-offending behavior is part of a pattern or process with definable antecedents and consequences. Each individual must plan, develop, and implement strategies to abort a re-offense. Offenders in the final stages of the treatment program at NFETC review the intervention strategies they develop in the relapse prevention module as preparation for reentry into society. Ideally, following discharge they would be able to enroll in a relapse prevention program for 52 weekly sessions as designed by the Florida Mental Health Institute.

Substance abuse module. Our substance abuse module, developed by a professional staff at the treatment center, combines didactic reading material with interactive group sessions. Developed from materials used by substance abuse programs throughout the country, this module incorporates relapse-prevention concepts found elsewhere in the treatment program. Since alcoholism and substance abuse include components of minimization and rationalization similar to sex offenses themselves, the module can be very challenging for sex offenders. Because the substance abuse module is extremely confrontational in nature, resistance to treatment surfaces. As with many of the treatment components at the center, this module stresses the necessity for lifelong commitment to a change in thinking and behavior.

Stress inoculation for anger and impulse control module. This module is adapted from a training manual developed by Novaco.[16]

It is used in the experimental treatment program for pedophiles at the Florida Mental Health Institute.

Designed for 12 sessions, it is a cognitive-behavioral therapy using a combination of didactic teaching, homework assignments, and practice sessions to improve anger management and increase impulse control. The three phases of the module are: "(1) cognitive preparation, (2) skill acquisition, and (3) application training"[15] (p. 27).

During the cognitive phase of the module, the therapist distributes handouts describing the rationale for the treatment, defining a common language for the purpose of clear communication, and educating the clients regarding the functions of their anger. Clients keep a diary during the course of the module which provides material for group discussion. This cognitive phase includes identification of persons and events that trigger anger, introduction of the concept of cognitive control of impulses, and introduction to the various skills used to better cope with anger and stress.

The skills acquisition component focuses on "cognitive arousal reduction" and "behavioral coping skills," using "self-instruction,"[15] which could be positive thinking or reframing and relaxation techniques. These techniques were taught the residents in the orientation and evaluation phase. This component combines cognitive and behavioral strategies. Assertive expression of emotions is taught and practiced. The underlying principle is to learn how to express emotions in a manner that will bring about constructive rather than destructive changes with the assertive behavior. It does not mean encouraging the residents to simply learn how to identify, feel, and express their anger without boundaries. Rather, the residents are assisted to learn how to modulate expression of their anger in an appropriate manner. In learning to manage the anger the resident is able to recognize and defuse the destructive patterns before they receive reinforcement.

The application training phase uses role play of imaginary and remembered experiences. Progressing from the mildest to the most triggering situation, the clients are gradually inoculated to the stressors.

These three phases are not in a rigid sequence and overlap during the course of the module.

Family visits/family therapy. Family therapy (especially the Giarretto model[8]) has been shown to be effective with child molesters, particularly in the treatment of incest offenders. Unfortunately, many offenders' families are not able to visit the Center regularly due to the Center's distance from their home. Only about 30% of the residents participate in family therapy. Some offenders have been incarcerated for a number of years and no longer have regular contact with their families. Others have been separated or divorced from their families. Family members may even have supported the offender's psychopathology by feeding into his disturbed beliefs and thoughts. Thus, family members may need help to modify their behavior in order to prevent remolesting. The offenders may have issues with their families of origin that can be addressed in family therapy. In this therapeutic setting the offender is encouraged to take responsibility for the sex offenses that he has committed and to learn ways to express his love or affection for his children in a nonsexual manner. Family therapy is seen as particularly important in the release planning for offenders and in helping to develop a healthy supportive environment within which the offender can return to society.

One of the crucial things that the family can do is to become part of the offender's "monitoring system." In the treatment modules the offender learns how to monitor his internal and external cues that in the past have been part of the process of chaining behaviors leading to child-molesting behavior. In family therapy other family members are made aware of this chaining process so they can be sensitive to events or stressors that might place the offender more at risk to molest. Since many offenders have unconscious denial processes, the family members who are aware of these mechanisms can intervene in an effective manner by sharing their observations with the offender *before* he engages in additional child-molesting behaviors.

Health/Education Modules

Personal health project. Every resident is required to develop a personal health project (PHP) with the help of his therapist, rehabilitation specialist, and health coordinator. The PHP is designed to provide an activity which is physically and emotionally rewarding. For example, yoga or jogging or running the "Vita Par Course" for 1 to 2 hours several times a week, are typically PHPs. For some, a structured weight-training program may be approved. Competitive sports are never approved for a PHP, although they are available for recreation. PHPs offer the resident an opportunity to engage in therapeutic activity on his own and may change numerous times during his course of treatment. Residents with chronic medical conditions may have certain limitations placed on their PHPs or may be asked to engage in specific activities recommended by the Center physician.

Sex education module. The healthy sexuality/sex education module was developed in response to studies suggesting that many offenders lacked effective sexual knowledge and engaged in sex offenses partly as a result of incorrect, distorted beliefs about human sexuality. A pretest is administered which, if passed, exempts the offender from taking this module. Upon completion of the module the resident is again tested. If he falls below 80%, he is required to retake the module. This module includes lectures, reading material, videotapes, audiotapes, and interactive group discussions. The offenders are encouraged to ask questions, to reveal in a noncritical environment their beliefs about sexuality, and to test these out in discussion with other offenders and with the staff facilitators. As with many of the modules of the Treatment Center, the reading material is aimed at approximately the fifth-grade reading level, due in part to the nature of the offenders who enter this treatment program.

Learning resources department (LRD)/adjunctive therapy. The learning resources department of NFETC offers a number of adjunctive services to the sex offender program. In the educational program, residents may earn their General Education Degree (GED). There are also vocational training components in video production, computer programming, and gardening. Adjunctive therapies provided by LRD include art therapy, music therapy, sports program, and woodworking and ceramics classes. A library of books and videotapes is also available for the residents' use.

PRERELEASE PLANNING

When the resident is three months from completion of the sex offender program he is transferred to the advanced resident housing unit. While in this building the resident is expected to take greater responsibility for his treatment plan and his treatment activities. Part of the resident's responsibilities include being a support person for new residents, co-facilitating new resident therapy groups with the professional therapist, and acting as a role model for new residents.

The primary treatment focus on the advanced resident unit is release planning. During this time, the resident reviews materials previously studied in the modules. Special emphasis is given to the relapse prevention module and covert sensitization modules. The resident is assisted in developing specific plans for release and encouraged to contact community resources.

The Treatment Center recommends that the offender continues in therapy for a minimum of three years following release from the program. Although not all offenders are mandated to participate in outpatient therapy as a follow-up to their inpatient treatment upon their release, some offenders have probation or parole sentence following their incarceration and continue with therapy for at least a brief period of time.

TRAINING OF THERAPISTS

Because few therapists receive training in their graduate programs specifically related to the treatment of sex offenders, new therapists require specialized training and a period of supervision. At NFETC a somewhat informal training period is tailored around the individual needs of the new therapist.

The new therapist sits in on the pod therapy groups of each of the other six therapists. Following each session, the new therapist discusses the session with the therapist in charge of the group. Since pod therapy groups are offered twice a week, this requires a period of three weeks. For the next month and a half, the director of the Sex Offender Treatment Unit facilitates the new therapist's therapy groups. Supervision and feedback follow each session. Usually at the end of a month and a half, the therapist has sufficient skills and confidence to direct the therapy sessions with weekly supervision by the director.

Because the modules are specific to the Center's program, a greater period of time is devoted to training the new therapists in their content and methods of use. Before running a module, the new therapist sits through the entire course of a module, studying its content and observing the manner in which it is given. Subsequently, the new therapist offers the module in conjunction with an experienced therapist. Only after two exposures to the module does the new therapist present the module to the residents on his own.

A new program just underway at the Center is the videotaping of both the pod therapy group and the module sessions for later viewing and critiquing by the other therapists. Because of time limitations, the therapist selects a 15-minute interval for viewing by the group. These videotapes offer great potential for training purposes. It is hoped that tapes of therapy and module sessions can be selected that will exemplify the best approach for interacting with the sex offender.

Therapists' Support Group

The need for support group sessions for the therapists in the Sex Offender Treatment Unit became evident some years ago. The therapists had their own personal problems that impacted on their work situation, as well as the frustrations of trying to maintain consistently quality therapeutic work with an extremely difficult population within a bureaucratic setting. The weekly sessions, not to be confused with consultative sessions where the therapists discuss their case loads and patients, are directed toward sharing with each other personal problems that might be affecting their relationships at work, tensions that might be developing through inadvertent behavior of other therapists or problems they might be experiencing in handling job-related stresses.

Closely resembling the encounter group model Carl Rogers employed with his therapy students, the support group is a leaderless group. No one person facilitates and caution is taken not to be overly facilitative at any given time. Whatever comes up is dealt with. Everyone has an opportunity to express concerns that are important to him or her and everyone tries to be as honest and open with each other as he or she is capable of being. While attendance is not mandatory, the group early on made the decision that if the support group were to survive, everyone would have to put energy into it and attend whenever possible. However, if one person or another cannot make it, the group is still held. There are two operating rules: (1) it is okay to disclose outside the group the work that you have done yourself; and (2) there will be no discussion with each other outside the group of the things that are revealed by other people in the group.

The therapists attribute enormous returns from their participation in the support group. It has helped them to be aware of each other's personal stresses and helped them to air differences in time to do something about them before they became more serious issues. It has contributed to the high morale that characterizes the treatment unit by drawing the therapists into a close, caring group.

REFERENCES

1. Abel, G. G., Becker, J. V., Cunningham-Rathner, J., Rouleau, J. L., Kaplan, M., & Reich, J. (1984). *The Treatment of Child Molesters*. Atlanta, GA: Behavioral Medicine Laboratory, Emory University.

2. Benson, H. (1975). *The Relaxation Response.* New York: Avon.
3. Carrington, P. (1977). *Freedom in Meditation.* Garden City, NY: Anchor Press.
4. Dychwald, K. (1978). *Body/Mind.* New York: Jove Publications.
5. Ellis, A. (1974). Rational-emotive therapy. In A. Burton (Ed.), *Operational Theories of Personality.* New York: Brunner/Mazel.
6. Ellis, A., & Geiger, R. (1977). *Handbook of Rational-Emotive Therapy.* New York: Springer.
7. George, W. H., & Marlatt, G. A. (1986). *Relapse Prevention with Sexual Offenders: A Treatment Manual.* Tampa, FL: Florida Mental Health Institute.
8. Giarretto, H. (1982). *Integrated Treatment of Child Sexual Abuse: A Treatment and Training Manual.* Palo Alto, CA: Science and Behavior Books.
9. Goleman, D. (1977). *The Varieties of Meditative Experience.* New York: Dutton.
10. Hittleman, R. (1983). *Yoga For Health.* New York: Ballantine.
11. Hittleman, R. (1973). *Yoga Twenty-Eight Day Exercise Plan.* New York: Bantam.
12. Knopp, F. H. (1984). *Retraining Adult Sex Offenders: Methods and Models.* Syracuse, NY: Safer Society Press.
13. Lange, A. (1986). *Rational-Emotive Therapy: A Treatment Manual.* Prepared as part of NIMH grant No. 1 RO1 MH42035, "Prevention of Relapse in Sex Offenders," D. R. Laws, Ph.D., Principal Investigator.
14. Lowen, A. (1975). *Bioenergetics.* New York: Coward, McCann, and Geoghegan.
15. Meichenbaum, D. (1974). *Cognitive Behavior Modification.* Morristown, NJ: General Learning Press.
16. Novaco, R. W. (1986). *Stress Inoculation for Anger and Impulse Control: A Treatment Manual.* Prepared as part of NIMH Grant No. 1 RO1 MH42035, "Prevention of Relapse in Sex Offenders," D. R. Laws, Ph.D., Principal Investigator.
17. Perls, F. S. (1947). *Ego, Hunger and Aggression.* London: Allen & Unwin (San Francisco: Orbit Graphic Arts, 1966).
18. Perls, F. S. (1969). *Gestalt Therapy Verbatim.* Moab, UT: Real People Press.
19. Wickramasekera, I. (1980). Aversive behavioral reversal. In D. J. Cox & R. J. Daitzman (Eds.), *Exhibitionism: Description, Assessment & Treatment.* New York: Garland Press.
20. Yochelson, S., & Samenow, S. E. (n.d.). *The Criminal Personality.* New York: Jason Aronson.

CHAPTER 8

History of a
Child Molester

Presented in this chapter is an interview with a 53-year-old white male child molester on the day before he was discharged from the treatment program at North Florida Evaluation and Treatment Center after three-and-a-quarter years in the treatment program. The interviewer, G.B., had never met the patient, R.I., prior to the interview and had no previous knowledge of him. This transcript is not meant to be representative of an intake interview. Instead, it serves two goals: to illustrate the events that seem to have contributed to the patient's development as a sex offender and to determine the molester's perception of the extent of his change while in the treatment program.

Although the interview was not conducted to demonstrate a particular theoretical model, we have used the rational-emotive therapy model to illustrate the chaining links of behavior–thoughts–feelings which led to the development of child-molesting behavior. In this sequence, which we label *"Process,"* one can easily see how, at times, a rather innocuous event can be misperceived so that the person is conditioned or affected in a significant manner. In order that the reader may follow the analysis more readily, we label the *"Process"* in boldface type with the following sequence:

A. *Activating Event*
B. *Distorted Belief*
C. *Emotional Consequence*
   A' *New Activating Event*

We then give the resident's comments from which we derived the basis for our analysis and, in parentheses, insert our interpretative remarks. Not everyone will agree with our interpretations, but the data are available for the reader to see how they were formulated.

In order to follow his resettlement in the community subsequent to his discharge, an abbreviated six-month interview is included.

INTERVIEW

G.B.: I appreciate your willingness to talk with me today. We wish to benefit from what you have learned while you have been here at the treatment center. When did you come into this program?

R.I.: I came in the first of December—in 1983; so a little over three years ago.

G.B.: I know you have been here a long time. Could you tell me what you were like when you first came here?

COGNITIVE DISTORTION AND RATIONALIZATION

R.I.: When I came I was fairly convinced that what I had done was really okay and that the law was really wrong, although I knew that it was against the law. I was convinced that I was really helping the kids. The sexual gratification was there, but the benefit that I was giving them was offsetting that.

G.B.: What were you doing to the children?

IDENTIFIES MULTIPLE VICTIMS: MALE AND FEMALE

R.I.: I was committing mutual oral sex acts with adolescent boys and a few girls. Mostly there were boys. There were a few girls. Over 35 years—from the time I was 15 until about age 50—I had around 280 victims. Only about 30 or so were female.

G.B.: How many different occasions do you estimate that you had sex with these victims?

RELATES MULTIPLE OCCASIONS WITH THE SAME VICTIM

R.I.: That would be very difficult because it was like hundreds of times. Some victims went along for a period of three years and it would be maybe three times a month I'd have some sexual act with them.

G.B.: Were you having sex with more than one victim at a time?

R.I.: Yeah. There were periods when it would just be one person but then there would be periods when there would be like 12. None of them really knew that I was doing it to the other. There were only a couple of occasions when there was more than one person involved.

G.B.: In your own mind you believed what you were doing was right. How was having sex with these victims justified?

> *Process:*
> A. *Activating Event: Learns of brother's death*
> B. *Distorted Belief: Thinks he is responsible*
> C. *Emotional Consequence: Experiences anger*
>   *A' New Activating Event: Engages in sex with cousins*

R.I.: This is one of the things I worked through in treatment. When I was seven, an event occurred that became very traumatic for me. One afternoon I was playing softball in the backyard with my mom and she wanted to quit. I pitched a fit because I didn't want to quit and so she said, "I'll have your dad take care of you when he gets home." He whipped me.

A month later my mom had a baby that was breech and it died a couple hours after birth. I didn't even know she was pregnant. My cousin knew about it, so he said, "Yeah, we knew she was pregnant. You didn't know?" *(learns of brother's death)* So, I realized how much was kept from me and I became very angry about that. *(becomes angry)* Not long after that I began to involve myself in sex play with my cousins both male and female. *(engages in sex with cousins)*

G.B.: So at this time you were about seven?

R.I.: About seven or eight. And then when I was eight I involved my sister in this and my sister and I had a sexual relationship of an exploratory nature. At age 13 we were caught and I was lectured by my father.

I really blamed myself for my brother's death because if I hadn't insisted that my mother play, he wouldn't have come breech. *(distorted belief: thinks he is responsible)*

G.B.: The first sexual contact you had in your life was with these cousins?

TRAUMATIC EXPERIENCE LINKED WITH FIRST SEXUAL MEMORY: THREAT OF CASTRATION

R.I.: No, there was an event that occurred in first grade when I first realized an attraction to another little boy in the class. Earlier than that, my first experience of a sexual nature was when my mother threatened to cut my penis off after I exposed myself to my aunt.

G.B.: How old were you then?

R.I.: Somewhere between four and five.

G.B.: What did you do in front of your aunt that caused your mother to be so upset?

Process:
A. *Threat of castration*
B. *Associates sex act as something that must be done in secret*
C. *Experiences fear and hides*
   A' *Substitutes sexual feelings for feelings of fear by engaging in sex act (fondles self)*
   B' *Hides feelings from himself with sex act*
   C' *Experiences pleasure*

R.I.: I had learned to play with myself and it felt good. I pulled my pants down and showed my aunt (saying), "See my thing." You know. . . .
   My mother had a butcher knife in her hand and she come running out there and said, "If you ever do that again I'll cut it off." *(threat of castration)* I ran and hid in my bedroom closet. It was really terrifying. *(experiences fear and hides)* I learned then that sexual acts had to be kept secret and you can't do them out in front of people. *(sex must be secret)*

G.B.: Is that your first sexual memory?

R.I.: Yes.

G.B.: Did you have an erection when you showed yourself to your aunt?

R.I.: Yes.

G.B.: When you went back to your bedroom you hid?

R.I.: Yeah. And I played with myself. *(fondles self)* I learned that I could hide those feelings of fear and terror by having sexual feelings. *(hides feelings by engaging in sex act)*

G.B.: Okay. So, you had the sexual feelings—had an erection. You showed it to your aunt and your mother says, "I'm going to cut it off if you do this again." You went back to your room and you then continued to have some sexual excitement.

R.I.: Yes. The terror was there and a lot of sobbing, a lot of crying. And I was covering myself over with some old clothes that were in there. Then after a little while, I began to play with myself again and it still felt good. *(experiences pleasure)* I made my mind up that from now on I couldn't tell anyone. If I did this, I had to keep it to myself.

G.B.: You had not played with yourself before that?

R.I.: That's my first memory of it.

G.B.: And then after that did you play with yourself other times?

R.I.: Yes.

G.B.: Was it always in secret?

R.I.: Yes. Until I was seven. About then I saw my cousins doing it in the barn. After that we did it in a group.

G.B.: So you played with each other?

R.I.: Yes.

G.B.: The sex play was with hands?

R.I.: Yes, until I was 10. At that time a (male) cousin who was three years younger than me taught me about oral sex. We did that for several years and we didn't let anyone else know that we were engaging in that.

G.B.: So that was a secret?

R.I.: Yes.

G.B.: When you were not doing it, did you have sexual fantasies?

R.I.: Yes, a lot. I had a lot of wishes for sex, talked about it at school, and had fantasies of having sex with girls.

G.B.: Can you remember the content of the sexual fantasies—what they were about?

R.I.: Being naked with girls and having intercourse.

G.B.: How old were the girls that you fantasized about?

FEELS SEXUALLY INADEQUATE WITH GIRLS AND ADEQUATE WITH BOYS

R.I.: I was 10, 11, 12, and they were nine, 10, 11—along there. There was some infatuation with classmates, but it seemed like none of those things materialized for me. I began to feel inadequate because I would have a girlfriend and pretty soon someone else (some other boy) would come along. I never was able to keep a girlfriend and that was my experience all through school.

G.B.: Were you more successful in sexual experiences with boys than you were with girls?

R.I.: Yeah.

G.B.: Apparently you and your cousin had been having some kind of sexual experience for a period of several years.

R.I.: Yeah. See, my cousin had often tried to make it with girls but we never could seem to be successful, so we just had it between ourselves.'

G.B.: When did the experience with your sister start?

R.I.: It started when I was eight and it continued until I was 13.

G.B.: What did you do with her?

R.I.: Mostly it was like "playing house" at first. And then, finally, I tried penetrating her once and wasn't able to do it. That was like unfinished business for me. I felt like something was wrong that I could not do that.

G.B.: What kept you from it?

R.I.: I just couldn't get lined up. I didn't know how to approach it, and it was like I should have been able to.

G.B.: How old were you when you were trying to have intercourse?

R.I.: Thirteen.

G.B.: And she was how old?

R.I.: She was 11.

G.B.: Were you having any oral sex with her?

R.I.: No.

G.B.: How old were you when you were caught having sex with your sister?

Process:
  A. *Receives lecture from father about sex*
  B. *Believes he can disgrace family*
  C. *Has fear of his father*
    A' *Avoids sex with girls*

R.I.: That was when I was 13 years old.

G.B.: Thirteen? And who caught you?

R.I.: My grandmother.

G.B.: And what did she do?

R.I.: Well, she said she would tell my mom. *(gets caught)* My daddy, of course, got involved. So from that point on, they didn't let us stay together anymore. Anytime we were left alone, I was put one place and my sister was put another place.

G.B.: Were you punished for that experience?

R.I.: I wasn't punished in the sense of getting a whipping. I was lectured. *(receives lecture from father)* My dad talked of the disgrace I could have caused my sister—getting her pregnant. *(believes he can disgrace family)* And that put a real fear in me of having sex with girls. And later I would be dating and I would have some chances to have sexual experiences, but I was afraid I would get them pregnant, so I stopped before intercourse. *(avoids sex with girls)* If I got a girl pregnant, my dad would do me in. *(has fear of father)*

G.B.: Earlier you mentioned giving up your sexual experience with your sister, some memories about your brother started coming back to you. How does this tie together?

R.I.: Because I was alone again.

G.B.: Alone again?

R.I.: My sister is not with me anymore. She won't have anything to do with me. My sister's friends won't have anything to do with me. Now I just need my little brother and if I had him it would be okay. I really became lonely. There was only one cousin that I was having oral sex with.

G.B.: So you were never without some kind of sexual partner then?

R.I.: No, from about eight on. . . .

SUBSTITUTES SEX FOR FEELINGS OF SADNESS

R.I.: I remember a lot of sad events when sexual thoughts came, and when I used sexual fantasies and masturbation to get away from the sadness. I remember the Christmas Day my great-grandfather died and all the sadness in the family that afternoon. I had sexual fantasies and masturbated.

G.B.: What were the fantasies?

R.I.: Of being with my sister. I even tried to engage in sex acts with my sister. When I was 10, a cousin who was really close to the family got married and moved away. I remember being real sad that she was going to be gone. Sexual thoughts came up that afternoon. I remember getting an erection; I remember going out to the barn and masturbating.

G.B.: If I am hearing you correctly, you are saying if you had a loss you became sexually excited, or when you became fearful you became sexually excited. Are you saying that you used sexual feelings which were pleasurable to replace the painful feelings of experiencing loss or feeling fear?

SEXUAL FEELINGS REPLACE OTHER FEELINGS

R.I.: Yes, sexual feelings replaced others. I could hide the sadness by having sexual excitement or I could hide fear or anger with sexual feelings.

G.B.: If you had an unpleasant feeling, you would do away with that by having sexual feelings?

R.I.: Yeah.

G.B.: Was this substitution a conscious thing that you were aware of?

R.I.: It wasn't a conscious process I went through. It's like you learn that if you're sad and you don't want to be sad, here's how you can do away with sadness.

G.B.: Sometimes you could enjoy sex without doing away with another feeling?

R.I.: Yeah. Because I enjoyed the sex part—I didn't do it only when I was sad.

G.B.: Did you have any other good feelings besides sexual ones? Like do you remember other positive feelings when you would say, "I like this!"?

Process:
  A. *Father initiates pleasurable activity with him, but then stops*
  B. *Believes father will abandon him*
  C. *Feels anger at father*

R.I.: It seems as though every time those kinds of feelings came, they didn't last long. There was something that happened that would stop them. And a lot of them are related to my dad. I felt he abandoned me and this brought anger. My dad worked a lot and when I was with him it was like cherished time. I wanted to be with him. I remember he bought a motorcycle once and I could ride on the back with him and the first time that he fell with it, he got rid of it. Just about the time that I got real close to him, he backed out and I lost that good feeling. I lost that closeness. If we went camping, things would get too rough—the mosquitoes would be too bad or the rain wouldn't stop—and we would come home. He would say, "Okay, I'll teach you how to fly model airplanes. I'll let you get into that hobby—that's something you will enjoy." When I got pretty good at it and wanted to go to competitive events, he wouldn't let me go. I was looking forward to playing football in high school but he said, "No, you can't play football."

G.B.: Why wouldn't your father let you play?

R.I.: Well, I lived three miles from school. He said he didn't have time to pick me up after practice, and it wasn't safe for me to hitchhike home. So I couldn't play.

G.B.: You mentioned the word "abandonment." Did your father actually leave?

COGNITIVE DISTORTION

R.I.: No. My father would give me an idea, and he would carry me so far. And then he would abandon me in it.

G.B.: Were you closer to your father or your mother?

R.I.: I was closer to my mother because she was always there. She was the one that took care of me; she was the one that saw that I had my clothes and saw that everything was done. He was the disciplinarian. The shifts that he worked made it very difficult for him to be with me.

G.B.: You mentioned that your father would bring you a good idea, but that he would never carry it through. Did you have good experiences with your mother?

Process:
A. *Brother dies*
B. *Thinks he was responsible*
C. *Feels guilty*
   A' *Does helpful things for mother*
   B' *Thinks himself indebted to mother*
   C' *Feels close to mother*

R.I.: Yes. I remember a lot of the things that she would do. Like we visited cousins sometimes in another city. Those were close times. I guess the most intimate time was shortly after my little brother's death. *(brother dies)* My mom developed a very severe skin condition. She had real long hair and she would put it up in braids. My sister and I took turns combing her hair for her every day and doing the things for her in the house that she couldn't do. *(does helpful things for mother)*

I had the sense that I owed her because it was my fault that this was happening. *(feels responsible for death, feels guilty, feels indebted)* The good feelings I had for my mother were somehow connected to this feeling of indebtedness. *(feels close to mother)*

G.B.: So this bad feeling you had when she threatened to cut off your penis if you exposed it anymore never kept you from being close to her?

R.I.: No, but it made me not want to be open. I remembered that threat and I shuddered. For a long time I had a body reaction when I remembered.

G.B.: You said you had some anger. Were you aware of any continuing anger toward her or was it to someone else?

R.I.: My greatest anger came toward my dad for backing out on everything and toward my peers for rejecting me.

G.B.: What peers?

R.I.: In school.

G.B.: Girls, boys, or both?

R.I.: Both. The deepest hurt was from being rejected by girls— and I felt angry about that.

G.B.: When did that feeling of rejection come about?

R.I.: Probably about 11 or 12. I would have a girlfriend in school and then she would take up with someone else.

G.B.: How did you understand that? Why were they leaving you for somebody else?

LIVES IN ISOLATED AREA, FEELING EXCLUDED
FROM PEERS

R.I.: Because other people were better than me. They had more stuff, bigger houses. They could do things. When I was in junior high and high school, I wasn't allowed to be with my peers after school hours. I went to school in a different community. I met friends there that I would like to have some interaction with, but there was no way for me to get back into that community and be involved in outside activities. I couldn't date or anything. We lived on a farm and then in a small rural community, and I went to school in town.

G.B.: So you couldn't get back for social activities with your classmates?

R.I.: Right. You know, the guys would get around and on Monday mornings in shop class they would tell about their sexual exploits over the weekend. The only thing I had to tell about was sex with my sister or sex with my male cousin and you don't talk about that, you know. It was like I was excluded. I never felt that I was in that group.

G.B.: From what age?

R.I.: I would say from sixth grade on and all the way up until I got into college. I never felt really a part of that group.

G.B.: So did you have any ongoing friends who were close?

R.I.: There were a couple of guys that I interacted with pretty much. At age 16 they got cars and could go off and do things. My mother told me that I couldn't go with them because 16 was too young to have a car and be out running around. So I couldn't go with them and I felt abandoned by them.

G.B.: What did you do with these feelings of being abandoned and alone?

R.I.: I just went home and had sex with my male cousin. Then I molested a little neighbor boy about that time.

G.B.: Is that when you first began to molest children?

COMMITS FIRST SEXUAL MOLESTATION WHEN FEELING
REJECTED AND ANGRY

R.I.: Yes. My first molestation was at about 15 when I molested a six-year-old boy next door. That's the molestation I really recognized as being connected with the anger.

G.B.: Tell me about that. What happened?

Process:
  A. *Girlfriend rejects him*
  B. *Thinks other people are better than he—*
     Feels abandoned by his girlfriend
  C. *Feels angry*
   A' *Commits sexual molestation*
   B' *Believes the child likes him*
   C' *Has positive feelings toward the child*
    A" *Turns to child for sex, even when not feeling rejected*

R.I.: When I was in high school I went with a girl who was in junior high school. One afternoon after I got home, she told me she didn't want to be my girlfriend anymore. *(girlfriend rejects him)* I really felt rejected and angry. *(feels angry and abandoned by girlfriend)* I always walked from school through the neighbor's yard. On this particular day, when I walked through the backyard, I found this little boy playing. I enticed him into an outdoor toilet where I played with him and had oral sex with him. That was my first molestation and it occurred when I was really angry. *(commits sexual molestation)*

G.B.: How did you connect the thought to your action?

R.I.: I just thought, "Well, at least Lester still likes me. At least, I've still got Lester. He's my friend. *(has positive feeling toward the child)* Ann doesn't want me no more, but Lester does." So the sexual relationship began between us that day. *(turns to child for sex)*

G.B.: But you were angry at her?

R.I.: Yes, angry at her, angry at the boy who became her boyfriend, and also angry at my parents. My anger was directed in all sorts of places.

G.B.: Were you angry at the child?

R.I.: I didn't think so, but I can see now where he received that anger.

G.B.: But you didn't feel any conscious anger toward him?

DENIAL OF ANGER TOWARD VICTIMS

R.I.: No. When I came to the Treatment Center the biggest thing was the denial of my anger toward my victims. It was misplaced aggression, but I didn't believe that it existed. Later I learned that is what it was.

G.B.: Back with Lester. What were you feeling toward him?

R.I.: Closeness.

G.B.: Closeness?

R.I.: Real closeness.

G.B.: So your sexual relationship with the boy was a positive thing?

R.I.: A positive thing.

G.B.: What was it about him that excited you?

FEELS IN CONTROL WITH A CHILD

R.I.: I was in control. I could just say, "Let's do this," and he did it. I felt real safe in that. We had this secret between us. It was a bond.

G.B.: Was there anything about his body that turned you on?

R.I.: I hadn't thought of it to this moment, but I can see an image of his penis being like Auburn's, a classmate in my first grade. Both Lester and Auburn were six. Lester wore short pants and was sitting on sand. He had no underwear on and I could see his penis. I just now remember that's the way Auburn looked and that's what intrigued me. So there's some connection there that I haven't even thought about.

G.B.: How long did the experience with Lester last?

R.I.: Off and on for 15 years, until he was about 21. I left to go to school, came back, renewed the relationship. It was pretty steady for five years.

G.B.: On that first day you turned to him because you were angry. After that what was your relationship with him?

RELATES FEELING INADEQUATE WITH GIRLS, THUS TURNING TO CHILD MOLESTING

R.I.: He was my playmate. With the sex we just added another aspect to our relationship and had something that we both enjoyed. I felt I was not adequate with girls. Nobody wanted me anyway, so Lester and I would do it and that would be sufficient.

G.B.: Later you did not have to be turned down by somebody to go back to him?

R.I.: Right.

G.B.: You just did it because of the positive feelings that existed with him?

SUBSEQUENT SEX WITH BOY DOES NOT RESULT FROM REJECTION BY GIRLS

R.I.: He would come over to the house and we would play. We'd wind up doing that (engaging in sex) even while I was in college.

G.B.: After you got older and he got older, what type of sex did you have?

R.I.: We had oral sex on each other.

G.B.: At a later time, when you were having sex with him, what were your thoughts and fantasies?

R.I.: I thought of him being old enough to be away from home and our not having to hide anymore. I would like for him to have a girlfriend and for me to see them having sex together. I would like to be a part of that.

G.B.: While you were having sex with him, did you also have other sex partners?

R.I.: Yes, a couple of male cousins. My cousins and I were really oriented toward having sex with girls, but we also enjoyed it among ourselves.

G.B.: But during those five years, these cousins were, more or less, your own age. It wasn't like you were using kids younger than you, right?

R.I.: From 15 to 17 the only significantly younger child was Lester. At 17 I met a girl and I stopped all the other sexual activity with my cousins and Lester. Then, at 20, this girl broke up with me.

G.B.: Were you having sex with her?

R.I.: No. I had a religious commitment that I made to the church. I cleaned out my closet of all the pornography that I'd collected and I'd quit sex with Lester. So there was no sex between 17 and 20.

G.B.: Did you masturbate?

R.I.: Yes, I masturbated and I had fantasies of having sex with my girlfriend Evilene during that time. I had committed my life to Christ and when I was 18 I entered college to study for the ministry.

It was when I was 20 that Evilene broke up with me. She wrote me a letter saying that she didn't want to go with me anymore.

G.B.: How did you take that?

FEELING REJECTED, HE MOLESTS AGAIN

R.I.: I felt very rejected. The first thing I did was molest a boy in the church. At that point in my life, I knew that it wasn't right.

G.B.: That's the first time you knew that?

REGRESSIVE TYPE RESPONSE

R.I.: Yeah. That's the first time. Before it was like this is okay, this is growing up. I stopped at 17, it was easy to stop. It was all over. I felt good about that. I felt that it was in my past. For those three years, I felt really moral. For the first time I had a girl who liked me, I was in pursuit of a career, I was going to college, and I was supporting myself. I really felt good about myself. Wham, it was like she took all that away from me, so I started molesting the kids in church.

G.B.: So you got the "Dear John" letter, and what were you feeling?

Repetitive Process:
A. *Girlfriend rejects him*
B. *He thinks no one likes him and he is unable to have a girlfriend*
C. *He feels hurt and anger*
  A' *He molests a boy*
  B' *Believes people his own age don't like him but kids do— he was born to be this way*
  C' *He has pleasurable feelings molesting children*
    A" *He continues the molestations*
    B" *The boys understand and accept him; he feels that this is the way it was meant to be*
    C" *The hurt is not there, he feels good*

R.I.: I was really torn up inside; there was a lot of pain in my heart and it was like my heart was breaking. Tears were burning my eyes and I cried. I just couldn't believe it. I felt anger toward her sister, who gave her the idea, who persuaded her. A lot of anger was directed toward her. *(girlfriend rejects him; he feels hurt and anger)*

G.B.: So you felt hurt and anger. What did you do?

R.I.: It preoccupied my mind. I felt I was no good. I couldn't go with anybody. *(thinks he is unable to have a girlfriend)* I thought I was okay and now—what was I going to do? At that point I couldn't tell anyone what was really going on. I can't say I'm not worth anything because my girlfriend broke up with me. I kept it inside. Very soon after that I started having sexual relationships with kids from the church. *(molests a child)*

G.B.: Before you had said that you were not going to do this. What changed? What allowed you to make this decision?

DISTORTED COGNITION AND RATIONALIZATION
FACILITATE MOLESTING

R.I.: Nobody my age liked me, but these kids liked me. *(kids liked him)* It looked like the only thing I was good for was to have relationships with kids. I've got this attraction for kids and I didn't put the attraction there. Maybe this was the way I was born. *(born to be this way)* Maybe this was the way it was supposed to be. Maybe those three years were just a dream and I was not supposed to be normal like everybody else.

G.B.: After three years of not having sex with children, how did you decide to have sex with this boy?

PARTIAL STIMULUS EVOKES FEELINGS

R.I.: I noticed a boy, Tim, who was 14 years old and was sexually developed. He reminded me of another guy, G.R., who I had sex with when I was 16 and he was 18. I saw that Tim's penis stood out and I was attracted to that. I reached over and felt it and my hands said, "This is G.R. This is just like the feeling that I had when I was 16." Inside there were the same feelings—now I've got somebody who understands me, because G.R. did, and so the hurt went away again.

G.B.: And with this boy you rediscovered G.R., so to speak. How long did that relationship continue?

R.I.: From the time I was 20 until I was 22.

G.B.: And did you have sex with other boys at the same time?

R.I.: Yes.

G.B.: What ages then did you choose?

MAINLY SELECTS PREPUBERTAL BOYS AS VICTIMS

R.I.: From that time, with the exception of four boys, my molesting was only with boys who had not reached puberty. In two years there were probably 30 boys that I made sexual contact with.

G.B.: What age were the boys?

R.I.: One was six. The rest were nine and 10 years old.

G.B.: Were you looking for a particular kind of body?

LIKES TO TAKE ROLE OF TEACHER

R.I.: I was looking for someone who had a sexual interest, where I could play the role of the teacher about sex and they could play the role of the student. Up to nine, 10, 11, and 12, it was very easy for me to entice them and say, "Here's something you can learn and it's okay."

COGNITIVE DISTORTION

R.I.: My religious thoughts began to play into my sexual activities with young boys. I thought God wouldn't have given me a penis to masturbate or manipulate if it was wrong. He *(God)* made the penis, so go ahead and enjoy it.

G.B.: The way you are saying this, it's more like you were looking for somebody to educate, but not like you were looking for a specific sized body. Was there anything about their bodies that was particularly exciting for you?

VICTIMS REMIND HIM OF PAST EXPERIENCES: FIVE DIFFERENT CATEGORIES

R.I.: Recently I did a study of all my victims to try to stereotype them. I came up with five different classifications of victims as far as appearance and age is concerned. I remembered that each of these five groups represented a group from my childhood who were almost identical in looks. There was the group that reminded me of Lester; there was a group that reminded me of Pete; there was a group that reminded me of G.R.; there were the athletic ones with dark hair who had many girlfriends and were real popular; then there were those that were ostracized by everybody, who were outside the group and were picked on. It was like each one of them had a root, something inside that was attractive to me. At that time, I didn't know why the attraction was there and I only learned later why I was attracted. It was because they reminded me of an earlier experience when sexual feelings and sexual relationships made me *(feel)* safe.

G.B.: Briefly describe the different five types.

R.I.: Okay. First there were girls between 12 and 14. That was one of the types. Then there were young boys, eight to 11, like Lester. And then, there were the boys who liked to do sex. They were the boys that if I touched them they would respond immediately. I'd find out they were already doing it with someone else. They liked it. They were in a group. There were the boys that were outside the group, like they were the outcasts. And then there were the popular ones who always excluded me from their group.

G.B.: Would you have different kinds of sexual activity with these different groups?

HIS VICTIMS SERVE DIFFERENT MOTIVES

R.I.: No. Ultimately it was all the same. It was like with one group there were no conflicts. It was readily available and it seemed like that's what they wanted. In another group I felt, "I'm going to seduce you whether you want to do this or not! You will want it so much that you will ask me to do it." That was the group that was popular with the girls, the ones that were the athletes. These were the guys in high school who had rejected me. I wanted to get back at them. One of the worst things you can do is question your sexuality and I could make them question theirs. After a while they began to wonder if they were homosexuals, or what, because they began to want the experience.

G.B.: So you were able to get different kinds of things out of these different relationships. You didn't get just the sexual experience?

MOTIVES: POWER, CONTROL, ANGER AND SEXUAL GRATIFICATION

R.I.: The most that I got from it was the control. I felt real powerful. I also got the sexual gratification out of it.

G.B.: Did you get something different from the boys who were lonely and outcast than from the ones who were popular?

R.I.: Yeah. The "get back" attitude was for the popular ones. The conquest was there. I knew I had control over those boys because I took them into something they detested and I turned them around and made them ask me to do it.

G.B.: And how about the outcasts?

R.I.: It was like they were victims. In all of my experiences, I thought they were the only victims. They were the guys that, when I wanted to have a sexual experience, I could have it with them because I felt that was what they were supposed to be for. They were poor; their mothers were prostitutes.

G.B.: What satisfaction did you get out of girls?

R.I.: I should have been able to have intercourse when I was an adolescent like everybody else who was doing it.

G.B.: So what did you do with the girls?

R.I.: I fondled them.

G.B.: What stopped you from having intercourse?

REASONS FOR CHOOSING MALE VICTIMS

R.I.: It was the fear of getting one of them pregnant. There's no way you can get a boy pregnant. There are no real consequences if something goes wrong with a boy. It was easier for me to have boys around me than girls. As an example, I had 12 boys working for me at one time. Their parents would let me take them anywhere I wanted to.

G.B.: Were you a scout leader?

R.I.: No. But I worked in the church. We would go to other cities to do electrical work. They would say to their parents that they were going to go with me to another city over the weekend to do a job. It would be okay with the parents. That wouldn't have worked for girls. All during this time of having the sexual acts with the boys, I really had a strong fantasy of young girls, like 14-year-old girls. Even after I came here for treatment these fantasies remained with me.

TYPE OF SEXUAL ACTIVITIES

G.B.: You were having mutual fondling with the girls and boys, right?

R.I.: Yes.

G.B.: And you were having oral sex with both of them?

R.I.: With the boys, not with the girls.

G.B.: Any anal sex?

R.I.: No.

G.B.: What kept you from doing that?

R.I.: When I was young, my cousin and I tried that and it was real painful and I said I don't want to do it.

G.B.: When did you begin to have intercourse with girls?

REPETITIVE PATTERN OF MOLESTATION

R.I.: At 24 when I married my wife. But before then I got caught for molesting. I graduated from college at age 22 with a degree in religion and went to work as a church youth director. When I was 23 I fondled several of the boys who went to the church. One of them told and I was asked to leave the church. The police were not notified. I got a job as youth director for another church after being turned down as a student in the seminary, but within nine months they caught me molesting some boys in the church. They also didn't want to have the police involved. Instead, I admitted myself to the hospital for psychiatric tests and then went to outpatient therapy for two months. During that time I enlisted in the Army. After basic training, I got married. I was 24 and she was 19.

G.B.: And that's your first sexual intercourse with a female?

R.I.: Yes.

G.B.: How did that go? What kind of an experience was it?

R.I.: It was very good. It didn't last long enough. We had a honeymoon and I left for overseas.

Process:
A. Separates from his wife
B. Believes his wife had trapped him into marriage
C. Feels resentment
A' Molests a child

R.I.: We were separated for eighteen months. While overseas I molested again.

G.B.: Did you have sex with any adults?

R.I.: No.

G.B.: Were there women available?

R.I.: Oh, yes. This is when I began to really develop issues with my wife that played a part in my molesting. I felt trapped by her. I had asked her what she thought of marriage. She took that as a proposal and told her mother I had proposed to her.

G.B.: Overseas, was your primary sexual interest in children or did you think that you were interested in adult women?

R.I.: Well, I was interested in having my wife with me. I explored every opportunity I could find to get her over there. It was a military occupation, so she was not allowed to come.

G.B.: If she had been available, would you have molested the children?

R.I.: I probably would have.

G.B.: Why?

COGNITIVE DISTORTIONS THAT FACILITATED MOLESTATION

R.I.: Because they provided me with the feeling that they cared about me, that we were close, and that we had something that was special. All of those feelings and all of those concepts I had with those kids.

G.B.: You didn't have that with your wife?

R.I.: I had it with her.

G.B.: Same feelings?

R.I.: I did until I got back home and then I began to lose them. But I had them during the courtship. During the courtship, we'd get very aroused. We'd masturbate each other. At one point she wanted to go ahead and have intercourse and I said, "No." I wanted to put it off until we got married. Then I went into the military and it wasn't an issue anymore.

HAS SEXUAL ATTRACTION FOR WIFE AND CHILDREN

R.I.: Then I came home and we were married. For a couple of weeks we had good feelings.

G.B.: Were the feelings different from those you had with the children?

R.I.: Yes. *(Being with my wife)* was like this is what it's supposed to be like.

G.B.: So, it was the same kind of feeling you had with the children?

R.I.: Yes. It was special with her, but it was more than that. With the children, there was always an awareness in my mind that this is not all that it can be.

SEXUAL REGRESSION—IMPOTENCE WITH ANGER

G.B.: The sexual relations with your wife were even better?

R.I.: This was better, but we didn't have enough time together to make a strong sexual bond. So when I had to spend 18 months away from her I started my old patterns again. By the time I returned home I had developed a conflict with her. I would send her money and she would spend it rather than saving it for us. She shouldn't have done that and at one level I hated her. So it wasn't long before I found that the only way I could maintain an erection was to fantasize about having sex with these kids. I just couldn't keep an erection.

G.B.: What thoughts did you have?

Process:
A. *Wife refuses oral sex*
B. *Doesn't understand her refusal*
C. *Feels anger and resentment*
  A' *Experiences impotence with wife*
  B' *Has fantasies of sex with children*
  C' *His anger is defused so he is able to maintain erection with his wife*

R.I.: I was anxious and eager to have a good sexual relationship with her. In the military I heard oral sex talked about a lot. I came back home and began to talk to her about oral sex. She was turned off by the idea. *(wife refuses oral sex)* Of course, I had oral sex with boys many times and I couldn't see why she objected. *(doesn't understand refusal)* So we began to have a struggle over what kind of sexual relationship we were going to have. I wanted us to perform oral sex on each other, but that was not something she wanted to do. So I began to lose sexual interest in her. There began to be a seed of discontent between us. *(feels anger and resentment)* Before long I was having to fantasize about past sexual experiences with boys in order to even maintain an erection. *(fantasizes sex with children)*

G.B.: What fantasies did you use?

R.I.: Of having a very erect penis and really having an orgasm that was powerful, a lot of movement in it, convulsions.

G.B.: During oral sex with them?

R.I.: Yes.

G.B.: What kind of sex would you be having with her at that time?

R.I.: I would be having intercourse with her while I had fantasies of sex with my cousins. *(anger is defused so he is able to have erection with his wife)*

G.B.: And how long did your marriage last?

R.I.: I'm still married to her.

G.B.: Well, what kept you together?

R.I.: The commitment to stay. We pledged we were going to stay through any problems we might have.

G.B.: Did she know about your committing more sexual offenses?

R.I.: No. She tells me now that she only suspected. A year after coming back from my overseas duty station I molested a boy from the church. So I reenlisted back in the service. I didn't tell my wife that I'd molested. I just lied to her. Shortly after we got to my new duty station, where I was the chaplain's assistant, I molested a boy. The chaplain kept it quiet and got me transferred to a new post where, again, I was the chaplain's assistant. I molested children there, too, and after five years, when I was 30, I was caught. This time they prosecuted me and I was sent to the military disciplinary barracks for 18 months.

G.B.: Did your wife stay with you?

R.I.: Yes. She was at the overseas base. The military paid for her trip back to Florida and she stayed with my parents. One son was born overseas and my wife was pregnant at this time with our second child. She came back to Florida and the military paid for his birth. After I was released from prison, I came home in 1965 and didn't molest again until 1968.

G.B.: How did you keep from doing it for that time?

R.I.: The deterrence of being a prisoner. The sound of the jail cells clanging. I had the urges, but I just held off from molesting.

G.B.: What happened after you were released from prison?

R.I.: I came out and went back to the same community that I grew up in. A lot of the people who were my friends came and said, "Come to our church." So, we finally went back to the church that I grew up in. During that time there were some events that happened that helped to erode away my deterrence.

Process:

A. *Several youths die*
B. *Believes himself to be responsible*
C. *Feels anger*
   A' *Molests boy*

R.I.: A girl had gotten into drugs. Her father came to me and said, "Ann always thought a lot of you. She'll listen to you. How about working with her?" I said, "No. I just can't do it." I knew that I still had these desires to be sexually engaged with children. Within a month after he asked me, Ann, driving under the influence of drugs, ran her car into a tree and killed herself. Shortly after that the pastor asked me to work with Lester. Lester had come into this church. He had started drinking real heavily. I said, "No. I'm not going to do it," because I knew what would happen with Lester and me. Not long after that Lester, while drunk, ran his car over the center line. A truck ran into him and killed him.

Again, I felt the same responsibility. I was angry at myself. If I had talked to him, even if I had sex with him, whatever it would have taken to get to him, maybe he would still be alive. So the next time someone asked me to help, I said, "Yes." A parent in the church asked me to take up some time with his oldest son who was having some problems with drugs. I started taking up time with him and before long we were having sex. He was off drugs, but he was on sex. I was back into it again.

G.B.: Did you feel that you were doing good and helping him?

COGNITIVE DISTORTION

R.I.: The rationale was that if I was not interested in him sexually, I would not have any interest at all, and he wouldn't be off drugs. I was the only one who could make any headway with other kids having problems. I finally began to own that I was sexually attracted to them, but also that I was helping them become better people. My rationale was that if I wasn't attracted to them sexually, that I would probably not be interested in them at all. That was how I rationalized having sex with them.

G.B.: Did you get caught anymore?

R.I.: In 1975, 10 years after I got out of prison, I was caught again. I was put on 15 years' probation and I served seven years of it. In 1982 I molested another boy and got caught and was arrested. My probation was revoked and I was sent to prison. I stayed there until I came here to the Treatment Center in 1983. Now I have 10 years probation waiting for me on that charge after I leave here tomorrow. The pattern just kept right on going on up to 1975.

G.B.: How old are you now?

R.I.: Fifty-two.

G.B.: Are you still married to the same woman?

R.I.: Yes. And have two sons, 23 and 25.

G.B.: Did you ever molest either one of them?

R.I.: No.

G.B.: Was there anything that kept you from doing that?

DISTORTED BELIEF ABOUT SEX WITH CHILDREN

R.I.: My rationale was that sex was a way to get to the kids and build a relationship that was more open. I thought it was actually a technique that could change their entire personality. I used it that way. I didn't have a problem with my sons. My sons and I were very close. We had a real good relationship, so there was no reason to molest them.

G.B.: Do you still have a good relationship with them?

R.I.: Not now. After I was arrested I was interviewed by a news-paper reporter who told me that she was doing a feature on child sexual abuse. She wanted to interview me. When the story came out, it was just a story about my crime: my whole history, being in prison before, my military record, the whole thing. I had made a statement that my family supported my work with kids, and the way she used the statement in the papers was that my family supported me molesting children. From that point on, my sons didn't want anything to do with me.

G.B.: But your wife did?

R.I.: My wife did.

G.B.: What has kept her with you?

R.I.: She said that when we were married that it was for as long as we lived. We have worked through other things, and we're going to work through this.

IRRATIONAL BELIEF ABOUT WIFE

R.I.: For a long time I had a lot of negative thoughts about her. I thought she stayed with me because she couldn't make it on her own. My wife is also in therapy and that has helped her to be able to deal with it. Finally, she has been able to say to people where I am.

G.B.: Are you able to see her at times?

R.I.: She has come to see me every other week all during these five years. She'll be picking me up tomorrow morning.

G.B.: What's the relationship with her like now?

RELATIONSHIP WITH WIFE CHANGED AFTER THERAPY

R.I.: It's a lot more honest. It's like I can say to her what I'm experiencing. I can tell her feelings I have. I can hear her. My being in control of the marriage is probably the hardest issue I had to work on. I began to do things like address her letters by her first name rather than Mrs. __, using my name. I did this to make her more of a person and not just subservient to me. We've worked on some of those issues. She is more assertive. She is able to take care of herself. She's independent. . . .

G.B.: Does she work outside the home?

R.I.: Yes. She's become very successful. She's gotten a lot of promotions and commendations. She is a highly respected worker. In the past I didn't respect her, but I do now. In the past I loved her in terms that I understood at that time, because she was always there for me. She would always do what I wanted her to do, and so she was really my servant. Now, she is a person to me, and I can see her as a person. We make decisions jointly. We are going to be in therapy together. I have an appointment with that therapist next Tuesday.

G.B.: Is this the therapist she has had all along or is this another one?

R.I.: Yes. The therapist she has had. I will also see a therapist for my sexual disorder. I'm attempting right now to get into an outpatient group once I am discharged.

DETAILS WHAT HE GOT OUT OF TREATMENT

G.B.: At this time I'd like to shift topics and to focus on what you got out of the treatment here. I know you have been here for three years, and I know the program has changed during that time. Let's go back to when you first came in. How did you adjust to the program? You were in prison before you came here, right?

R.I.: Yes, for a year.

G.B.: What was that like? How was that prison experience?

R.I.: In prison I was able to use all the skills I learned to keep a real secure exterior. I was a master electrician on the street. When I came to prison I was sure I had a copy of that certification in my records, and right away I became the electrician for the institution. It wasn't long until I walked around the institution like one of the staff members. That made me feel like a really strong person there.

IN TREATMENT HE IS DIRECTED TO LOOK AT HIS CHILD-MOLESTING BEHAVIOR

R.I.: When I came here I found out quickly that none of that mattered, and it was very difficult to realize that here I would have to work on the weaknesses and not my strengths. None of the strong things in my life counted for anything.

G.B.: Like what?

R.I.: I was never going to be allowed to touch any tools here. I was never going to be allowed to be in the control room. I was just going to be brought face-to-face with the fact that I was a child molester. We were going to get to the root of my being a child molester.

G.B.: Why did you volunteer for treatment? What were you interested in getting out of treatment?

R.I.: When I was in jail I thought I was at an age I couldn't do anything to change. I thought I would just commit suicide. And then I decided that there is still a lot that I have not attained.

I've looked for a good life and somehow it has eluded me. This is the last time and the last chance I'll ever get. It is either change it now or die.

DECISION TO ENTER TREATMENT

R.I.: So I made the decision to pursue treatment opportunities. I heard about this program and I made it known from the very beginning that I wanted to get in here. This is really the first time I could go into therapy to work this out. The change was very hard for me, because when I came here I did not separate what I felt were pure motives for helping kids with deviant motives. They were all mixed up together. I could not tell one from the other. The first thing I was told was that there were no pure motives, that all my motives were deviant, that I just used these apparently pure concepts to support the deviancy, that the deviancy was the primary thing. I fought that.

G.B.: You fought it?

RESISTANCE AND DENIAL

R.I.: I fought it. I resisted that for a good part of treatment. I refused to believe that I was a seductive person. My politeness and courtesies were taught to me from my childhood and I did not believe they were seductive. I said the smile on my face was because I was happy and it had nothing to do with hiding anger. I refused to believe that the smile had anything to do with hiding or being seductive. I refused to accept that I was a seductive person. I was not acquainted with anger. I said, "I am not going to be angry. You can't make me angry, because I'm in control." I denied anger. It took two years in treatment to make a lot of changes. Every treatment assignment I did to the best of my ability and did exceptionally well. I did everything top notch, except to experience the change.

When I finally got to K.'s pod, I thought I was ready to go home. I had learned a lot of things. I felt good about myself. I didn't have fantasies of sex with children anymore. I was ready to go.

CONFRONTATION BY THERAPISTS

R.I.: And K., the therapist, says, "You haven't started yet. You don't even trust anybody. You won't listen to anybody. You're here. You're going nowhere." It was like a slap in the face. Then on rounds Dr. N. said, "Listen to these people. Every therapist you've had has been exasperated with you." Well, I didn't know that. I mean, I thought they were pleased with my progress.

G.B.: They were not giving you any feedback?

R.I.: No. I had a lot of different events happen and I felt the therapists were working with me. But K. said, "You never let go of one thing. You never trusted. You never just turned it loose." I really didn't know what he meant, but I told him on rounds that day, "Let's go for it. From now on I will do whatever is told to me to do."

IRRATIONAL BELIEF AND DENIAL OF ANGER

R.I.: I thought it was good that if somebody said something to you that made you angry, it was good not to blow your cool and cuss them out and let all that out. I always said if I ever get angry, I'll be honest, I'll express it. They were saying to me, "You are denying anger; you've got a denial process." I'm saying, "I'm not denying it. I don't feel it." I wasn't aware that denial is a subconscious mechanism that you use. I thought they were accusing me of being dishonest.

RESISTANCE TO CONTROL DECREASES

R.I.: I began to realize that there was a point that I got to where I refused to turn loose and go beyond because I didn't know what was going to happen, what would happen, if I just let my control go. So I decided to let it go. When I would do a role play in a group of some of the traumatic events in my childhood, whatever happened, I just let it go.

BEGINS TO TRUST GROUP

R.I.: My group was there to support me. I began to grow. . . .

G.B.: When you say "letting go," what does that mean?

R.I.: If you were to do a role play with me, and you are going to be my father, and you lecture me for having sexual intercourse with my sister, I'm going to get angry with you, and I'm going to tell you off. I'll just let it go. I won't try to hold back. I looked back at the work I had done previously and realized there was a point where I stopped everything.

G.B.: You mentioned traumatic events, were you ever sexually abused as a child?

R.I.: No. The only traumatic event involved with sex is a threat by my mother. As far as a grandfather or a father molesting me, I've never experienced anything. My cousins and I were all in that together and I didn't ever think of that as any kind of abuse. The basic problem was the rejection by peers. Being ostracized and made fun of was traumatic for me.

G.B.: So most of your work here—has it been done in groups?

R.I.: Yes. By the time the new program started I had done in a group setting most everything that is now done in the modules. I had done a lot of role plays. I worked with traumatic events. I had also done assertiveness training and communication skills. All those things are now modules—so I got credit for several modules. I did take several behavioral modules. I did the cognitive restructuring, relapse prevention, and sensitivity training.

G.B.: How about masturbatory satiation and covert sensitization?

R.I.: Yes, I did those.

G.B.: Since you've been here, have you continued to have fantasies of molesting children?

PARTIAL STIMULI EVOKE MEMORIES

R.I.: When I came here it would be safe to say that from 50–100 things a day would trigger a memory of a past sexual experience. I could hardly see a name of a person or a town, but that I hadn't molested somebody by that name or in that town. I was constantly being bombarded by stimuli that triggered memories of these kids. I cut it off, right there. I said, "I'm not going to think about it. I'll think about something else." I felt really good. That was the period of time that I said, "I'm ready to go and not have any fantasies anymore. It's not there."

G.B.: You felt back in control?

RELATES AROUSAL TO DEVIANT STIMULI

R.I.: The urge was gone. When the lab was set up, I was selected with three other residents to go over and view the deviant slides which were to be used with the plethysmograph. When I got through, I knew I was still attracted to children.

G.B.: Did you get sexually aroused while viewing the slides?

R.I.: I got really aroused. I wanted to go outside and commit sex acts with kids. I isolated myself and later that day I told my therapist about my experience. He said that's what happens when you suppress it. I realized I hadn't changed anything. I had just buried it for a while. It was still there. K. said, "You are a very dangerous person." I said, "I'm not dangerous, I'm not going to hurt anybody."

INSIGHT INTO HIS DANGEROUSNESS

R.I.: Then I realized what my dangerousness really was: I was a child molester. I still had the urges to molest children. I knew thoughts of molesting children could still be exciting to me. I had denied that, and that's what made me dangerous. Because I could easily be in a situation again where I perceive this child as though he wants to have sex. And if he should want to, why not—just this once; it would be safe. I could easily see where I could get back into that.

DEVIANT BEHAVIOR MONITORING SYSTEM

R.I.: We developed a deviant behavior monitoring system where you think of all the behaviors you did on the street and the behaviors you do here in the Center, and you make comparisons between them and how they fit into your crime. We call that the Daily Manifestation of Psychosexual Disorder.

G.B.: Tell me about this.

R.I.: It's a planned treatment assignment, and you monitor everything you do, all the significant interactions that you have for like three days. You write them down and the behaviors that are involved in those interactions. Then another part of it is that you go back to any week prior to your arrest and monitor all your behaviors and interactions. What did you do? work? family? alcohol? drugs? All those kind of things you put down. Then you make a comparison to the things you did then that led up to your crime to the things you do now. This allows you to see how your psychosexual disorder is kept going here. I became aware of a lot of behavior that I do. This is when I began to work on the seductiveness. When I began, I monitored about 24 behaviors that I thought supported my psychosexual disorder.

CENTRAL PROCESS

R.I.: We have a concept that we call Central Process. This means how you operate as a molester from the time that you get triggered until you actually molest.

G.B.: You said for you rejection is a core theme.

R.I.: Right. That would be the part of the process that I focused on. I had to focus on when I was rejected, what did I do next? Then next, then next, then next—until there is a victim.

ANTECEDENT BEHAVIORS TO MOLESTATION

R.I.: The important thing for me was when K. said, "You know what your process is from the time you get rejected to the time of acting out, but you are not aware of how you set this whole thing up to be rejected." He told me to look at what I do to make myself be rejected by peers. He said that is what I will be doing on the street.

G.B.: So you looked at behavior coming before and after the rejection?

R.I.: Before and after. My problem was that I corrected people. If you said the University of Southern California built the swimming pool for the Olympics, I'd say, "No. MacDonalds built it." I knew MacDonalds built it. I had the evidence. I read it in the paper. I could go and pick up the paper and prove my point. No one really likes to be proved wrong all the time. So people didn't like me because I was proving them wrong. I was correcting people over insignificant things. So that's a behavior that I monitored and I just stopped doing it. Another behavior was the smile when I was not happy, or the "thank you" when I didn't feel any gratitude. All of those behaviors were part of the seduction. So we began to focus on behaviors that I, as a child molester, used to set myself up to be in a relationship with victims, to make them feel safe with me.

G.B.: You are mixing two things.

INSIGHT INTO HIS REJECTION

R.I.: Okay. I was responsible for being rejected, because I engaged in behavior that pushed adults away from me. And at the same time I engaged in behaviors that made children come toward me.

G.B.: So, two different things. You were responsible for adults rejecting you and for making the children come.

INSIGHT INTO HIS SEDUCTIVE BEHAVIORS

R.I.: The magic that I thought I had with children was magic I created by making children feel safe with me. All the little behaviors that I would do, taking interest in them, finding out about them, buying them things—if I brought a child something long enough, he became dependent on me. Once he was dependent upon me, he thought twice about pulling away from me. Eventually, he gave me the sex in order to keep getting what he was getting.

G.B.: You mentioned one of your central processes has been the theme of rejection. Have there been other themes that you have found?

TWO CENTRAL PROCESS THEMES: REJECTION AND LOSING CONTROL

R.I.: Being rejected has been the biggest one for me. Losing control has been another one of the themes. Rejection and losing control.

G.B.: There are two different themes?

ACTIVATING EVENT

R.I.: Right. They work hand-in-hand. Say, if you were my boss, and I worked very hard for you but you didn't show approval and you criticized me. For example, I bring in this plan for you. I'm going to show you how we can save $5,000 on this job by doing it this particular way. You tell me that you are not going to do it that way.

IRRATIONAL BELIEF ABOUT REJECTION

R.I.: Now what that means to me is that you've rejected me. You didn't reject my plan, you rejected me.

HIGHLY CHARGED EMOTIONAL CONSEQUENCES OF ANGER AND SHAME

R.I.: Then I become angry and lose control. I argue with you and lose control. And I'm going to try to get my point across. When I walk out of that office, I say, "I shouldn't have done that. I'm going to be ashamed, and I'm going to be embarrassed."

STAGES

R.I.: So feeling the rejection comes first, and then losing control, and then being ashamed. So that's the core, right there.

NEW ACTIVATING EVENT

R.I.: From then on it's just finding the victim. The fantasies come back up. That part I learned how to deal with.

G.B.: How did you do that?

R.I.: In groups we spent a lot of time going over crime descriptions of things that happened over and over in order to find these key steps.

DROPS IRRATIONAL BELIEF

R.I.: Later I began to think that people's behaviors do not necessarily mean rejection. If you said, "I don't like this idea," you didn't say you didn't like me. My ideas and I are not the same. You can disagree with an idea without disagreeing about me. It was a self-esteem issue. So I worked on that.

G.B.: How would you gauge your self-esteem across the years?

GAINS INSIGHT ABOUT FEELINGS AND SELF-ESTEEM

R.I.: I thought I had a really high self-esteem. Then I came here and found this was one of the denial things. My therapist said I didn't really have very much self-esteem. I said, "Well, I do." He said, "Well, it's not showing up." So we started looking at words I used that meant that I had low-esteem, such as writing in a passive voice. If I said, "I feel angry," that was not as direct as saying, "I am angry." If I said, "My thoughts are angry," I am putting it even further away. So, I began to be aware that my emotions were removed from me. I then saw I did not have much esteem for myself.

R.I.: Then I began to own things, "I am angry." I began to use a very active voice in speaking and writing. Through this process I began to develop some esteem, and I began to interact with people. I worked into other areas of therapy and I tried some things, such as football, that I hadn't done before.

LIVES OUT A FANTASY

R.I.: You know, I mentioned that my dad never let me play football. All these years I had the fantasy and dreams of running a touchdown and hearing the crowd cheer as I made a touchdown. In 1984 I went out for a football team here in intramurals and I made the first touchdown of the season. Everyone was cheering and I had lived my fantasy. After that, I haven't had that dream again. It actually lived itself out.

CORRECTED DISTORTED BELIEF

R.I.: I tried to figure out this process of the things that triggered me. One was my interest in sex with a 14-year-old girl. Not having sex with her was an unfinished issue because I did not have anything to talk about with the guys. I went on and looked at this in relationship to my wife. I began to see how they were not the same. I saw how I have a wife that still stays with me. My wife comes to see me, and it's an exciting experience when she comes.

WORKS ON IMPOTENCE

R.I.: I worked on my problem with my impotence by trying to be aware of genital sensations. My assignment was after every visit I had to tell about the sexual sensations that I felt during the visit. This was connected to my fantasy with the 14-year-old girl.

AWARE OF DISTORTED BELIEF

R.I.: With her (the 14-year-old girl) I was saying I had unfinished business. There was something unresolved. I should have had an experience back when I was 15 and then been able to tell my friends. I thought if I had been able to do so, I would have been accepted into their group. I couldn't do that, so in my adult life I was continuously trying to do that.

G.B.: Trying to do what?

SEEKS ACCEPTANCE

R.I.: As a child molester, I was continuously trying to go back and be in high school again, and have sex with a 14-year-old girl so that I could talk about it to my friends and my friends would accept me.

G.B.: How did that relate to your wife?

CORRECTED DISTORTED BELIEF

R.I.: In therapy I found out that I already had a sexual conquest with my wife. My wife comes to see me and we have a romantic experience. There is an excitement in the visit. There are sexual stimulations that happen inside of me during the visit. So I can come back and say, "See group, I am one of you." And it was like fulfilling an unfulfilled wish.

G.B.: Are you now able to have some sexual excitement with your wife?

R.I.: Yes.

G.B.: Do you get erections?

R.I.: Well, some. I became totally impotent on the street. You know, I mentioned when I came back home from service in 1960 that I began to fantasize about sexual experiences in order to maintain erections. That was like an off-and-on thing, but it progressively grew worse. I could still have erections like in the morning wake-up. It was not something physical, but it was a psychological thing.

DOES BIOENERGETIC EXERCISES

R.I.: I began to do a lot of bioenergetic exercises, focusing on the pelvic area, trying to get energy released in the pelvic area.

G.B.: You did this while here in treatment?

REGAINS GENITAL SENSATIONS

R.I.: Here in treatment. I began to be aware of sensations. I could feel sensations in my genitals. I hadn't done that for years. Before treatment I walked around like I didn't even have any genitals. In therapy I was able to explore a lot of the things from my childhood that I kept trying to fulfill with these kids. Then I saw how I already had fulfilled them, or I was able to fulfill them here.

G.B.: Are you now beginning to get some erections?

R.I.: Yes. As I wake up in the morning I have erections.

G.B.: Do you have erections when you are with your wife?

R.I.: Yes. In the visiting park, we can talk about being together. I want to be with her. I can rub her shoulders and massage her.

BEGINS TO HAVE ERECTION WITH WIFE

R.I.: At the Center, touch is limited, but in the little amount of touch that we have I can begin to feel an erection. This hadn't happened before.

G.B.: So you don't know yet if you are going to be impotent with her?

R.I.: No. I don't know.

G.B.: Do you ever get a full erection when you are with her?

R.I.: No. Before coming to prison, sometimes I would really have a strong urge to have a sexual experience with her, but have no sensations in the genitals. The urge was inside; mentally and physically I was ready, but my body would not cooperate. It was just like cut off. Feelings have come back, so tomorrow when I'm with her we have a plan. After we shop we plan to stay in Gainesville overnight at a motel.

PLANS PATIENCE

R.I.: We are going to take things really slow and there is absolutely no expectation of whether everything will work or whether it won't work.

G.B.: On the part of you?

R.I.: On the part of me and her.

G.B.: Have you talked about it?

R.I.: Yes, we talked about it. We will be together and see what happens. A lot of times now I can get an erection. In the past, if I had an erection, as soon as I penetrated I lost it immediately. That was part of the impotence.

G.B.: So tomorrow you are going to go off with your wife, and after going shopping, then you will have sex with her?

R.I.: We'll go to a motel room and just be with each other. Both of us have the intention that we would like to have a sexual experience and we've talked about it.

LOWERS EXPECTATIONS OF SELF

R.I.: We are aware that I may not even be able to get an erection, but I will hold her and she will hold me and we'll be together.

ATTEMPTS TO CHANGE OLD DISTORTED BELIEF

R.I.: If I can't get an erection, I will not say that I'm inferior. I will not say that I am no good. I will say that this is another issue, but now we have the time to work with it. Previously, when I knew that I couldn't get an erection, I wouldn't even tell her that I wanted to have sex. Instead, I went and found a victim. This played directly into my child molesting.

CORRECTS DISTORTED BELIEF—SEES WIFE AS SUPPORTIVE

R.I.: Tomorrow she will be there with me one way or the other. We will face it together. We will be in therapy together and we will work out whatever psychological issue there is that is keeping me from having an erection. We will discover it together and we will build that part back.

G.B.: I know you have told me some of the things you have learned, but tell me, if you will, what you got out of the program. What has it done for you?

R.I.: The way I experienced things is different.

EARLY IN THERAPY HE HAD NO EMPATHY FOR VICTIM

R.I.: For example, when I first came here, if I saw someone do a role play of molesting a child, I would get aroused. I would say to myself if he had done this he would have never got caught. I could do this better. I would get caught up in that part of the role play.

LATE IN THERAPY HE HAS EMPATHY FOR VICTIM

R.I.: Tuesday we saw a role play of someone molesting a child, and my experience was different. I felt a sick stomach. That first happened during the masturbatory satiation module. When I think of that aversive scene I get nauseated. In the role play the image that came to my mind happened to be an image of one of my victims, a young girl: dark skin, long brown hair, and real huge dark eyes. In the role play there were huge tears in the girl's eyes and an awareness that she didn't want to do this; she was holding back. That was not my experience. Something along the way changed the way I experienced it.

G.B.: And this is a new scene that never existed for you?

R.I.: I was watching a videotape of someone else's role play. There was no girl in the role play, but I put a girl in the role play and the image that I saw happened to be a 12-year-old girl that I had molested my own self years before.

G.B.: Did the real girl cry?

R.I.: She did not cry.

G.B.: But in your fantasies she did?

R.I.: On Tuesday she did. Tuesday there was the hurt and the fear in her. I know that my victim was afraid, too. Before I refused to see it. She didn't cry, but I know she held the tears back. I began to see a lot of hurt in my victims.

EARLY HE HAD DISTORTED BELIEF
THAT MOLESTING WAS OKAY

R.I.: When I came here I believed that molesting was all right. I thought eventually society would agree with me and say that kids should have the right to have sex with whomever they want. I thought the kids weren't being hurt by having sex with adults.

CORRECTS DISTORTED BELIEF

R.I.: Now, I no longer believe this. I get sad when I think about it—kids having sex with adults.

G.B.: Let's move to a different subject. What is to keep you from molesting again? You've got a long history of it. You've learned some things, but as you project yourself forward, what is to keep you from remolesting?

SUPPORT SYSTEM TO BE USED AS DETERRENT

R.I.: One thing that is going to help is the fact that I have people out here that still support me. Some are former residents from here. I will have contact with them. When I came here there wasn't anyone I could ever tell that would understand. Now, if an urge comes up, there is somebody out there that will be with me during that time. I do not have to go out and molest.

USE OF AVERSIVE FANTASIES AS DETERRENT

R.I.: If I feel rejected by my boss and I feel the urge to molest, then an aversive fantasy will come into my mind. That's going to be a temporary deterrent. That's going to give me time to pick up the phone and call someone. I will call back here if I have to.

G.B.: Whom are you going to call?

R.I.: I can call my wife. I can tell her that I am experiencing urges to molest. Or I can tell the person that I'm living with temporarily. He was a former resident here.

G.B.: So you are not going to go back to your wife right away?

R.I.: No. We are going to live separately. We are going to have a courtship again and build it back real slowly.

G.B.: Why is that?

R.I.: Because we want to go through therapy and we want to be able to work out all of the differences. We also have financial reasons. It's not wise to go back to the community where I molested and we can't afford two houses.

G.B.: Will you be in the same community with her?

R.I.: No. About 30 miles away.

G.B.: Do you have a job?

R.I.: No. But I have an ex-offender placement program lined up to help me get employment.

G.B.: How much probation will you have?

R.I.: I have 10 years of probation.

G.B.: Besides your wife, who can you call?

SUPPORT NETWORK

R.I.: Any of the former residents here. We've got a network. We've got phone numbers.

G.B.: How close are they to where you will be living?

R.I.: They are in several nearby cities.

G.B.: Do you know these guys?

R.I.: I know them. I've been in therapy with them. They've cradled me. They've held me and I've held them. We support each other in treatment.

G.B.: What else?

NO LONGER USES DEFENSES THAT ISOLATE HIM

R.I.: The other thing is that the behaviors which I used to set myself up to be rejected, I don't use them anymore. I've got friends. I'm creating more honest friends. The way I respond to people is different. I don't push people away with some of the behaviors I used to do. So those would be a good deterrent. *(will have outpatient treatment)* I'll continue in therapy on the outside.

G.B.: In individual therapy as well as couple therapy with your wife?

MEDITATES AND DOES BIOENERGETIC EXERCISES

R.I.: Yes. So that will be a strong point. The other thing is that physically I've learned to be more in touch with my body. I meditate and relax myself. When I came into prison I had a blood pressure around 150 over 110. Now it's down to a normal range, like 120 over 76. I did that with no medication or anything.

G.B.: Did you lose weight?

R.I.: When I came into prison I weighed 256 lbs. and I weigh 210 now. I'm struggling to get it below that.

G.B.: So you lost weight and you meditate.

R.I.: I meditate and do exercises every day. I do bioenergetic exercises to keep myself grounded. I changed my breathing structure. I do deep breathing exercises. I breathe from the abdomen. I do deep breathing exercises. I don't rush around.

CAN USE ASSERTIVE SKILLS

R.I.: If things start going too fast for me and people start loading too many things on me, I have learned assertive skills so that I can say stop when I'm getting overwhelmed. Those are some of the skills that I learned here.

When I was on the street, I could not stand to be alone. I had to have someone with me. I could have hired adult people from the company I worked with, but instead I hired kids because I was in control. They were with me and I felt superior to them.

CAN TOLERATE BEING ALONE

R.I.: Now, I can be alone.

G.B.: What are your plans about being with kids?

WILL AVOID CONTACT WITH CHILDREN

R.I.: I won't have any contact with kids. I know there are kids in the environment and they're going to be there.

HAS LEARNED BEHAVIORS TO AVOID POTENTIAL VICTIMS

R.I.: Now, I know if I go home in the afternoon and I go past the 7 Eleven and there is a bunch of kids hanging around, I'll just go to the next one. That's step number one. If I get down to the very last store before I get home and there is something that I have to have before I go home, then I will go in the store, but I will not establish eye contact with the child. I'll walk in and make sure that our faces don't meet. These are the skills I've learned how to use.

G.B.: How about your contact with the church? It seems to have been important in the past. You have done a lot of molesting with the contacts you made in church.

R.I.: This is a harder situation. I knew this is a place of risk for me. So I plan to avoid it.

PLANS TO AVOID MINISTRY WITH CHILDREN; INSTEAD WILL WORK WITH PRISONERS

R.I.: Right now my thinking and my plan is that I want to get involved in a prison ministry.

G.B.: With adults?

R.I.: With adults inside of a prison. I'm going to explore the possibility of fulfilling my religious aspirations within the context of ministering to inmates.

G.B.: You don't see yourself really having contact with kids at all?

R.I.: Not in the kinds of ways I did before. I mean I can't say I won't have contact with kids because they are everywhere you go.

G.B.: Do you still feel at risk with that?

R.I.: That's been the hardest thing to let go.

G.B.: Do you think this will ever change, that you will not be at risk?

ACCEPTS IDEA THAT KIDS ARE A RISK FOR HIM

R.I.: At this point, I'm going to say it will always be a risk for me. I've reconciled the fact that no matter what my past was and no matter how much good I might have done, I am not going to debate that anymore. It's a risk for me and I have to go in other directions.

G.B.: What do you think is the most dangerous thing about you that you need to look out for?

AWARE THAT DEFENSE OF DENIAL IS STILL PRESENT

R.I.: Denial. I still have a problem with denial. I still deny feelings. Recently I remembered the experience of the female reporter writing the article. I was really angry at her. I denied the anger and focused on my fear of what she could do to me. In the process of running away from these feelings of anger, I speeded. I walked out of the building without signing out. The moment I did that I knew that I had already committed an offense.

G.B.: So it took your committing an offense in order to be aware of denying your anger. Is that what you are saying?

R.I.: I did the offense and then I was aware of the anger.

G.B.: What made you become aware of it?

ABLE TO ANALYZE CENTRAL PROCESS

Process:
A. *Remembers reporter writing article*
B. *Believes consequences will be awful*
C. *Feels angry and fearful*
   A' *Violates rules*
   B' *Sees his action was inappropriate*
   C' *Becomes aware of the anger feelings*

R.I.: Okay, I processed it out. I analyzed what was going on with me, and that's when I began to look at the process. I saw the reporter writing the article was the triggering event, and then I focused on the inappropriate behavior of not signing out of the building. Then I would just go back and process out and work back until I saw, "Hey, I'm angry at that reporter."

G.B.: How do the new residents learn about process thinking?

R.I.: That's taught in the new resident module while they are in orientation and before they even get accepted in the treatment program. They are taught about process thinking and how to monitor behavior. They begin to identify the behaviors: anger behaviors, avoidance behaviors, denial behaviors.

G.B.: With the new program coming in within the last year, have any parts of the old been lost which in your viewpoint should have been kept?

R.I.: I miss the close contact we had in the working through of traumatic events with peers. We had four intense groups with a primary therapist each week. Now we have two groups per week. The new program is built around learning in the modules. I do know that if a guy goes through all the modules and applies himself he will walk out of here with a briefcase full of answers or tools for every situation. If he does the modules, he will learn how to develop the skill to use those tools and everything he needs to keep from reoffending. I don't know about his suffering as a human being. I don't know about the things that still go on inside of him. The suffering may still be there.

G.B.: You sound as if you feel that finding the reasons for suffering is a good thing to do?

R.I.: When I was really small I had a bad throat, bad teeth, bad ears, a lot of pain. I would toss and turn at night and my mother would come and put what she called a "sugar teat," a little piece of cloth with sugar in it, tied up, and put that in my mouth for me to suck on. That would relieve the pain.

G.B.: When you were how old?

R.I.: Maybe two, three, or four years old. The first thing I did when I got home from school was to get a piece of honeycomb with the honey still in it and chew that.

AS INFANT HE USED ORAL GRATIFICATION
TO RELIEVE PAIN

AS ADOLESCENT AND ADULT HE USED ORAL SEX
MOLESTATION TO RELIEVE PAIN AND GIVE PLEASURE

R.I.: Most of my offending occurred around that time in the afternoon. I believe there are some connections there. I believe that if I can better resolve and understand some of those connections, it lessens the dangerousness.

G.B.: Speaking of your dangerousness, have you ever done any acts of violence in your child molesting?

R.I.: Not as far as physical violence or actually doing physical damage to the victim. I hate to say that I have never done anything violent to the victim because I don't think that there is anything more violent than molesting a child. But like breaking an arm or bashing their head in or something like that, I never did those things. I seduced my victims.

G.B.: You caused no physical pain?

R.I.: No.

G.B.: Did you have thoughts of causing pain but didn't do so?

R.I.: Yes. Especially as the relationship began to wane. As the child grew and developed, the things that I provided in this relationship no longer satisfied him. As he developed other interests, it became harder to maintain the relationship. I have had many violent fantasies involving killing the victims. I did a lot of work on that in my treatment.

G.B.: Are you still having fantasies of child molesting?

R.I.: No. I still have memories that are triggered by certain things. When a memory occurs, I say: this is a memory; this is a time when I molested a child; this is the trauma I caused for that child; and this is the result to my own life. Then I try not to dwell on those memories.

G.B.: Have you become sexually aroused with the memories?

R.I.: If I fantasize, I will become sexually aroused. So I cut them off.

G.B.: Well, we've gone through a lot of things and I don't want to stop without making it open for you to be able to say any additional things you may wish.

R.I.: Well, I know I want to be involved in the prevention of sexual abuse. I feel I have put a lot of money and a lot of energy into abusing. Now I have an interest in being on the other side and working in some way to prevent abuse.

G.B.: Along those lines, what can you tell parents about prevention of child molestation?

R.I.: The first thing is to make kids sexually aware, to teach them about sexuality in the home from the earliest age. Parents should be available so the child can come and talk about things. They should let children know there are some people in the world who, although they seem to be good people, will play up to them and take advantage of them sexually. If that occurs, while it may seem to be all right for them at the moment and they might be excited about it, there are adverse consequences down the road. Parents should be told if sex does occur between the child and the molester it is not their fault or the child's fault, because most child molesters are able to con children and overpower them emotionally. They should give the children the word that if someone comes on to them and they believe that they are going to be touched inappropriately, they should tell that person they will inform their parents if he does something to them. If the kids had told me that they would tell their parents I would have quit right there.

FOLLOW-UP INTERVIEW

This interview took place six months following R.I.'s discharge from the Sex Offender Treatment Unit of North Florida Evaluation and Treatment Center.

G.B.: Now that you have been back in the community for about six months, I would like to find out how things have been going for you.

R.I.: Initially, I had difficulty in finding work. Not so much because I was an ex-felon, but because of my age. I found a real good job as an electrician in about six weeks. I got a raise last week so I think the employment aspect of my life is coming along real well. I had always worried about getting a bond, but I just walked into the insurance office and told them I needed a bond and they just filled it right out. As far as treatment is concerned, I'm still in the outpatient treatment program in a nearby city.

G.B.: How is it going?

R.I.: It's going really well. We're using a treatment module, rational-emotive therapy (RET). I'm going deeper into my beliefs about sex with children. I have had a lot of apprehension being near new people because I eventually have to tell them my past. I've been able to use RET for that real well.

G.B.: Can you give an example of something you have found out about yourself in this treatment?

R.I.: My superiority thing has always separated me from other people. Like I don't drink, don't smoke, and don't use profanity. I always felt as if I were the odd person in the peer group because of that. A situation existed at work where the guys would get together and drink a few beers after work in the parking lot. Some of my closest peers, guys that I've come to know real well, are in that group. I was reluctant to associate with them because I didn't drink. In RET we talked about past experiences being some of the things that cause us to think in certain ways. I challenged my old belief that the guys would see me as odd if I didn't drink. I challenged that by going out with the guys and talking without drinking. I found out that I was respected and not put down. Also, I found out that they didn't feel I was putting them down.

In another situation, a newspaper reporter who covered my case when I was arrested has been after me quite a bit. She's asking everybody she can for information about where I live. She finally found my home telephone number. Everybody has told her I don't want to talk with her, but she's bound and determined to stir it up. This is another opportunity to use RET. I don't feel the anxiety to the extent that I did before I was in prison.

G.B.: Has she been in touch with you since your release?

R.I.: Just recently she tried to locate me when a former victim of mine called the local police department and said that I tried to run him down in a car. As a matter of fact, I was at treatment that night, and I had documentation that established that I was a considerable distance away when it occurred. But he swears that I am the one.

Some of the probation officers wanted to take me before the judge, but my probation officer, who has been extremely supportive, thought something could be arranged through petitioning the judge. As a result of the petition, part of the conditions of my probation are that I will not have any contact with my former victim. I had no intention of contacting him anyway.

G.B.: What do you think is going on with your former victim to say something like that?

R.I.: His family and the newspaper reporter are working hand-in-hand to keep this thing alive. They regard me as a very dangerous person who should not be on the street. They're doing everything they can to see that I get put back.

G.B.: But you've not had any contact with your former victim?

R.I.: No. I wouldn't even know what he looked like now.

G.B.: You have been able to document your movements?

R.I.: Yes, I keep a log of my travel movements. That particular night that he claims I tried to run over him I was on my way back home. I had stopped at a convenience store to buy a few groceries. The cash register receipt had the time on it. In addition, I had paid with a check and the back of the check had the time stamped on it. That established that I was at a distance of 35–40 miles, 45 minutes prior to the time of occurrence. At the exact time it reportedly occurred, I was buying gas at a gas station 12 miles away from the scene. I had no receipt, however, to substantiate the time or place of this purchase.

So now I routinely ask for a cash receipt on which I have the clerk write the time, the date, and his initials. In this way I document my movements. In addition, I keep a speedometer log so that I have a record of where I've been. In this way, I'm taking care of myself.

G.B.: And you're doing it without feeling too apprehensive?

R.I.: Right. I'm not going to let them force me into doing things out of fear.

G.B.: How are things going with you socially?

R.I.: I've been to the Sexual Compulsive Anonymous Group which provides some social activities.

G.B.: Have you had any social contact with children?

R.I.: No. The only contact I've had with children was when some children came to the door selling candy on a school money-raising project. I was not here at the time, but my roommate was. Without thinking, he ordered some candy. This meant the children had to come back to deliver the candy. Well, they came back the next afternoon when I was home alone. I managed to get rid of them and avoided a situation. Since then he's taken steps to see that they don't come around. I see children at church and I see children when I shop. I must say that the urge to have sex with children is still present. Sometimes it's stronger than at other times.

G.B.: Have you figured out what triggers it?

R.I.: Being alone. It is also associated with stress and fatigue.

G.B.: How do you handle it when it is there?

R.I.: I know that it will pass. I just say, "Well, I don't have to engage . . ." and I tell myself that while I might enjoy the experience for a few moments, there are consequences: the consequences to the victim and the consequences to myself. I tell myself that I have goals now, and any contact with children would cause an adverse effect on the goals I'm pursuing.

G.B.: So you're putting into application some of the things you've learned.

R.I.: Yes. I'm really enjoying having money in my pocket now. Before, I blew all my money on molesting children. I know I'll have to give up the financial freedom I now have if I engage in sex with children. The other thing I do, something I learned in the relapse prevention module, is to reward myself. If I see a kid hitchhiking, many times I'll have the urge to pick him up. But I don't pick him up and I feel personally rewarded. As soon as I pass him by, I feel a real charge inside, knowing that I beat the urge one more time.

G.B.: It's a positive kind of reward, emotionally?

R.I.: Yes. My former experience was that if I passed a kid by, I would ruminate about what it would have been like. And sometimes I would even turn around and go back for another try. For a few days it would go through my mind how the contact would have been. I would feel sorry that I hadn't gone ahead and picked him up. Now, as I pass the child up, my experience is different. I think about how glad I am that I withstood the urge one more time, and that it didn't kill me not to pick him up. Even though I'm alone, I have support. If I'm extremely lonely, there are people I can call. I don't need children for that anymore.

G.B.: How about your adult sexual contact now?

R.I.: I found that I can maintain an erection, but not every time. My wife has been very understanding; if it doesn't occur this time, maybe it will occur next time. We still have interaction. I don't feel less than a man if we begin a sexual experience and I lose the erection. We can touch without having to go for intercourse, and that's taken the pressure off. I've had many successful sexual experiences with her since I've been home.

G.B.: Have you had anything that you could not handle? Any major obstacles that you couldn't handle?

R.I.: No, I've been able to handle each one.

G.B.: I hope you can keep things under control and continue without further obstacles or hassles. Thanks for talking with me.

OVERVIEW

This child molester, like most other child molesters, has a history that indicates a multifactor genesis of his deviant behavior. Unlike many child molesters who give a history of having been sexually abused during childhood, however, R.I. was not sexually abused as a child. What does appear in his early socialization was a series of incidents to which he responded with cognitive distortions. These distorted beliefs, in turn, became linked with sexual behavior.

An example of this is the distorted belief of his responsibility for his brother's death and the subsequent sexual experience with his cousin. Another was his distorted belief that he could disgrace his family through sexual activity with girls. As a result of this thinking, he avoided sexual contact with girls, a pattern he followed throughout his life.

After his mother threatened to castrate him for displaying his erect penis to his aunt, he learned to hide his feelings of fear and terror by having masturbatory sexual experiences. He learned to hide his sexual thoughts and activities from others. As an adolescent he tells of relieving the pain of being rejected by his girlfriend by molesting a young boy. Thus, he turned from finding pleasure in fondling himself to that of fondling a younger boy. He found that boys were accepting of him. This behavior developed into a repetitive pattern of molestation.

As an adult when he became impotent with his wife, he used fantasies of having sex with children to partially diffuse the anger he felt toward his wife so that he could maintain an erection.

He reported that while in treatment he was initially resistant and used a lot of denial. It was only after he had been in treatment for a while that he was able to look at the antecedents of his child-molesting behavior and to work effectively to correct some of his distorted beliefs that supported his deviant behavior.

A six-month follow-up interview following his release from the treatment program indicates that he is continuing in outpatient therapy. He has been able to cope effectively with the stressors confronting him in the community and has not reoffended. He reported that he still has the urges to become sexually involved with children, but he has used the skills acquired in therapy to avoid acting on these deviant thoughts and feelings. He stated that he has had sexual satisfaction in sexual intercourse with his wife.

It is obvious that this individual is not "cured" as a child molester in terms of being free of the desires and thoughts of molesting, but rather, he is in remission from acting overtly on his impulses. The fact that he continues to have the urges to molest children points to the need for extended outpatient treatment. Continued therapy reinforces the gains that the molester has obtained in one phase of his treatment and reduces the likelihood for further offenses.

III. LEGAL, ETHICAL, AND TREATMENT ISSUES

CHAPTER 9
Legal and Forensic Issues

In contrast to the cooperative model of the helping professions, the legal system is predicated on an adversarial model. The shades of grey that clinicians customarily consider when handling the complex and often individualized elements of patient treatment do not work within the black-and-white framework of the legal system. However, when evaluating and treating the child molester, the clinician must interface with the law and may get caught between conflicting forces—for example, the duty of confidentiality to the patient versus the duty to protect foreseeable victims. A background knowledge of the laws governing the obligations to both the patient and society, as well as an understanding of some of the ethical and legal issues that can arise when evaluating and treating a child molester, are prerequisites to effectively carry out clinical practice and to avoid lawsuits.

TORT LAW

The purpose of *tort law* is to help an injured party become whole again by receiving remuneration for the injury, usually adjudicated as a monetary award. A *tort*, or civil wrong, can be divided into two categories: intentional or unintentional. Although clinicians are rarely confronted with intentional tort actions, physicians occasionally must face the unintentional variety, or negligence—commonly referred to as "malpractice" when the medical profession is involved. In a medical malpractice suit, the patient (or plaintiff) seeks damages for injuries which allegedly have been caused by the negligence of a physician (or defendant). In order to win the lawsuit, the plaintiff bears the burden of proving that the injuries are the result of either an act which a duly careful member of the medical profession would not have done, or an omission of an act which a reasonable and prudent clinician would have done under similar circumstances.[10]

Malpractice actions against the physician are usually viewed as tortuous in nature and must be fully substantiated. In order to establish a successful tort action in a negligence suit, the plaintiff must show that the following essential features (known as the four "Ds") are involved:[10]

> *Duty*—the defendant owed the plaintiff a specific duty.
> *Dereliction*—the defendant breached his duty to the plaintiff, or committed a dereliction of the duty.
> *Damages*—the plaintiff suffered injuries with damages.
> *Direct Causation*—there was proximate or direct causation between the breach of duty by the defendant and the injury suffered by the plaintiff.

In medical malpractice terms, the plaintiff's case must show by a preponderance of evidence (at least 51%) that the physician's negligence of duty to use reasonable care resulted in injuries to the patient.[9]

DUTY AND THE FIDUCIARY RELATIONSHIP

The concept of *duty* cannot be fully appreciated without understanding how the law views the physician-patient relationship. While this relationship is a contractual agreement and is governed by special laws in each state, it is also a *fiduciary relationship* in which the clinician has special obligations based on the patient's trust and confidence in the physician.[10] The obligatory and affirmative duty or duties placed upon the clinician are controlled, in part, by the physician's knowledgeable, skilled, and experienced authority in important matters about which the patient is not well versed. Physicians have the responsibility to use their medical skill and knowledge with *reasonable care* or *due care*, which are standards expected to compare with any established member in the medical profession working under similar circumstances. Some of the basic principles of the due care concept were set forth in the 1898 New York case of Pike v. Honsinger.[10]

Most areas, however, have either modified or abandoned the locality specification, and this locality rule is not usually applicable for specialists, who are compared with their peers at a national level. The general physician is compared to the standard of care delivered by other reasonable and prudent generalists, whereas the specialist is held to the standard of care by other specialists in his area of expertise.[19]

BREACH OF DUTY AND PROXIMATE CAUSATION

In a malpractice suit, when negligence is proven to exist (when there has been a *breach of duty* to provide skill and care to the patient), and when this negligence is verified to have proximately caused injury to the patient, then malpractice damages may be awarded. Except in states where the comparative negligence theory is honored, the patient, as plaintiff, must prove that he or she is free of contributing negligence, and must show that the physician departed from acceptable standards of practice which caused the injury. As highlighted earlier, the plaintiff's burden is fourfold:

1. To indicate what the applicable standards of care entail.
2. To show that the defendant did not meet the standards.
3. To prove proximate causation between the injury and the defendant's failure to meet the plaintiff's acceptable standard of care.
4. To show that injury or damages resulted.

Since these essential elements are believed to be beyond the common knowledge of the trier of fact, an expert witness is often called in to give testimony, and is expected to provide opinions as to what the standard of medical care under similar cases and conditions would have been, and how the defendant-physician deviated from the standard. Just as the "preponderance" of evidence is needed to prove that negligence has occurred in a tort action, in general, the terms which the expert must affirm—*with reasonable medical certainty* or *with reasonable medical probability*—are taken to mean the experience in the majority of cases, or 51%. While the expert witness may give opinions on these issues, in the final analysis it is the responsibility of the jury to determine whether the plaintiff has proven that the defendant was negligent.

INFORMED CONSENT AND THE RIGHT TO REFUSE TREATMENT

When the concept of duty inherent in the fiduciary nature of the physician-patient relationship is linked to the legal right of a competent adult to determine what should be done with his or her body, there emerges a powerful doctrine of *informed consent.*[10,11] This doctrine places an affirmative obligation on the physician to inform the patient about the planned course of diagnostic and/or therapeutic procedures, and to warn the patient of any possible complications. The doctor also has the duty to tell the patient of alternate courses of action. Once the patient has been *duly informed,* the right remains to accept or reject the plan proposed by the physician. However, the law does not specifically delineate what information physicians should give their patients. This qualifying "should" must be evaluated and compared to what other competent physicians would do under similar circumstances.

The doctrine of *informed consent* essentially stresses the two-way nature of the physician-patient relationship. If the physician proceeds without obtaining the patient's informed consent, and if the procedures result in injury to the patient, then the doctor may be liable for the damages. For example, if a physician follows a treatment plan in which the patient's body is touched (e.g., electroconvulsive therapy), even if an injury has not occurred, this action is considered a battery unless the informed consent of the patient is obtained prior to the procedure. In another instance, if a psychiatrist gives a sex offender an antiandrogen drug (e.g., Depo-Provera), the patient must be informed of the risks and benefits of the medication and of alternate treatments and give consent. In order to have a valid consent, it is important to remember that three conditions must be present: the individual must be a competent adult; he or she must be aware of the facts and alternatives of the proposed therapeutic or medical procedures; and the treatment must be voluntary.

The right to refuse treatment has long been recognized in common law as the right to autonomy over one's body. It has constitutional basis in the first, fourth, eighth, and fourteenth amendments as well as a basis in decisions of the Supreme Court that have supported the individual's right to privacy.[8] This is not an absolute right, but rather is conditional and does not apply when the life of the patient (or the lives of others who are endangered because of the patient's condition) is threatened. The right to refuse treatment becomes a particularly complicated issue in cases of mental illness. In the absence of emergencies, the courts have ruled that mental patients have the right to refuse treatment.[4,13,16,17] States have varied in terms of the protective measures used to enforce these rights. For example, in some states it has been determined that the courts must be petitioned for a hearing, and the court then decides whether the patient may refuse medication, whereas in other states the courts have ruled that certain administrative procedures can be established that do not require a judicial hearing to determine individual cases.

In the past, the voluntary component of informed consent has raised some complex issues concerning the treatment of prisoners and committed mental patients. In some cases, the court has ruled that an involuntarily detained patient is capable of giving informed consent for routine procedures in which the risk and the benefits are fairly well known, but that this patient is not able to give informed consent for experimental procedures in which the risks and benefits are less certain.[3] The court reasoned that experimental procedures performed on the involuntarily detained patient are not "voluntary" since the right of consent would be given within the context of coercive institutional forces; for instance, the patient might "choose" experimental treatments, without fully understanding the risks involved, to appease the authorities, or because he or she hoped to shorten the length of the detainment.

CONFIDENTIALITY

The right to *confidentiality* is founded in both ethical principles and contractual law.[7] While the concept of the right to privacy is important in all branches of medicine, it is especially crucial in psychiatry. If the patient is to develop the sense of trust that is necessary in therapy, he or she must feel assured that what is discussed with the therapist is held in confidence, and that without the proper authorization, this information will not be shared elsewhere. The patient's right to confidentiality is established as the backbone of the medical profession. The Hippocratic oath states, "And whatsoever I shall see or hear in the course of my profession, as well as outside my profession in my intercourse with men, if it be what should not be published abroad, I will never divulge, holding such things to be holy secrets"[15] (p. 5). Both the American Medical Association and the American Psychiatric Association also have a code of ethics which requires that a physician protect the rights of patients and the confidentiality implicit in the transactions.

In addition to ethical considerations, most states have specific statutes which protect the confidentiality of the patient. "Confidentiality" does not mean, however, that information relayed to a psychiatrist by the patient cannot go beyond the sanctity of the therapeutic relationship. The law specifies certain stipulations when this information can be shared. For example, the patient can sign a release of information form that permits the physician to show medical records to a third party, or the judge can subpoena the physician to release the medical records to the court. However, if the physician provides information concerning the patient's condition or in any way violates the privacy of a therapy session in an unauthorized manner, the therapist can be sued for negligence in breaking his duty to maintain patient confidentiality.

THE DUTY TO WARN AND PROTECT THIRD PARTIES

At times the psychiatrist is caught on the horns of a dilemma, pulled between a conflict of duty: If the therapist believes that the patient is likely to harm a third party, is it the therapist's duty to protect the confidentiality of the patient and remain silent, or to break the implicit agreement and warn the third party of the potential danger?

This dilemma was illustrated in the well known case of Tarasoff v. Board of Regents of the University of California.[12,21] In 1968 Prosenjit Poddar met Tatiana Tarasoff while he was a graduate student at the University of California. When Ms. Tarasoff rejected his interest in her, Poddar became depressed and withdrawn, and subsequently entered psychotherapy. After learning that Poddar expressed fantasies of harming the young woman and intended to purchase a gun, the psychotherapist consulted a psychiatrist about the danger. The psychiatrist, in turn, requested that the campus police take Poddar to the hospital for commitment. However, when the campus police spoke with him, Poddar assured them that he had no intention of harming the woman. Convinced that he was not dangerous, the campus police did not take him to the hospital. A short while later, Poddar killed Tatiana Tarasoff. Her parents then brought suit against the University, the therapist, and the campus police, charging them with negligence.

Tarasoff v. Board of Regents of the University of California[21] worked its way to the Supreme Court of California twice, and received two separate rulings: one decision involved the *duty to warn*, while the other pertained to the *duty to protect*. Tarasoff I stated:

> When a doctor or a psychotherapist, in the exercise of his professional skill and knowledge, determines, or should determine, that a warning is essential to avert danger arising from the medical or psychological condition of his patient, he incurs a legal obligation to give that warning.[20] (p. 914)

Whereas Tarasoff II stated:

> When the therapist determines or pursuant to the standards of his profession should determine that his patient presents a serious danger of violence to another he *incurs an obligation to use reasonable care to protect* (author's italics) the intended victim against such danger.[22] (p. 346)

The Supreme Court of California failed to define what it meant by *duty to protect*. Subsequent courts have interpreted the Tarasoff principle differently and have not been consistent in upholding it. The doctrine is also not law in all states. However, Beck, who reported on *The Potentially Violent Patient and the Tarasoff Decision in Psychiatric Practice*,[2] regards the Tarasoff *rule to protect* as the National Standard of Practice.

Although this duty to the third party is usually taken to mean a known, foreseeable victim, there have been several cases in California in which hospitals were found liable for not taking reasonable precautions to protect nonspecific victims who might be injured because of a dangerous patient. But, according to Beck, with the exception of California, there have been no other cases involving outpatient therapy in which, based on the Tarasoff principle, the court has actually ruled on hospital liability.[2] However, clinicians are well advised to honor the National Standard of Practice and to take the necessary precautions to protect themselves from a negligence suit.

For clinicians, an irony remains: it has been repeatedly demonstrated that psychiatrists and other psychiatric professionals are unable to predict satisfactorily the long-term dangerousness of a patient.[5,6,14] However, while admitting that it is difficult, the court still holds that the clinician is responsible to use *due care* in assessing patients to determine whether any potential danger exists toward a foreseeable victim, and to warn or protect the targeted person.[1] Applebaum suggests that there are three steps that a clinician can follow when faced with Tarasoff-like situations.[1] He lists that the therapist should,

1. Assess the patient's degree of dangerousness;
2. Select a course of action to deal with the threat represented by the patient; and
3. Implement the course of action appropriately.

Since the clinician cannot anticipate what some future court will judge as proper precautions, the best course of action to follow is one of *due care*—to determine what the reasonable clinician would do in a similar circumstance.

Taking a thorough patient history is one of the best ways to meet this requirement. The clinician should check the patient's past history of adaptation and response to stress. An assessment of past incidences of violence is also extremely important. Although a therapist may initially feel some discomfort, there are several ways to phrase questions about past violent behavior that should be directly asked: "What's the most violent action that you have ever done in your life?" or "How seriously have you ever injured another person? Have you had thoughts or fantasies of harming someone? If so, under what circumstances?" If there has been a history of past violence, the therapist should try to find out the factors that contributed to the violent behavior, and more specifically, whether the use of alcohol or drugs lowered the patient's inhibitions.

When assessing the dangerousness of a patient, although the clinician is not expected to be free from error, the therapist should remember the specifications defined by the Tarasoff court: "the therapist need exercise that reasonable degree of skill, knowledge, and care ordinarily possessed and exercised by members of (that professional specialty) under similar circumstances"[2] (p. 99). The best course of action is to understand the complexities of the situation, to use rational thinking when trying to make an assessment, and then to document the reasoning processes used to discern the patient's dangerousness. If the therapist is uncertain about the situation, a safe, reasonable approach would be to bring in another clinician for consultation.

Applebaum suggests that, as a general principle, in cases where the clinician wishes to warn a targeted victim, the decision should be discussed with the patient first.[1] The warning should then be communicated to the potential victim by telephone if possible, and if he or she cannot be reached, then Applebaum recommends that a special delivery letter be mailed. However, warning the potential victim, in and of itself, may not protect the victim sufficiently; other steps may be necessary—for example, initiate involuntary hospitalization of the dangerous patient; alert the police or relatives who might exercise control over the patient; prescribe medication to curtail impulses or psychotic behavior; call in social service interventions; or use other means to assist the patient in taking more responsibility for his or her own behavior.

When the targeted victim is a child, there is a duty to warn the parents of the potential danger. The following case illustrates how one such situation was handled:

Case #1: The Duty to Warn Parents of Potential Child Victim About Child Offender's Dangerousness

When Donny was 28 years old, he was transferred from the Department of Corrections to NFETC following a conviction on a charge of lascivious or indecent assault upon a child. The victim in the instant offense was a six-year-old boy. Donny remained in the Mentally Disordered Sex Offender program only slightly longer than the 90-day evaluation period, because he was judged as unamenable for treatment in the program and was returned to Corrections to finish his five-year sentence.

According to Donny's past history, he had sexually victimized minor children since the age of 14. He first noticed his attraction toward young children when, as a babysitter, he would feel sexually excited while changing their diapers. He reported becoming even more aroused when he smeared their feces on their bodies and spanked them. He would sometimes pinch their genitals, and at other times, he would have them pinch his genitals.

During his evaluation period, Donny spoke repeatedly of his anger and resentment toward his six-year-old victim for talking to investigators. He also shared thoughts about killing the boy when he was freed from prison. Although these feelings and fantasies were addressed by professionals during his stay, Donny remained unmodified in his stance toward the victim. Accordingly, the psychiatrist and the staff attorney, after lengthy consultation, composed a Tarasoff-type warning letter to the parents of the boy, warning them of Donny's statements, the unpredictability of his behavior, and his expected release date.

At the time of his transfer to the Department of Corrections, Donny was considered to have Borderline Personality Disorder as well as the manifestations of Pedophilia. Because of his potential dangerousness to the child, a copy of the warning letter was sent to the prison administrator and the prison psychologist so that further evaluation and appropriate interventions could be made.

DUTY TO REPORT SUSPECTED CHILD ABUSE

All 50 states in the United States have child abuse reporting laws.[18] Typically, the various statutes require that health care officials, teachers, social workers, and other clinicians report suspected cases of child abuse, including child sexual molestation. A few jurisdictions require that anyone who has knowledge of a child abuse incident must report the case. Generally, professionals who report cases of child abuse are given civil immunity.[18]

While most clinicians believe that breaking the confidential patient-clinician relationship should be avoided if possible, the clinician must break this confidentiality if there is good reason to believe that the patient will harm a known third party. Both the American Medical Association and the American Psychiatric Association endorse this breach in confidentiality when it is necessary to protect the patient or society.[18]

As reiterated earlier, the abuse must first be suspected and then the situation must be assessed before the mental health professional can proceed to make a reasonable decision about whether or not the likelihood of abuse is present. If abuse is suspected, the clinician then has several responsibilities: to make the diagnosis of suspected child sexual abuse and then to take action to protect the victim. Any case of suspected child sexual abuse must be reported to the appropriate department of social services and child protection agency, or to a central registry.

The therapist may be faced with a particularly difficult dilemma when it is conveyed to the clinician during a therapy session that the patient had committed an act of child molestation. Unless one is faced with an actual situation it is difficult to realize the conflict experienced by the clinician when faced with this dilemma. On the one hand he feels a loyalty to the patient to protect his rights to privacy and confidentiality, but on the other hand he is bound by his duty to the state to report child sexual abuse. In order that the reader may understand this conflict, we ask you to put yourself in the role of the clinician and assume the following facts:

Case #2: Duty to State Versus Duty to Patient

Tim, a 32-year-old, white single man sought therapy because of a severe depression which had lasted for one month's duration. He experienced a loss of sleep and a lowered appetite; in the one month, he had lost 10 pounds and experienced anhedonia. After Tim had been in treatment for one month, he told you as his therapist that he was sexually abused as a child by a female babysitter. Since he had not shared this experience with anyone before, he temporarily experienced relief from his depressive symptoms. In a subsequent visit, however, he told you that over the past six months he had sexually abused his sister's son on several occasions while babysitting and had kept the abuse a secret from his sister.

The reader as therapist is now confronted with an ethical and legal dilemma involving several choices: (a) Should you remain silent and not report the abuse to anyone? (b) Should the sister be notified of the past abuse and warned about the potential for further abuse? (c) Should you notify the authorities directly without involving the sister? (d) Should you notify the sister and the authorities?

What is your decision and what are your reasons for making this choice?

While you as therapist may not want to report the case to the authorities, you are obligated to do so by the laws of most states. You have no duty to inform the patient's sister directly. In fact, if you do so without obtaining the patient's permission you are violating his rights of confidentiality. As therapist you should discuss the matter thoroughly with the patient so that he is aware of your decisions and has opportunity to discuss the issues.

In addition to facing conflicts arising from duty to the state versus duty to the patient, the clinician must also wrestle with problems involving a duty to the patient versus duty to the victim. Again, in order that the reader may better understand the dilemma, you are asked to be the clinician and assume the following facts:

Case #3: Duty to Patient Versus Duty to Victim

John, a 42-year-old married man and father of three teenagers (two daughters and a son), had been in treatment for about nine months. After pleading nolo contendere to a charge of sexually molesting his 15-year-old daughter, John was placed on probation and was ordered into outpatient group therapy along with other men accused of incest. Following his arrest, the court also ordered him out of the home, and he moved to a furnished apartment in the same city. However, after he had been in treatment for some months, with the approval of the Court, he returned home to live with his wife and children.

After what appeared to be satisfactory progress in group therapy, John suddenly became withdrawn and his participation dwindled during the group sessions. When asked about his withdrawal, at first he denied that anything was wrong, but after further exploration, he expressed that he was fearful about the possibility of molesting his younger 13-year-old daughter. After realizing that the group support alone was not sufficient, the clinician recommended that John move out of the house and live in an apartment. He also recommended that John and his wife begin conjoint therapy. In this manner the wife could be aware of John's struggles and could lend her support.

Despite the willingness of his wife to attend the therapy sessions, John continued to experience sexual fantasies about his younger daughter and became even more depressed, verbalizing thoughts of suicide. After accepting the therapist's recommendation for hospitalization, John was started on antidepressant medication and received individual therapy. With treatment, John showed improvement; he stated that his sexual fantasies had decreased and he felt that he had gained more control of his sexual urges.

At the time of discharge, the therapist met with both John and his wife to discuss John's struggle to control his sexual urges toward the daughter. The wife shared her concerns about the financial hardship that was imposed on her and her children because of the expense of John's apartment, and asked that her husband be allowed to return home to live. She claimed that she was aware of the risks involved and was willing to assume the responsibility of monitoring John's behavior in order to maintain family stability. John expressed his desire to return home. He felt that he had improved sufficiently so that he would not be a danger to his daughter.

In making your decision as therapist, it is important to take into consideration the fact that John had not acted on his impulses but rather, became fearful and guilty about the fantasies, and the fact that he was open to discuss his urges with his wife. As therapist, assess John's ability to cope with stress at the present time. Consider how the monitoring of John's behavior would be imposed.

If you choose to recommend he return home, prior to his discharge, as therapist you may wish to meet with John and his wife, along with the 13-year-old daughter. At this meeting you may inform them that John was not "cured," but that his sexual urges seemed to be under reasonable control. You may wish to instruct the mother to monitor all interactions between the father and daughter and to make sure that the two are never left alone together. You may inform the daughter to tell her mother, and her therapist, if the father showed any behavior toward her—even the most subtle sexual innuendos—which made her feel uncomfortable.

If you choose not to recommend that John return home at this time, you should give a thorough explanation to the patient and his wife. In your discussions, be as explicit as possible about the behaviors you will need to see before you can agree with the patient and his wife for him to return home. You may wish to tell them that while he has improved, you want to see how he will be after discharge when he is not in the structured environment provided by the hospital. You may wish to have him continue in outpatient treatment and visit his daughter under the wife's supervision. This will provide the opportunity to see how he, his wife, and daughter feel after this social interaction. If this type of visit goes well, additional ones could be carried out so that his return to the family unit is a gradual one, predicated on the comfort of him, his wife, and his daughter.

CLINICIAN LEARNS TO LIVE WITH UNCERTAINTY

By this time clinicians must realize that working with child molesters requires the specialized knowledge and skills of their own profession as well as the legal profession. What may not be appreciated is the fact that even the best of clinicians will be unable to control the attitudes and behavior of the child molester. The clinician can influence the child molester, but in the final analysis it is the molester, not the clinician, who determines if an act of child molestation will occur. This means that the clinician must develop the trait of tolerating the unknown; that is, "Will my patient reoffend?" Faced with this dilemma, the clinician must be aware of those aspects of the law that protect the interests of the patient, the interests of society, and the interests of the clinician.

REFERENCES

1. Applebaum, P. S. (1985). Implications of Tarasoff for clinical practice. In J. C. Beck (Ed.), *The Potentially Violent Patient and the Tarasoff*

Decision in Psychiatric Practice. Washington, D.C.: American Psychiatric Press.

2. Beck, J. C. (1985). The psychotherapist and the violent patient: Recent case law. In J. C. Beck (Ed.), *The Potentially Violent Patient and the Tarasoff Decision in Psychiatric Practice.* Washington, D.C.: American Psychiatric Press.

3. Brooks, A. D. (1974). *Law, Psychiatry and the Mental Health System.* Boston: Little, Brown.

4. Callahan, L. A., & Longmire, D. R. (1983). Psychiatric patients' right to refuse psychotropic medication: A national survey. *Mental Disability Case Reporter, 7,* 494.

5. Cocozza, J., & Steadman, H. (1976). The failure of psychiatric predictions of dangerousness: Clear and convincing evidence. *Rutgers Law Review, 29,* 1048.

6. Diamond, B. (1974). The psychiatric prediction of dangerousness. *University of Pennsylvania Law Review, 123,* 439.

7. Engelhardt, H. T., Jr. (1986). *The Foundations of Bioethics.* New York: Oxford University Press.

8. Gutheil, T. G., & Appelbaum, P. S. (1982). *Clinical Handbook of Psychiatry and the Law.* New York: McGraw-Hill.

9. Halleck, S. L. (1980). *Law in the Practice of Psychiatry: A Handbook for Clinicians.* New York: Plenum Medical Book Company.

10. Holder, A. R. (1975). *Medical Malpractice Law.* New York: John Wiley.

11. Lidz, C. W., Meisel, A., Zerubavel, E., Carter, M., Sestak, R. M., & Roth, L. H. (1984). *Informed Consent: A Study of Decisionmaking in Psychiatry.* New York: Guilford Press.

12. Mills, M. J., & Beck, J. C. (1985). The Tarasoff Case. In J. C. Beck (Ed.), *The Potentially Violent Patient and the Tarasoff Decision in Psychiatric Practice.* Washington, D.C.: American Psychiatric Press.

13. Mills, M. J., Yesavage, J. A., & Gutheil, T. G. (1983). Continuing case law development in the right to refuse treatment. *American Journal of Psychiatry, 140,* 715.

14. Monahan, J. (1981). *The Clinical Prediction of Violent Behavior.* Rockville, MD: Crime and Delinquency Issues: A Monograph Series. U.S. Department of Health and Human Services.

15. Reiser, S. J., Dyck, A. J., & Curran, W. J. (Ed.) (1977). *Ethics in Medicine: Historical Perspectives and Contemporary Concerns.* Cambridge, MA: MIT Press.

16. *Rennie v. Klein,* 462 F.Supp. 1131 (D.N.J., 1978). 653 F.2d 836 (3rd Cir. 1981): *Rennie v. Klein,* Cert. granted, judgment vacated and remanded, 50 U.S. Law Week 3998.27 (1982) 720 F.2nd (3rd Cir. 1983).

17. *Rogers v. Okin,* 478 F.Supp. 1342 (D.Mass. 1979), affirmed in part, reversed in part, vacated and remanded, *Rogers v. Okin* 634 F.2d 650 (1st Cir. 1980).

18. Slovenko, R., & Grossman, M. (1985). Confidentiality and testimonial privilege. In R. Michels, J. O. Cavenar, H. K. Brodie, A. M. Cooper, S. B. Guze, L. L. Judd, G. L. Klerman, & A. J. Solnit (Eds.), *Psychiatry.* Philadelphia: J. B. Lippincott.

19. Standard of Care for Specialists, Parts I and II. (1973). *Journal of the American Medical Association, 226,* 251, 395.

20. *Tarassof v. Regents of the University of California*, 118 Cal. Rptr. 129, 529 P.2d 553 (1974).
21. *Tarasoff v. Regents of the University of California*, 108 Cal. Rptr. 878 (1973).
22. *Tarasoff v. Regents of the University of California*, 17 Cal. 3d 425, 551 P.2d 334 (1976).

CHAPTER 10

Forensic Evaluation and Report Writing

It cannot be emphasized enough that the most crucial factor in the entire evaluative process is the credibility, or the basic integrity, of the clinician. Although all clinicians have certain unconscious biases that will affect their assessment, the psychiatric professional should strive to maintain the most objective and neutral posture as possible throughout the evaluative process, no matter who requests or pays for the examination.

This adherence to a comprehensive and objective procedure will prove especially invaluable when a clinical report must be submitted to the court. Because the state and the defense attorneys take oppositional and adversarial perspectives, the report cannot satisfy both sides. Whether it is favorable to the defense or the prosecution, the report must inevitably withstand the vigorous grilling that occurs in the legal arena from whichever side that is not benefited by the clinician's evaluation. This chapter will help to provide a model for conducting an objective examination and for writing a professional quality clinical report for forensic purposes.

STAGES IN THE FORENSIC PROCESS

Referral Phase

When a clinician is asked to perform a psychiatric evaluation for forensic purposes, the referral may come from the court, the defense attorney, or the state attorney. At times a letter will accompany the request outlining the purpose of the examination, and at other times the reason will not be defined. If an explanation does not accompany the request, the clinician should contact the referring attorney and clarify exactly what information is desired from the evaluative process.

At other times, the referral will come in the form of a court order, and the purpose of the examination will be clearly defined, including the criteria stipulated by the state law and/or the state's rules regarding criminal procedure. For example, the request may say: "The purpose of the evaluation is to determine if the defendant is competent to stand trial, pursuant to the criteria set forth in 916.12(1),F.S.&, FRCRP 3.211 (a), and also to determine whether he was insane at the time of the commission of the crime pursuant to FRCRP 3.216(E)."

Although competency to stand trial requirements vary from state to state, many states use the following McGarry criteria:[2]

1. Consider realistically the possible legal defenses.
2. Manage one's own behavior to avoid trial disruptions.
3. Relate to attorney.
4. Participate with attorney in planning legal strategy.
5. Understand the roles of various participants in the trial.
6. Understand court procedure.
7. Appreciate the charges.
8. Appreciate the range and nature of possible penalties.
9. Perceive realistically the likely outcome of the trial.
10. Provide attorney with available pertinent facts concerning the offense.
11. Challenge prosecution witnesses.
12. Testify relevantly.
13. Be motivated toward self-defense. (p. 74)

The regulations regarding the legal standard of insanity also vary from state to state. If the M'Naghten Rule is operative, the regulation will probably be stated in the following manner:[1]

. . . it must be clearly proved that at the time of the committing of the act, the party accused was labouring under such defect of reason, from disease of the mind, as not to know the nature and quality of the act he was doing, or if he did know it, that he did not know he was doing what was wrong. (p. 44)

In addition to the M'Naghten Rule, the Model Penal Code (1962) of the American Law Institute states that "a person is not responsible for criminal conduct if at the time of such conduct as a result of mental disease or defect he lacks substantial capacity either to appreciate the wrongfulness of his conduct or to conform his conduct to the requirements of the law" (p. 55). In the past year or so, several states have removed the section that pertains to the defendant's inability "to conform his conduct to the requirement of the law"; in these cases, since the only section that remains emphasizes the defendant's lack of substantial capacity to appreciate the wrongness of his conduct, the Model Penal Code essentially restates the M'Naghten Rule. Also note that the above terms, "mental disease or defect," in the Model Penal Code do not stipulate an abnormality that is manifested only by repeated criminal conduct or otherwise antisocial behavior.

In instances where the referral order requests the examiner to consider whether an incompetent defendant meets the criteria for involuntary hospitalization, the order may request an assessment of the following information: (a) the nature and extent of the mental illness suffered by the defendant; (b) whether the defendant, because of such mental illness, meets the requirements for involuntary hospitalization or placement; (c) whether there is substantial probability that the defendant will attain competence to stand trial within the foreseeable future; (d) the nature of the care and treatment to be afforded to the defendant and its probable duration; and (e) alternatives other than involuntary hospitalization which might be less restrictive on the defendant's liberty.

Beginning the Examination Process

Because the defendant may still be incarcerated at the time of a forensic evaluation, the assessment will frequently be done in the local jail or in a place other than the clinician's office. In these cases, the noise level may be high, and it may be difficult to find a place where the clinician and the defendant can feel comfortable during the examination. Despite this less-than-ideal setting, when greeting the defendant, it is important for the clinician to introduce himself or herself and to fully explain the nature and the purpose of the evaluation. It is also essential to inform the defendant whether or not the examiner's confidentiality is assured, and to whom the report or evaluation will be sent. Although there is no standardized way to conduct an evaluation, it is suggested that the examination follow the same outline sequence as the written report, presented below.

The Examination and Report Writing

Before the actual report writing, the clinician should receive a signed release of information form from the defendant so that previous medical records can be obtained and reviewed. The clinician also should make an effort to contact the state or defense attorney to obtain other pertinent records, including police reports and deposition statements from individuals who had contact with the defendant close to the time of the alleged crime. After assessing the medical and police records, as well as the evaluation notes, the clinician is then prepared to write the actual report and to send it to the appropriate legal authorities—either to the defense attorney only, or, in some instances, also to the state attorney and the judge.

A sample forensic report will be provided at the end of this chapter; however, the following format both outlines the necessary information that comprises a forensic report and integrates the authors' suggested interview technique for the evaluation process.

THE EVALUATION PROCESS OF THE ALLEGED CHILD MOLESTER

Identifying Information and Source of Referral

In this section the age, race, sex, and marital status of the defendant is listed. As examiner, the clinician should give the date on which the evaluation was held and the person who requested the examination—either the defendant, the defense attorney, the prosecuting attorney, or the judge. Specify the legal purpose of the examination—for example, to determine the competency of the defendant to stand trial; to assess the defendant's legal insanity; to evaluate if involuntary hospitalization is necessary; to ascertain if the defendant is a sex offender; or some other purpose. Finally, note that the defendant was informed about the confidentiality or nonconfidentiality of the examination and also was told who would receive the report.

Defendant's Account of Legal Charges

The purpose of this section is *not* to present the defendant's story of what actually took place at the time of the alleged crime—

this information is recorded later. Rather, in this section include the defendant's understanding of the actual charge(s) that he was accused of committing, and the date on which the crime was said to have occurred. Information should also be obtained from the defendant pertaining to when he was arrested, and in his own words, the criminal action he has been charged with committing.

The information garnered from the defendant about the alleged charge(s) is particularly important if the purpose of the evaluation is to determine whether the defendant is competent to stand trial. In this type of case, a crucial factor contributing to the overall picture of the defendant's capacity to stand trial is his ability to understand the legal charges that are held against him.

Defendant's Account of the Alleged Crime

This section is one of the most crucial parts of the evaluation process because it presents an opportunity to see how the defendant perceived the events that led to his arrest and subsequent criminal charge. These observations are critical to substantiate the clinician's judgment about the defendant's legal sanity or insanity on the day of the criminal events. In the case of child molestation, ask the defendant to relate what his relationship was with the victim, and in particular, what transactions happened between the victim and the defendant on the day of the alleged offense. Keep in mind that the information supplied by the defendant will have self-serving purposes and may not be a true account.

The chronological description of the defendant's activities on the day of the alleged molestation should be noted here as well; begin with the morning and track the events that occurred throughout the day and night. In this manner, the clinician can ascertain the defendant's perceptions, thinking, and behavior. In sex offense cases, the clinician should seek to find out who initiated the events that transpired between the defendant and the victim, what kinds of sexual behavior were manifested, and whether there were threats or use of force. If violence is indicated, determine what method was used—for example, whether the defendant used his hands or whether there was a weapon involved. Since many offenders frequently use drugs and alcohol, inquire whether alcohol and/or illicit drugs, as well as prescribed medication, were taken on the day of the alleged crime, and, if so, indicate whether the effect of these substances may have influenced the defendant's awareness of what transpired.

Defendant's Account of His Adjustment Since the Time of Arrest

Whether the defendant has been in jail since the time of the arrest, or whether he was released on bond should be noted in this section. Assess the impact that the arrest has had on the defendant; focus on his adjustment, especially whether any tendency toward acts of violence, either to harm himself or others, has been expressed since the time of the arrest; and indicate whether, for any physical or emotional reason, an examination by a general physician or a psychiatrist was required following the arrest. Also note whether the defendant was on any medication at the time of the evaluation.

Previous Criminal Record

Establish the defendant's chronological history of prior arrests. Include the defendant's age at the time of each arrest, the formal charges indicated, and the outcome of the arrest—for example, whether the charges were dropped; whether the defendant was placed on probation or fined; or whether a definite sentence was determined. If the defendant is accused of a sex offense, focus on the various manifestations of previous sex charges to examine whether a definite pattern for any one type of offense is indicated, or whether there has been an escalation in terms of severity.

Past History

Family history. Include in this section the birth place and the birth date of the defendant, the number of siblings and the defendant's birth order within the family. Determine whether the parents are still living; if so, indicate their state of health and current marital status. Record if the parents have a history of criminal activity, mental health problems, or substance abuse. Provide a developmental history of the defendant that details how the accused got along with different family members, whether the defendant experienced, or perceived experiencing, mental or physical abuse, and whether there was a history of running away from home.

Educational history. Include the highest level of education and whether the defendant's performance was so poor that he repeated any years of school. In addition, comment on whether he had learning or adjustment problems that necessitated intervention with special education classes. Record his behavioral adjustment in school. In particular, note if there were hyperactivity or antisocial behavior that caused suspension or expulsion from school.

Military history. If the defendant served in the military, note the length of time, his level of adjustment, and whether he had any disciplinary problems during his enlistment. Also indicate whether the defendant experienced combat duty. Include in this section the type of discharge that the defendant received—for example, honorable, undesirable, general, or administrative.

Employment history. To establish some indication of the stability, or lack of stability, in the defendant's work habits, include the nature and length of the jobs the accused held, and the reasons that he terminated employment.

Sexual history. Include his age at the onset of puberty. Record the age when the defendant's first sexual contact with another person occurred, the age and the sex of the partner, and the type of sexual behavior that took place. Establish his age when sexual intercourse began to occur on a regular basis, and the details concerning the age and the sex of his partners as well as the nature of the relationships.

It is important to determine if the defendant was sexually abused as a child. Determine his age at the first and last occurrence of sexual abuse. The clinician should be cognizant of the defensive nature of many individuals to admit that they were sexually abused as children. Sometimes this nonadmission is due to repression or denial whereas other times the person remembers having been abused but is unwilling to share this with someone he does not know well. It is quite common after an offender is in treatment and has established trust in the therapist to remember and share the memories of having been abused during childhood. Find out his relationship to the abuser(s) (relative, acquaintance, stranger) and the type of sexual abuse he experienced. It is equally important to document his abusive history toward others. Record his age when he became the abuser, as well as the age and sex of his victims and the type of behavior. Ascertain whether the primary sex objects have been heterosexual or homosexual in nature, and the variety of sexual behaviors he has experienced. Record any sexual dysfunction that the defendant may have experienced (e.g., impotence or premature ejaculation).

Marital history. Indicate whether the defendant has ever been married, and, if so, the number of times. If the molester is currently or has previously been married, discuss the defendant's observations about the relationship and the stability of the marriage. Specifically address any sexual problems that the defendant may have experienced with his wife. If the defendant has children, any sexual contact between the offender and his children, or stepchildren, should be directly inquired about and commented upon in this section. Some discussion should also be included that pertains to the defendant's parenting behavior in general.

Violence history. Although information concerning the defendant's past history of violence may have been included in the "Previous criminal record" section, review in this section any violent behavior that did not result in a subsequent arrest. Look particularly for indications of whether the defendant has a repetitive history of violence toward others; if so, determine toward whom and under what circumstances. In sexual abuse cases, focus on whether the defendant had sexually forced (i.e., raped) or inflicted other violent sexual behavior on others.

Surgical history. In this section record the types of operations, if any, that were performed on the defendant, and whether there had been complications.

Physical trauma history. Note the kinds of accidents and injuries that the defendant had suffered, and the types of treatment that were provided.

Medical history. Do a quick systemic review to identify any serious medical problems that have not already been covered, specifically information pertaining to seizures, loss of consciousness, and venereal disease.

Psychiatric history. Indicate whether the defendant has had any inpatient or outpatient psychiatric treatment. If so, indicate the symptoms and circumstances that led to the treatment. It is important to record whether the defendant has had a history of hallucinations, either visual or auditory, as well as suicidal thoughts and attempts.

Alcohol and drug history. If there is a history of drug or alcohol use, note when the defendant first began to use either of these substances, and whether there has been a pattern to their use, both over an extended period of time and particularly during the year prior to the arrest. Also indicate whether the defendant was ever treated for substance abuse and include any actual signs or symptoms of abuse—for example, blackouts, the shakes, delirium tremens, or alcohol-related arrests such as driving while intoxicated.

Mental Status Examination

In this section, the examiner reports on the general description of the behavior of the defendant. After it has been ascertained whether the accused is oriented to time, person, place, and situation, make an assessment of the defendant's fund of knowledge, as well as a clinical evaluation of his level of intelligence. Draw upon standardized data to check immediate and recent past memory. Notice speech patterns and whether any abnormalities exist. Also focus on thought and perception processes to assess whether disorders are indicated—for example, loosened association, delusions, or flight of ideas. Evaluate the defendant's mood, feelings, and affect, as well as his judgment and insight in a given situation.

Collateral Sources of Information

In this section, routinely try to review other sources of data concerning the defendant—for example, prior medical records, police arrest reports, statements and depositions of individuals who were in contact with the defendant around or close to the time of the alleged crime, and other material that either the defense attorney or the prosecuting attorney feels is pertinent to consider.

Opinions and Diagnostic Impressions

The psychiatric diagnosis, as well as any indication of the presence or absence of a specific mental disorder or defect, are included in this section. The clinician is also expected to render his or her opinion based upon the indicated purpose of the evaluation—for instance, the opinion may involve the issue as to whether the defendant is competent to stand trial (in which case the McGarry[3] items that are considered for competency to stand trial may be noted here); whether involuntary hospitalization is mandated; or, in a situation where criminal responsibility is being determined, whether the defendant is assessed as fitting that particular state's legal requirements for insanity (e.g., the M'Naghten Rule in the case of Florida). If the request for the examination asks for other opinions that relate to issues of sex offenses, the information is supplied in this section as well. Finally, while stating these opinions, it is very important not only to summarize the supporting reasoning behind the opinions, but to provide a well-formulated assessment that will hold up against any attack on the credibility of the report.

Depositions

After the evaluation has been submitted to the party requesting the examination, either the defense or the prosecution may wish to use the report in court. The opposing attorney may not want to rely on the written report alone, but may wish to interrogate the clinician in more depth. This interrogation process is done through the form of a deposition.

At the time of the deposition, a court reporter will swear in the clinician. Both the attorney for the plaintiff as well as for the defense will be present; however, most of the questions that are asked will come from the opposing attorney. Since it is a general rule of strategy to avoid surprises at the time of the trial, the adversary will try to gain as much information as possible.

Prior to the deposition, it is beneficial to hold a predeposition conference; during this time, the attorney who is using the report can prepare the clinician for some of the anticipated line of questioning that the opposing side may pursue. Also prior to the deposition, the clinician should review all the data in order to be well prepared.

Like the stages of testimony in an actual trial, the stages of a deposition include: direct examination and then cross-examination, followed by redirect examination and then recross-examination. The clinician should not be caught off guard at the time of the deposition by the casual demeanor and innocuous questions that are sometimes posed by attorneys. Remember that the answers provided may be used to impeach the clinician at the time of the trial. The clinician should read the typed deposition prior to the trial.

Testimony at the Trial

At the trial, the evaluator may be asked to testify as an expert witness. An expert witness is valuable to a case because he or she is permitted to give an opinion testimony at the time of the trial, whereas other witnesses are permitted to state only factual testimony.

After being sworn in, the clinician, as an expert witness, should be aware that how he or she makes the presentation may be as important as what is said during the testimony. The demeanor, dress, and mannerisms of the witness are very important. It is advisable to dress conservatively, to make eye contact with the examining attorney, and to make occasional eye contact with the jury. It is also important to testify in an objective and unbiased manner. The testimony should be offered in a clear, audible manner using as little technical language or jargon as possible. The witness should answer questions directly, but if a question cannot be answered, the clinician should state this fact. The clinician must be aware of the strategy of some attorneys to lead the witness so as to give answers favorable to his side. The witness should realize also that the opposing attorney will try to discredit the testimony and that the best thing to do in these circumstances is to remain cool and unmuddled.

FORENSIC REPORT: AN EXAMPLE

John Doe
Alachua County Case #87–000.

Identifying Information and Source of Referral

This 39-year-old white, married, male defendant was seen in psychiatric evaluation on February 14, 1987. The examination had been requested by the defense attorney, W. D. The purpose of the evaluation was to determine the defendant's competency to stand trial, to assess his sanity at the time of the alleged offense, and to make treatment recommendations. The defendant was informed that a copy of the psychiatric report would be sent to his defense attorney, but would not be released to other parties without proper authorization.

Defendant's Account of Legal Charges

Mr. Doe said that he was arrested on January 2, 1987, and was charged with the sexual battery of his 15-year-old stepdaughter, Holly. The defendant reported that he was charged with having sexual activity with his stepdaughter intermittently over the past three years, with the last occurrence taking place one day prior to the arrest.

Defendant's Account of the Alleged Crimes

Mr. Doe said that he had his first sexual contact with his step-daughter, Holly, two-and-a-half years ago when his wife left Holly alone with him while she went on a week-long business buying trip. One night after he had drunk an excessive amount of alcohol, he asked Holly if she would give him a back rub. While she was rubbing his back, he opened a sex magazine and showed her some of the pictures. He then put his hand down her panties and fondled her genitals. At the time he didn't think that Holly seemed frightened or upset. However, the next day he apologized for his behavior and told her that it would not occur again. He cautioned Holly not to say anything to her mother because it would only upset her. For a number of months he did not have a further desire to approach Holly sexually, but then he began to have fantasies of experimenting with other forms of sexual behavior with her.

About six months later, his wife again had to be away from home for several days on a business trip. The defendant promised himself that he would not become involved with his stepdaughter sexually, and the first day that his wife was gone, he did not make sexual advances. However, the second day of his wife's absence, after drinking steadily throughout the day, Mr. Doe approached his stepdaughter after she had showered and gone to bed. He got into bed with her; after mutual fondling, he asked her to perform oral sex on him, which she did, but not to the point of ejaculation. On other occasions when his wife was absent from home, he and his stepdaughter engaged in fondling and oral-genital sexual activity. During the six months prior to his arrest, he penetrated her with his finger, and on two occasions with his penis. The pattern of the sexual behavior was basically always the same: his wife was away on a business trip; thus, he was alone with his stepdaughter, and he was drinking heavily. The defendant denied that he had ever used any force, threats, or bribes. He reported that his arrest came about after his stepdaughter saw a television movie about incest and talked with a school counselor about her step-father's behavior.

Defendant's Account of His Adjustment Since His Arrest

Mr. Doe said that following his arrest he was in jail for five days before he was released on bond. While in jail he had difficulty sleeping and experienced a loss of appetite. He felt depressed, but denied that he had any suicidal ideation. His wife visited him in jail, and they have continued to communicate following his release;

however, he has not seen his stepdaughter. He has moved into a furnished apartment, since he was under a court order not to return to his home. He has not tried to harm either himself or others. The defendant continues to feel depressed, but not as severely as he felt while in jail. He has not received any psychiatric treatment to help him work through his depression, and at the present time, he is not on psychiatric medication.

Previous Criminal Record

The defendant had no arrests as a juvenile, but in the past three years he has been arrested on two occasions and charged with "driving while intoxicated" (DWI).

Past History

Family history. Mr. Doe was born in Baltimore, Maryland, on June 12, 1947. His biological father, a house painter, is 64 years old and his mother is 62 years old. The defendant's parents separated and divorced when he was 10 years old. He reported that his father was, and continues to be, an alcoholic. The excessive drinking caused trouble between his father and mother, which eventually resulted in divorce. On many occasions, his father came home and beat him, his mother, and his older brother, but never beat his older sister. The defendant described his relationship with his father as a fearful one, and said that following his parents' divorce, he had little contact with his biological father. After the divorce, he lived with his mother and two siblings. His mother remarried when he was 12; however, she divorced his stepfather after three years of marriage because of the stepfather's extramarital activities. His mother never remarried, and worked as a librarian to support the family. The defendant said that he got along well with his stepfather and was sad when his mother and stepfather divorced. He related that he always felt close to his mother, but that she had a way of making him feel guilty whenever he disagreed with her.

Educational history. Mr. Doe graduated from high school at the age of 18. He was a good student and never failed a grade. In high school he was a member of the band and sang in the school chorus. He had no disciplinary problem and was never expelled or suspended from school. He considered himself to be somewhat shy, but had a few good friends with whom he got along well. After a tour of duty in the Army, he enrolled in college, where he did well academically. He received his BA degree from the University of Florida and his MA degree in Education at Florida State University.

Military history. Mr. Doe was in the Army from 1965 to 1967 and had no disciplinary problems while in the service. He was in combat in Vietnam, where he received a shrapnel wound in the right leg and was unable to return to duty. He was given a medical discharge under honorable conditions.

Employment history. Mr. Doe held several part-time jobs while in high school and college. Since graduating from college he has been employed as a high-school teacher in several schools; his longest period of employment at any one school has been 10 years. Mr. Doe said that at his most recent school he had a good relationship with the principal, his colleagues, and his students. Prior to his arrest on the current charges, he had never been fired from a job; however, when the principal learned of the charges, he informed the defendant that he did not think that Mr. Doe should be teaching high-school students and dismissed him. Mr. Doe found a job clerking in a store, where he is currently employed.

Sexual history. The defendant's first sexual contact occurred at the age of 10 with his 15-year-old sister. He maintains that it was his sister who initiated the sexual contact and that their sexual activity was limited to mutual masturbation. They continued to have sexual contact intermittently over the next three years until she moved away from home. He denied any sexual contact with his brother.

He began to date girls when he was 15 years old. He engaged in petting, but did not have intercourse until he was 17 years old, when he had sex with a girl in his junior class. Although he had sexual intercourse with several other girls, he never had sex regularly until he married. He denied any sexual interaction with males—either boys or men. He also denied sexual attraction toward children in general, and specifically denied any sexual activity with any children other than his stepdaughter.

He reported that his sexual life with his wife was very satisfactory until about four years ago. At that time he and his wife began to have an increasing number of arguments about his drinking; following one stormy scene, she walked out on him. Although they had a reconciliation, their sexual life never again seemed to be as enjoyable to him. From time to time the defendant has experienced difficulty getting an erection and occasionally has premature ejaculations. He denied any extramarital affairs. He reported that he did not think that his wife had had any affairs either.

Marital history. When he was 23 years old, he married a 25-year-old woman who had a daughter from a previous marriage. Following the marriage, his wife returned to college and earned a degree in marketing. Later she worked as a buyer for a department store—a position that necessitated considerable traveling. It was during these business trips that the sexual activity between her daughter and husband occurred. Mr. Doe denied that there were any serious conflicts between him and his wife, other than those related to his drinking problem. However, at the same time, he alluded to some feelings of jealousy over his wife's frequent buying trips which took her to the northeastern cities. Although he longed to travel, it was not economically feasible for him to do so.

Violence history. The defendant reported that his only history of violence had been during his Vietnam tour of duty in the Army. When on combat duty he had killed several Viet Cong, firing at close range. On the patrol in which he received a shrapnel wound in the leg, he saw several buddies blown up from detonated booby traps. He was sent back to the United States for medical treatment, where he experienced deeply disturbing dreams during which time he relived his combat experiences.

He denied that he had ever threatened or committed any form of violence outside of the military experience. Specifically, he denied that he had ever forced himself sexually on anyone. While he denied he had used physical force to have sex with his stepdaughter, he admitted that he used his parental authority.

Physical trauma and surgical history. Mr. Doe's most serious traumatic event, as well as his only surgical procedure, involves the shrapnel wounds that he received during his combat experience in Vietnam. He received a severe wound to his right leg, which required several surgical procedures. He currently experiences chronic pain from the injury, and has a noticeable limp.

Medical history. The defendant has had no serious medical illnesses. Specifically, he has had no periods of unconsciousness and no seizures or venereal disease.

Psychiatric history. For two years following his return from Vietnam, Mr. Doe had nightmares, reliving his wartime experiences, and he would awaken in a cold sweat. He denied any flashback experiences, but said that for several years following his Vietnam experience he had startle reactions to loud noises. He denied ever having auditory or visual hallucinations, and reported that he had never had serious feelings of depression, with the exception of the period during which he was separated from his wife, some four years ago. He has never had any psychiatric treatment. The defendant also denied that he had ever had any serious thoughts of suicide or had ever made a suicidal attempt.

Alcohol and drug history. Mr. Doe had his first drink of alcohol when he was 15 years old, but did not get drunk until he was in the Army, when he was 18 years old. His use of alcohol began on a regular basis, however, after his discharge from the Army. While he was in college, he drank three or four beers a day; after graduation he drank about six beers a night during the week, and more on the weekend. When his wife was away on her trips, his alcoholic consumption was 12–24 beers per day.

During the past three years, Mr. Doe has had blackouts on four or five occasions. He denied experiencing the shakes or delirium tremens and denied receiving treatment for his alcohol abuse. He said that since his arrest on the current charges, he has not drunk any alcohol and has joined Alcoholic Anonymous (AA).

The defendant denied the use of illicit drugs, but stated that several years ago when he was in chronic pain and had difficulty sleeping, he became dependent on the use of a prescribed medication that he took to control his pain and to help him sleep. After about a year, he became concerned about abusing the prescribed drug and discontinued its use. Since that time, when he experienced problems with pain or sleeping, he relied on alcohol to gain relief.

Mental Status Examination

Mr. Doe appears to be his stated age. He is oriented to person, time, place, and situation. Clinically he is judged to be in the bright-normal level of intelligence. There is no indication of a thought disorder, and specifically, there is no loosening of association, delusions, or flight of ideas. There is no indication of abnormalities in his perception in the form of hallucinations or illusions. He is able to abstract five out of five proverbs. Both recent and remote memory are intact. His affect is appropriate. There is no sign of increased anxiety; however, he appears mildly depressed. He cries when he discusses missing his wife and stepdaughter, and over the pain that he has caused them as well as himself. He denies suicidal or homicidal ideas. No unusual behaviors are noted during the examination. He has limited understanding about the factors that contributed to the incestuous behavior, and expresses a desire for treatment.

Collateral Source of Information

In addition to my psychiatric examination of the defendant, I interviewed Mr. Doe's wife. She reported feeling very angry and resentful toward her husband when she first learned of his incestuous behavior toward her daughter. Initially, she sought to cut off any further contact with him, but after visiting him in jail and ventilating her feelings toward him, she found herself ambivalent about a divorce. She now reports that she is moving more in the direction of wanting to salvage her marriage and is willing to enter into conjoint therapy with her husband. She related that her daughter has been seeing a therapist to help resolve conflictual feelings about herself and her stepfather.

Diagnostic Impressions

1. Pedophilia, nonexclusive type, opposite sex, limited to incest. DSM-III-R—302.20.
2. Alcohol Abuse, episodic. DSM-III-R—305.00.

Opinions

At the present time, I do not see an indication of any major thought, affective, or perceptual disorder. The defendant has an appreciation of the alleged charges, as well as an appreciation of the range and nature of the possible penalties. He understands the adversary nature of the legal process, and is aware of the role of the judge, jury, state attorney, and defense lawyer.

Since he has the capacity to relate to me his thoughts, feelings, perceptions, and actions at the time of the offenses, I think that he has the capacity to disclose to his attorney pertinent facts about his alleged crimes. He responds appropriately to my questions, which leads me to think that he has the ability to relate to his attorney. Based on his ability to reason in a logical and sequential manner, I believe that he has the ability to assist his attorney in planning his defense and/or to realistically challenge prosecution witnesses. His stable behavior patterns during the interview also lead me to believe that he has the ability to manifest appropriate courtroom behavior. There is no sign of abnormal thought processes during examination, which indicates to me that he has the ability to testify relevantly. It is my medical opinion that the defendant is presently competent to stand trial.

It is also my opinion with reasonable medical certainty that at the time of the alleged crimes the defendant knew what he was doing, knew what would result from his actions, and realized the wrongfulness of his actions. I base this opinion on two facts: the defendant gives no history of having at any time lost contact with reality, and there is nothing to suggest that he ever experienced psychosis. The defendant has a long history of alcohol abuse, and in the past has experienced blackouts; but the blackouts were not present during the times of the alleged sexual offenses. He reports that on all of the occasions that he engaged in sexual relations with the stepdaughter, he was drinking heavily. Although the alcohol may have decreased his inhibitions and lowered his judgments, he still seemed aware of the nature of his actions and the wrongfulness of his behavior.

The defendant expresses remorse for his incestuous behavior toward his stepdaughter, and expresses a strong desire to rejoin his family. At the same time, he realizes that neither his wife nor his stepdaughter would feel comfortable with his living in the household at the present time. He also has no idea how long it will take, if ever, for his wife and stepdaughter to feel comfortable with his rejoining them at home. In my opinion, because the wife and stepdaughter feel as they do, Mr. Doe should not return to the home at the present time. Although he does not have much understanding about the dynamics that led him to engage in sexual behavior with his stepdaughter, the defendant is interested in gaining insight into these dynamics and has expressed a willingness and desire to begin a treatment program.

It is my medical opinion, at the present time, that the defendant does not meet the criteria for involuntary hospitalization, and I do not see the need for an inpatient form of treatment. I recommend that he and his wife enter into outpatient conjoint marital therapy, and that he simultaneously enter group therapy with other men who are receiving treatment because of their incestuous behavior. Also, I recommend that he abstain from the use of alcohol and remain in Alcoholics Anonymous.

George W. Barnard, M.D.

240 The Child Molester

REFERENCES

1. Bromberg, W. (1979). *The Uses of Psychiatry in the Law: A Clinical View of Forensic Psychiatry.* Westport, CT: Quorum Books.
2. Grisso, T. (1986). *Evaluating Competencies: Forensic Assessments and Instruments.* New York: Plenum.
3. Laboratory of Community Psychiatry, Harvard Medical School (1973). *Competency to Stand Trial and Mental Illness.* (DHEW Publication No. ADM 77–103). Rockville, MD: NIMH, Department of Health, Education and Welfare.

CHAPTER 11
Clinical Implications for the Therapist

Up to this point the focus has been on providing factual information and an intellectual understanding of the child molester. In this chapter we will acquaint clinicians with some of the emotional issues they may encounter when dealing with these offenders. Although these problems may seem unique to clinicians specializing in the treatment of sex offenders, those with only occasional contact with a child molester patient may be just as likely to experience the dilemmas discussed.

THERAPISTS OF SEX OFFENDERS MAY BE HELD IN LOW REGARD

Although many people recognize the importance of treating sex offenders, there is a significant number of people who believe that sex offenders do not deserve treatment, but rather the only intervention should be punishment or isolation from others. Some professionals have difficulty treating sex offenders because they feel their work is not always understood or appreciated by the public or their colleagues, some of whom may even question the clinician's motivation for going into that line of therapy. The therapist who works with sex offenders is sometimes regarded by others as a sex offender advocate. The therapist may face criticism and at times even ostracism by other mental health professionals in the community, particularly by clinicians who work with victims.

NEED TO CONFRONT THE DEFENSES OF THE CHILD MOLESTER MAY BE CONTRADICTORY TO PREVIOUS TRAINING

A clinician's previous training often serves as a disadvantage in dealing with the child molester. Many therapists are taught to be accepting and to allow the patient the opportunity to move at his own pace, without confronting his defenses. However, this non-confrontational approach does not work with most child molesters who may take advantage of the situation and make little or no effort to change. Many child molesters are excellent "con artists" who manipulate the naive clinician into dealing with aspects of his life that are not directly related to his sexual pathology vis-à-vis children. Unless clinicians modify their technique with this group of individuals, many of whom have severe characterological disorders, they may experience frustration and a sense of impotence in their inability to address the core issues of sexual molestation.

As a form of their resistance, most child molesters employ defense mechanisms of denial, rationalization, minimization, displacement, and intellectualization to avoid recognizing and admitting the consequences of their pathology. These coping mechanisms serve to distance the therapist from the patient. The therapist must confront the defenses to the degree that is necessary for the child molester to recognize and admit to himself the destructive elements of his behavior that lead to victimization of children.

The clinician can also expect different levels of resistance in the treatment process. Initially, the child molester may say that he did not abuse the child. Later, he may admit molesting the youngster but maintain that he was seduced by the child. At a still later stage, he may acknowledge having committed the offense but claim it was because he himself was sexually abused as a child or was mistreated in life by a meaningful person such as his mother or his wife. It is important for clinicians to recognize that once a layer of resistance is overcome (e.g., the offender's denial of a process) the child molester probably will expose other layers of defenses. He will usually remain on a plateau and rely on a particular defense mechanism until he is willing to move to another level of understanding about himself.

The resistances of the offender tend to keep both the child molester and the therapist from learning about the molester's sexually deviant pathological acts. And yet, acknowledging these acts is essential if the offender is to become aware of the precursors to his offending behavior. It is rare that the act of child molesting is committed spontaneously. There is a complex chain of behavioral events that leads to an offender completing a child-molesting act. At NFETC this chaining of behavioral events is called "process." There are many examples of this in Chapters 7 and 8. The child molester may or may not be able to gain insight or understanding about how the chain of events leading to molestation is tied in with traumatic events from his own childhood.

The child molester may maintain these resistances because he fears that once his pathology is revealed to the clinician, the clinician will reject him. The therapist's job is to learn about the sexually deviant acts and thoughts and, in a nonjudgmental manner, maintain empathy toward the child molester.

PROBLEMS OF THE THERAPIST IN EMPATHIZING WITH THE CHILD MOLESTER

Therapist's Bias Toward the Child Molester

An additional complication confronting many clinicians is that they often initially find little about the child molester with which to empathize, are repulsed by the offender's behavior, and struggle to find a way to connect with him as a human being. Clinicians must come to grips with their own biases concerning child molesters. They must look at their own background and belief systems. These belief systems may include seeing the child molester as someone who is so weird and different from themselves that they want to have nothing to do with him. If clinicians are to be effective clinically they must get beyond this prejudice. In some way the therapist must get beyond the magical belief that says, "If I have anything to do with the child molester, he will contaminate me and alter my value system."

If clinicians are able to develop an empathic and understanding relationship, they often find an individual who, like most patients, has specific strengths and vulnerabilities. Many child molesters come from very disturbed families and have experienced a limited number of positive life experiences and an abundance of negative ones. By focusing on the offender's life experiences in which he has been the victim, it is easier to empathize with him as a person.

The Repulsive Nature of the Child Molester's Acts

Clinicians visiting at NFETC who have no experience with sex offenders are often emotionally upset when they watch the offenders reenact their offenses in the therapy groups. Some are so repulsed by the child molesters' accounts of their sexually abusive behavior toward children that they cannot remain through the entire group therapy session. They are forced to acknowledge that they would be unable to use this technique. It takes a certain degree of detachment on the part of the therapist to be able to participate in these reenactments. Not all therapists are emotionally able to do this. Because of the emotional drain on the therapist, a clinician should learn this form of treatment under the guidance of an experienced therapist.

Complex Personality Structure of the Child Molester

At times, treatment is further complicated because the child molester may present as a combination of opposing characteristics. On the one hand he may present himself as a lying, deceitful, manipulative, uncaring, unfeeling, and cruel person. Conversely, he may appear quite "normal," displaying attitudes and behaviors of an individual concerned about others. When this persona is shown, one would not suspect him of being a child molester. The capacity for change and growth may be seen when the therapeutic process is successful and the child molester emerges as a person who recognizes and respects the rights and feelings of others, who can be more open and honest in his own feelings and behaviors, and who has learned ways to control and prevent further child molestation.

Exploitation of the Therapist's Trust

However, as all experienced clinicians know, this growth and change in individuals with personality disorders is difficult and slow to bring about. If change is to occur, it will only be by overcoming the offender's many layers of resistance. One of the primary resistances of the child molester is to agree verbally with the therapist, but not to implement behavioral changes. This resistance may continue because the child molester's unconscious defense mechanism of intellectualization is operative or because he is consciously being manipulative. Through this ploy the therapist may be led to believe that the child molester is doing more than he actually is. A child molester may say, "I'm doing all I can and I need you to make me different." Such passivity and plea for the clinician to take control should not be accepted. Rather, the offender should be reminded that he is in control of his own behavior and is responsible for any changes that may occur. Clinicians should realize that many molesters have lifetime experiences of successfully misleading others or having others take over for them so that their passivity is reinforced.

In working with the offender, a therapist will experience the tensions of the ebb and flow of trust and mistrust in their relationship to the offender. At times, the clinician will have his trust violated by the offender. One therapist working with child molesters told the following story:

> We were doing a large group at holiday time and invited the men to share their sadness or hurt feelings due to being incarcerated during the holidays under the strong arm of the law. A child molester offered to do some work (we were doing Gestalt therapy in that particular group) and he wanted to work on the hurt he felt over his dog dying during the holidays when he was younger. As I did this work with him, he cried. I remember feeling a lot of hurt myself and feeling a very close connection with him. Then in front of all the men in the group he made a statement like, "Gee, I feel really guilty. I made that all up. I never had a dog or anything." I remember feeling betrayed and embarrassed. I asked myself whether a better therapist would have recognized this resistance. Later, when I recovered from the trauma, I felt good that even though he was manipulative, he had owned up afterwards. He was honest enough to say that he had made it up. It stayed with me for years as the kind of situation that I rarely experienced in therapy with less-disturbed clients.

This clinician blamed himself and thought "a good therapist" would have seen through the con. He failed to realize that most therapists working with individuals who have personality disorders will be misled occasionally. As in all psychotherapy, clinicians make themselves vulnerable when they empathize with the child molester, but it may be better to be fooled from time to time than not to have a caring relationship with the patient.

This relationship between therapist and patient is often in delicate balance. Therapists may experience a struggle within themselves in determining the degree of involvement they will allow with the child-molester patient. They must learn how to be "involved" with the child molester without being "overly involved." Clinicians need to detach themselves from the manipulative maneuvers of the patient. If they cannot make this detachment, clinicians are at risk to feel guilty and devalued.

BREAKING THE RESISTANCE BARRIERS OF THE CHILD MOLESTER

Having discussed the many layers of the resistance that the sex offender presents to the therapist, we offer the following guidelines on overcoming or at least attempting to overcome these resistances:

1. Work in a Group Setting

We strongly recommend that a clinician works with child molesters in a group setting, especially for the initial therapy sessions. By doing so, a therapist shares with others the emotional depletion that comes from working with a child molester. Those members who are in advanced stages of therapy, aware of the types of resistances offenders use, will be able to share their insights and lessen the burden for the therapist. Group members can model appropriate group behavior, including self-disclosure, and at other times challenge or confront the offender's resistance. It may be easier for the child molester to accept what a fellow offender is telling him than to believe the therapist. In this way the group members help the molester to become a more active and disclosing participant.

2. Work with a Co-therapist

For many of the above reasons, we strongly recommend working with a co-therapist. Working as a therapeutic team reduces the amount of anxiety that the individual therapist experiences. Also, when co-therapists engage in post-group discussions, they have an outlet for the tensions induced in the therapy.

3. Define the Terms and Conditions of Therapy

At the onset of therapy the clinician should meet with the child molester and clearly define the requirements and expectations of therapy. This is essential for child molesters who come to therapy under duress, such as a condition of probation or an agreement with a spouse. Some of the offenders who come into therapy at the insistence of others have no intention of bringing about changes in their belief system and behaviors. Rather, their aim is to defeat the purpose of therapy by going through the motions, without having to experience any of the discomfort that accompanies the therapeutic work. Some therapists accept these involuntary patients on a conditional basis and instruct the offenders that unless they demonstrate a willingness to actively participate they will not be retained in the program.

Detailing the conditions of therapy involves arriving at an agreement with the patient about the circumstances of confidentiality. If the child molester voluntarily seeks treatment, no reports about his progress or lack of progress is reported to other parties. If the offender has entered treatment under a court order, however, the clinician is usually required to send periodic progress reports to the court or to the probation officer. This stipulation can exert pressure on the offender to abide by the conditions of probation; if the child molester has violated the condition of probation, the offender can be asked to appear before the judge for a hearing. In traditional forms of therapy the therapist is allied only with the patient. In working with child molesters, however, the therapist operates under a dual alliance—partly toward the patient and the relief of symptoms and partly toward society and the prevention of violent behavior. A clinician who is not accustomed to working with sex offenders may feel uncomfortable having an alliance to a party other than a patient.

Some therapists openly communicate this split alliance at the beginning of therapy and delineate the special limits to confidentiality. As long as the patient works with the therapist toward preventing the victimization of others, they are on the same team. Should the therapist consider that the offender is not working toward this goal, the therapist becomes an extension of the arm of society and does what is necessary and practical to protect society from the individual and his deviant behaviors.

The experienced clinician will recognize that a split alliance does not fall in the exclusive domain of working with child molesters. Therapists of patients threatening suicide, homicide, or other dangerous, acting-out behavior must wrestle with these same issues relating to the control of aggressive behavior. With these patients most clinicians do not passively stand behind the bond of confidentiality and permit the patient to kill either himself or another.

Since the Tarasoff ruling, the legal system has insisted that in a situation of danger to a known victim the therapist's first allegiance is to the potential victim and thus to the community at large. This realignment of allegiance from patient to community when "the chips are down" represents a radical departure from the customary thinking of most therapists. The clinician working with the child molester must actively intervene if the patient is unable to control his deviant sexual behavior with children.

4. Expect Graduated Openness from the Child Molester

There must be an agreement between the patient and the therapist that the offender will communicate more openly than he has in the past. This means that he will share certain types of information not only with the therapist but also with such key people as family members and probation officers, who, in turn, are asked to share their observations of the offender's behavior with the therapist. In essence, it is essential for the child molester to be more open about his deviant thoughts and acts than he has been in the past because this secrecy contributed to his deviancy. While the therapist may desire and expect the child molester to be more open, he or she should not expect the openness to come about all at once. Being secretive probably has been a way of life for the child molester and he is not likely to change rapidly.

5. Expect the Child Molester to Disclose All Incidents of Child Molestation

Commitment to treatment requires that all previously undisclosed acts of molestation be shared. The patient will probably want to reveal new information privately to the therapist first, before then admitting it to the group, and finally to his family.

6. Engage the Family in the Therapeutic Process

The therapist should recognize that it may be especially difficult for parents of a juvenile offender to learn the degree of deviant urges and behaviors that their child has. One of the best ways of preventing future offenses is to inform the custodians of the seriousness of the problems that the offender faces. If the family is to be helpful in the treatment, it is necessary that they learn about the offender's past behaviors. Past deviant behaviors may have been allowed to continue because it appeared no one in the family knew what was going on.

Whether the offender is a juvenile or an adult, it is essential that the offender, his family, and the probation officer understand the high-risk situations which set the stage for him to reoffend. Questions helpful to answer when working with the molester and his custodians are: What types of precursor behaviors exist? What are the patterns of reoffending? What are the circumstances that may precipitate the reoffense?

Recently, therapists have found it is often beneficial to have support groups consisting of family members of the child molesters.

The support groups offer a source for concrete advice and comfort during the times of crisis with the offender.

7. Alert Key Persons to Risk Factors

The treatment of child molesters is not simple; it cannot be made to adhere to rigid formulas. Situations will occur for the child molester that will put him more at risk to reoffend. The actual circumstances will vary from offender to offender, but the patient, his therapist, key family members and, if relevant, the probation officer should all be alerted to the uniqueness of his dynamics and the nature of his high risk situations. For example, if in the past an offender has committed his offense only during the times when he was under interpersonal stress and was abusing alcohol, the family can target behavior and intervene. These educated family members can also be extremely useful when the offender goes through crises. A family member may join the offender in therapy sessions with the clinician to discuss what is going on and what can be done to remedy a problem before the child molester reoffends.

STRATEGIES FOR HANDLING CRISES

Clinicians who have experience in working with child molesters know that they are frequently in some form of crisis. They may use the crisis as an excuse for engaging in child-molesting behavior. Thus, the clinician must maintain flexibility in his or her approach to treatment and employ a variety of therapeutic tools to assist the offender through the crisis.

The crisis may take the form of losing a job, being in conflict with a family member, or having a disagreement with an authority figure such as a probation officer. It may be a direct outgrowth of therapy insofar as the child molester may become anxious when he uncovers previously unknown sexual desires. At any point in therapy, if the child molester experiences obsessive sexual desires directed toward children, he may experience anxiety over losing control and reoffending.

If the clinician has developed a positive therapeutic relationship with the child molester, it makes it easier to handle these times of crises. The clinician should expect that as the offender is confronted with crises, whatever the cause, he probably will show some form of regressive behavior and may lose some of the ground he had gained in previous therapeutic sessions. This is only a temporary setback, however, and does not mean all the effort has been wasted.

Typical crisis strategies include: eliminating alcoholic intake; using Antabuse to lower the probability of alcohol intake; using Depo-Provera to reduce intense sexual urges; using a neuroleptic agent to reduce or calm impulsive behaviors; providing daily psychotherapy; and, in some cases, placing the offender in a secured environment such as a hospital, crisis center, or other form of structured environment in which he will be prevented from acting on destructive impulses.

CLOSING REMARKS

Clinicians differ as to the type of individuals and problems with which they can work best. By now some readers will appropriately say, "This type of work is not for me." For those of you who do not share this perspective, we think you will find assisting the child molester to change his attitudes and behaviors to be a rewarding challenge.

Our belief is that the goals or expectations of therapy should not be for a complete cure in the sense that the internal character structure will be changed significantly and the molester will lose all desire to molest. Rather, more limited goals should be defined: the achievement of some degree of characterological, cognitive, and behavioral change that will enable the molester to control his deviant impulses with some peace of mind and to live a more productive life.

Our experience, like that of other sex offender therapists, has been that a high percentage of child molesters who remain in therapy show considerable change during the treatment process. Although their deviant arousal patterns are not totally eliminated, they gain a measure of control over their lives. They learn to recognize their errors of thinking and perception that set the complex behavior chains into motion, leading to their child-molesting process. They learn to recognize situations that put them at risk to act out on their cognitive distortions and to take subsequent interventions. They learn how they dehumanized their victims and how this dehumanization process facilitated their molesting children. Through learning to see their victims as people whom they hurt, they learn the process of empathy. Gaining an acquaintance with their past, they discover some of the origins of their psychosexual disorder and how they acquired the low self-esteem that made it easier to look to children as sexual objects rather than to adults. Through treatment, many are able to increase their feelings of self-respect.

Child molesters, like other patients who are in therapy, experience crises in their lives which may result in temporary setbacks in their therapy. This does not mean, however, that the gains previously made are lost forever. Rather, the therapist and the patient must reassess the situation that led to the relapse and determine the therapeutic intervention that will prevent similar events from triggering a relapse in the future.

Index